PARAPSYCHOLOGY

Containing contributions from leading paranormal researchers, this edition of *Parapsychology* continues to challenge and provoke readers with some of psychology's most puzzling phenomena. Whether believers or sceptics, the book provides readers with the opportunity to further their understanding of the paranormal, bridging the gap between traditional psychology and its so-called fringe areas.

Featuring updates to many of the original chapters, this book brings readers up to date with the wealth of radical research in the field. This edition also includes several new chapters, covering subjects as diverse as possession and exorcism, conspiracy theories, reincarnation, and religious belief, many of which are extremely relevant in the world today. Drawing on a range of research, the book provides a balanced introduction to parapsychology, exploring the strengths and limitations of scientific investigation itself.

Parapsychology is for readers from a variety of backgrounds: professionals in the field, students, lay readers and anyone who wants to understand what the paranormal can tell us about ourselves. A variety of viewpoints are on offer, with the emphasis on the reader to make up their own mind. Prepare to be unsettled, again...

David Groome was formerly Principal Lecturer in Psychology at the University of Westminster, UK, where he retains a research connection. In 2009 he received the BPS Award for Excellence in the Teaching of Psychology.

Ron Roberts was formerly Senior Lecturer in Psychology at Kingston University, UK, where he now holds an honorary position. He is an Associate Fellow of the British Psychological Society.

PARAPSYCHOLOGY

The Science of Unusual Experience

Second edition

Edited by
David Groome and Ronald Roberts

Routledge
Taylor & Francis Group
LONDON AND NEW YORK

First published 2017
by Routledge
2 Park Square, Milton Park, Abingdon, Oxon OX14 4RN

and by Routledge
711 Third Avenue, New York, NY 10017

Routledge is an imprint of the Taylor & Francis Group, an informa business

First edition published by Routledge, 2001

British Library Cataloguing in Publication Data
A catalogue record for this book is available from the British Library

Library of Congress Cataloging in Publication Data
Names: Groome, David, 1946- author, editor. | Roberts, Ronald, 1955 Dec. 9-author, editor.
Title: Parapsychology : the science of unusual experience / edited by David Groome and Ronald Roberts.
Description: Second edition. | New York, NY : Routledge, 2017. | Includes bibliographical references.
Identifiers: LCCN 2016021156| ISBN 9781138916401 (hardback : alk. paper) |
ISBN 9781138916418 (pbk. : alk. paper) | ISBN 9781315689678 (e-book)
Subjects: LCSH: Parapsychology.
Classification: LCC BF1031 .P337 2017 | DDC 130—dc23
LC record available at https://lccn.loc.gov/2016021156

ISBN: 978-1-138-91640-1 (hbk)
ISBN: 978-1-138-91641-8 (pbk)
ISBN: 978-1-315-68967-8 (ebk)

Typeset in Bembo
by diacriTech, Chennai

In memory of Svetlana Boym,
and for Merry, Subi, Wandia & Alice (RR)

For Glenys as always,
and Izaak who may one day read this book.
And in memory of my dear friend Hazel Dewart (DG)

CONTENTS

CONTRIBUTORS

David Groome was formerly Senior Academic at the University of Westminster, London, UK. He retired in 2011, but still retains a research connection with the University.

Ron Roberts was formerly Senior Lecturer in Psychology at Kingston University, UK, where he now holds an honorary position.

Robert Brotherton is Research Fellow in the Department of Psychology at Goldsmiths College, University of London, UK.

Michael W. Eysenck is Professorial Fellow at the University of Roehampton, UK, and Emeritus Professor and Honorary Fellow at Royal Holloway University of London, UK.

Christopher C. French is Head of the Anomalistic Psychology Research Unit in the Department of Psychology at Goldsmiths College, University of London, UK.

Robin Law is a lecturer in the Department of Psychology at the University of Westminster, London, UK.

Chris Roe is Professor of Psychology and Director of the Centre for the Study of Anomalous Psychological Processes at the Department of Psychology at the University of Northampton, UK.

Caroline Watt is Koestler Chair of Parapsychology at the University of Edinburgh, UK.

Richard Wiseman is Professor of the Public Understanding of Psychology at the University of Hertfordshire, UK.

PREFACE

The first edition of this book appeared in 2001, and was written in an attempt to provide a scientific view of the many claims that have been made for the occurrence of paranormal experiences.

Experiences are said to be paranormal when they cannot be readily explained by normal processes or mechanisms in accordance with our existing scientific knowledge. For many centuries people have reported various different types of paranormal experiences, such as extra-sensory perception, communication with the deceased, possession by spirits and demons, and abduction by aliens. In many cases large numbers of the general public have come to believe in these phenomena, because they apparently found such claims to be convincing. Given the startling nature of many paranormal claims, scientists take a more sceptical view and require convincing objective evidence before they will accept them as genuine. Over the last century or so there have been extensive scientific studies of paranormal phenomena, and we are now in a much better position to make a considered judgement about whether the various claims of paranormal phenomena are real or not. This book was written in an attempt to summarise what these scientific studies have told us about the paranormal.

In writing the second edition of this book, our main aim has been to bring our review of the literature up to date, as there has been a good deal of new research since the first edition was published. However, we have also taken the opportunity to incorporate the suggestions made by reviewers and readers who felt that some important and relevant topics had been left out. In response to their comments and suggestions we have therefore added several new chapters, to cover areas which we neglected in the first edition. Our second edition therefore includes chapters on several new topics: mediums and survival, possession and exorcism, reincarnation, religious belief, and conspiracy theories. These new chapters hopefully provide a welcome addition to updated material from the first edition, which covered paranormal cognition, alien contact, near-death experiences, astrology, and psychic fraud.

Some may consider the decision to include astrology in this volume as controversial since strictly speaking astrology is not really a paranormal phenomenon, as it does not involve any personal experience of events which defy explanation. However, we have decided to keep astrology in the book for two reasons. First, because it does involve claims and beliefs regarding causal influences which are not supported by scientific evidence, and second, because belief in astrology is widespread among the general public.

As our book deals in large measure with various beliefs and the reasons underlying them, we took the decision to include a chapter on religious belief as there are clearly parallels to be found with the other types of belief covered in the book. We should make it clear that this chapter is intended to be an objective and scientific study of religious belief, rather than an attempt to attack or discredit any particular religious view. Our intention is simply to explain what scientists have to say on this issue.

There are several reasons why the study of paranormal beliefs can be of value. In the first place, it is important to establish whether or not paranormal phenomena are genuine, so that we know whether we can make use of them or whether they should be disregarded. A further reason for studying belief in paranormal phenomena is that in cases where the evidence fails to support the validity of these phenomena, we can learn a great deal about human cognition and how beliefs are established. Such studies can shed light on the reasons why people believe in something despite the lack of supporting evidence. A further benefit in studying paranormal phenomena scientifically is that it may help us to improve our investigative techniques. Paranormal research presents a particularly strong challenge against which we can sharpen and refine our testing methods and control procedures. In fact we believe that the study of paranormal claims offers an excellent basis for the analysis of scientific design and control procedures, and for the improvement of one's critical thinking capabilities. In the world we live in today this is of immense importance.

Most of the chapters in this book consider the scientific evidence relating to a particular type of paranormal belief, such as the evidence for paranormal cognition or alien contact. The last few chapters, however, deal with the nature of belief, and consider some of the possible mechanisms which may underlie paranormal beliefs. This part of the book includes chapters on the techniques used by conjurors and fraudulent psychics, the influence of conspiracy theories and social pressures on belief, and finally a chapter on the cognitive factors which might help to explain the formation of paranormal beliefs.

Whether a believer or a sceptic, we hope that you will find material here which will help you to acquire a more informed opinion and a heightened level of critical thinking. There is much here to challenge pre-existing opinions on either side of the debate. For those readers who are studying this subject matter as part of an academic course, we hope that you will gain not only an understanding of the breadth of ostensibly paranormal phenomenon and the challenges these pose for scientific investigation, but also an appreciation of the strengths and the limitations of scientific investigation itself.

David Groome and Ron Roberts
London
March 2016

ACKNOWLEDGEMENTS

We would like to thank everyone who has contributed to this book, and who suggested ideas about what to include. In particular we would like to thank Geoffrey Dean, Nancy Zingrone, and Gerd Hövelmann for their valuable comments and suggestions. Our sincere thanks also go to Ceri Griffiths and Michael Strang at Psychology Press, who somehow turned our thoughts into a book.

1

INTRODUCTION

David Groome and Ron Roberts

Unusual and paranormal experiences

We live in an age of science. However, there are many types of human experience which continue to defy any scientific explanation, at least in terms of the scientific knowledge we have at the present time. In some cases we may have a partial explanation, but in others even this is lacking. These cases which continue to deny any conventional scientific explanation are referred to as "paranormal" phenomena. However, in practice there is considerable overlap between what is regarded as "paranormal" and what is considered to be merely "unusual". Because of this, the present book will review both categories without necessarily making a distinction between them. The purpose of this book is to review the scientific evidence we have about unusual and paranormal experiences. The main categories of unusual and paranormal experience are listed below, and they will all be examined in detail later in the book.

Paranormal cognition means the perception of input through some channel other than the five principal senses. It includes such claimed phenomena as "extrasensory perception (ESP)", "telepathy" or the use of a "sixth sense". All of these terms basically denote a capacity for the brain to receive information from other sources by some unknown mechanism of transmission.

Mediums and survival. Mediums claim to be able to contact the spirits of the dead, a claim which further assumes that those who have died continue to survive in spirit form, and are able to interact with some living people.

Exorcism and possession. Possession refers to the belief that people can be taken over by evil spirits, which need to be driven out or "exorcised".

Alien contacts and abductions refer to purported encounters with extraterrestrial visitors. Some people believe they have encountered such visitors from other worlds, while some believe that they have been the victims of alien abduction.

These experiences are generally classified as paranormal because as yet there is no convincing evidence that this planet has been visited by aliens.

Near-death experiences. Many people who are close to death (or who are resuscitated after being declared clinically dead) describe experiences which seem to defy any straightforward scientific explanation. These may include visions of the afterlife and out-of-body experiences.

Reincarnation refers to the belief that after death a person's spirit is reborn in a new body or in some different form.

Dreams are the mental experiences we have during sleep, and although they are well established as real phenomena, there is as yet no scientific consensus on their underlying mechanism or the functions they serve.

Astrology is based on the belief that the stars have an influence over people's lives, their character, and their destiny. Again the mechanism by which this might occur remains unknown. Some authorities argue that, strictly speaking, astrology is not a paranormal phenomenon, as it does not involve a paranormal experience as such. However, we have included a chapter on astrology in this book because it does involve a belief in unexplained phenomena, a belief moreover which is very widely held by members of the public.

These are some of the more commonly reported forms of unusual experience and belief which continue to puzzle the scientific world. They are all linked by one common factor, which is that in each case the mechanisms underlying the phenomenon remain unknown. However, these phenomena have all been subjected to scientific investigation, and the findings of this research will be considered in the remaining chapters of this book. Each of the phenomena listed above will be dealt with in a separate chapter. There are additional chapters principally concerned with the nature of beliefs about paranormal phenomena and the various factors which may influence them. These additional chapters deal with *religious beliefs, psychic fraud, conspiracy theories, science and experience*, and *cognition and belief*. These have been included because they discuss concepts and ideas which may help us to explain why paranormal phenomena are so ubiquitous despite a lack of scientific evidence to support them.

Belief in the paranormal

Although we live in an age of science, belief in the paranormal remains surprisingly widespread. For example, a survey carried out in the UK (Theos, 2009) of 2,060 British adults found that 39 per cent believe in ghosts, 27 per cent believe in reincarnation, and 22 per cent believe in astrology. Similarly, a survey carried out in the USA (Harris Poll, 2013) of 2,250 American adults found that 42 per cent believe in ghosts, 36 per cent believe in UFOs and alien contact, 29 per cent believe in astrology, and 24 per cent believe in reincarnation.

With such widespread belief in the paranormal, it is obviously important for scientists to investigate the validity of these phenomena. For some people an interest in the paranormal is little more than harmless fun, but for many others it determines the decisions they may make about important events in their lives. Some people decide to get married or change their job on the advice of an astrologer, or move house to escape the presence of a ghost or poltergeist. Some take significant actions on the basis of information they believe they have obtained by telepathy or clairvoyance. Beliefs about paranormal phenomena may also be associated with considerable fears and anxieties as is the case with many of the people who report concerns or actual experiences of alien abduction. Likewise, people may live in fear of ghosts, demons, or the devil. There may be other more subtle consequences of beliefs about the paranormal, for example when people blame their own failures and misjudgements on paranormal phenomena. After an accident or catastrophe has taken place, it is sometimes tempting to blame the influence of some unknown force. The disaster was "fated", its origin lay "in the stars", or was brought about by demons or ghosts of the vengeful dead. This kind of attribution can often provide a convenient excuse for not accepting our responsibility for events. This is important, because where we fail to face up to reality we miss the opportunity to learn from our mistakes.

Testing the validity of paranormal phenomena

One obvious reason for studying paranormal phenomena is to find out whether they are in fact real and valid effects in the world in which we live. As suggested above, many people hold beliefs regarding the paranormal which have a very real influence over their lives. If these beliefs are based on valid phenomena, then not only might they provide useful knowledge and insights into our decision-making processes, but they may tell us something startling about the nature of reality. Telepathy, clairvoyance, and astrology might all have the potential to enrich and improve our lives, if they can be shown to be genuine phenomena. However, if it turns out that such phenomena are not genuine, then they represent a source of considerable confusion, misjudgement, and misapprehension, and possibly poor decision making. A person who bases their major life decisions on false beliefs will probably not be very effective in dealing with the considerable challenges and demands which life places on each of us. This is one very good reason why it is so important that paranormal phenomena should be subjected to scientific investigation, and much of this book is concerned with the use of scientific investigation in ascertaining whether claims for the reality of paranormal phenomena are well founded.

Explaining belief in the paranormal

Besides investigating the actual validity of paranormal phenomena, a second reason why psychologists are interested in paranormal research is that we can learn a great deal about the nature of belief systems in general from such studies. Many people continue to believe in things for which there is no credible evidence. There must be reasons why they show such unshakable faith, and by investigating why some people cling so steadfastly to such beliefs we can gain insights into the way our beliefs are created and maintained.

A further aspect of such investigations of paranormal beliefs concerns individual differences – what kind of people are likely to believe in the paranormal? Perhaps a proneness to adopt paranormal beliefs might be linked with certain personality factors, cognitive styles, prior experiences, or the kind of upbringing people have had. Research into the influence of individual differences on paranormal belief is again likely to help our understanding of the nature of belief in a more general sense, with possible relevance to other belief systems such as religious and political beliefs. Possible explanations for believing in the paranormal, and the influence of individual differences in personality and cognition, will be considered in the later chapters of this book.

Experimental design

Another good reason for studying the paranormal is that work in this area can help to improve the way we design and conduct scientific research. Studying the paranormal offers a particularly difficult challenge to experimenters, because there are so many potential influences and variables which need to be controlled for, often including unknown variables which would be overlooked in most other fields of research. For example, if you are trying to investigate the validity of extrasensory perception (i.e. communication between individuals by psychic means rather than using the known senses), then you need to control for a whole range of possible cues which might enable one person to inadvertently communicate with another. Information can be communicated from the "sender" to the "receiver" by subtle and relatively insignificant responses such as coughing, smiling, or eye blinking, which might occur quite unconsciously and without any deliberate intention on the part of the research participant. But even if the sender and the receiver are kept in entirely separate rooms or buildings, there is still a risk that the experimenters themselves might unwittingly provide feedback at a similarly unconscious level. Psychologists who wish to investigate paranormal phenomena must control for all of these possibilities and many more which may be even less obvious. The precautions required in the design of paranormal experiments are certainly exacting, but as such they can alert us to the possible shortcomings of experimental design in other fields of psychological research.

One crucial feature of the scientific approach is that it should be possible for other researchers to replicate the findings of any scientific experiment. However, many studies which have been carried out in the past and published in leading scientific journals have proved to be impossible to replicate. This has now been identified as a major problem for psychology (Roediger, 2012), and is currently attracting considerable attention. However, replication failure has proved to be particularly prevalent in studies of paranormal effects, and again there is a possibility that we can learn something from examining such failures. For example, a recent study carried out by a reputable psychologist (Bem, 2011) claimed to have found clear scientific evidence of precognition. Bem's participants showed superior recall of items which were to be tested at a later stage, compared with items which would not be tested, even though the participants did not know at the time which items would be included in the test. Three other psychologists (Stuart Ritchie, Richard Wiseman, and Chris French) subsequently tried to replicate these findings by carrying out a number of experiments using the identical procedure and materials as used in the original study by Bem. Their experiments all failed to produce evidence in support of Bem's precognition effect, but none of the leading journals were prepared to publish these findings. In fact, though their study was eventually published in an online journal (Ritchie, Wiseman, & French, 2012), it remained the case that none of the mainstream printed journals were interested in publishing it.

It would appear that journal editors are only really interested in publishing novel findings, in accordance with their own beliefs about what is worthy science. Subsequent studies which fail to replicate existing findings are therefore unlikely to be published. Clearly, if journals are only prepared to publish positive findings, whilst refusing to publish negative results (such as replication failures), this will create a publication bias in favour of positive results. This is sometimes referred to as the "desk drawer problem", whereby positive findings are published in journals whilst negative findings languish in someone's desk drawer, never to see the light of day. Publication bias of this kind has created a serious problem affecting all fields of psychology, and indeed all of science. However, it is probably a more serious problem for studies of the paranormal than in any other field.

Fortunately, the problem of publication bias has now been identified, and scientists are looking for ways to overcome it (Roediger, 2012; de Bruin & Della Sala, 2016). Given that journals are unlikely to change their publication policies in the near future, the best solution suggested so far involves the setting up of research repositories where replications (including failures to replicate previous findings) are recorded and held in a place that is accessible to researchers and academics, who will thus be in a position to draw conclusions based on a full review of all of the available findings.

Summary – reasons for studying paranormal phenomena

As outlined above, there are three main reasons why it is valuable to study paranormal phenomena. First, we need to find out whether these phenomena are valid, and whether they really happen or not. Second, by studying people who believe in paranormal phenomena we can learn a great deal about the nature of belief, and the reasons why some people acquire and maintain beliefs even in the absence of supporting evidence. And third, studies of the paranormal provide a very strict test of the effectiveness of experimental design, and may illuminate the presence of uncontrolled variables which would otherwise go unnoticed. Investigations of the paranormal can therefore provide us with some valuable insights into the nature of belief systems, and how best to study them. Such investigations provide the subject matter of the rest of this book.

2

PARANORMAL COGNITION

Caroline Watt

Introduction: the what, why and how of research into paranormal cognition

What are paranormal phenomena? UFOs? Bigfoot? Mind reading? Ghosts? Spoon bending? By "paranormal", I do not mean "supernatural" or "beyond nature" where the reported phenomena are by definition incompatible with scientific theorising and investigation. Rather, I mean that the phenomena appear to suggest organisms can interact with their environment in ways that are not explicable within *current* scientific understanding. This does not mean that paranormal phenomena can never be understood, but it may mean that some of our present scientific knowledge and theories would need to be adjusted to accommodate them. We don't yet know exactly how paranormal phenomena operate, indeed there is still some debate over whether such phenomena even exist, so it is more accurate (but cumbersome) to describe these as *seemingly* paranormal phenomena. The particular phenomenon that I will concentrate on in this chapter is extrasensory perception (ESP), with further definition and examples given below.

We can distinguish between paranormal *phenomena*, where there is a claim that a real anomalous effect is occurring, and paranormal *experiences*. In the latter case, there may or may not be a real anomalous effect; however, the individual has interpreted their experience as a paranormal one. Even if paranormal phenomena do not exist, paranormal experiences do, as surveys have shown that a considerable number of people report experiences that they interpret as paranormal in nature.

This chapter is about "paranormal cognition", a term that implies some kind of information processing model of paranormal phenomena. That is, the term suggests that individuals are somehow perceiving, processing, and responding to information that is acquired without the mediation of their known senses. I will consider research in parapsychology that throws some light on paranormal phenomena from a cognitive perspective and set out some of the evidence that parapsychologists claim supports the existence of genuine paranormal phenomena. Even if it turns out that paranormal phenomena can be explained through normal mechanisms, because many people have experiences that they interpret as paranormal, scientists have a responsibility to try and understand them. This is *why* parapsychologists conduct research into paranormal phenomena; what about the *how*?

Before proceeding further, let me define some technical terms. Parapsychology is the scientific study of paranormal phenomena and experiences. The neutral term "psi" is often used to describe these phenomena and experiences, which may be further subdivided into two main categories: extrasensory perception (ESP) and psychokinesis (PK). ESP refers to apparent mind-to-mind communication (sometimes the term "telepathy" is used to refer to the same phenomenon). For example, when you are asleep you may have a dream about your sister in Australia and when you wake up the phone rings and it is your sister, saying she had been in an accident and had been thinking about you. Some people would interpret this anecdote as an example of extrasensory communication between you and your sister; others would say the coincidence between the dream and the phone call is just down to chance (see Chapters 8 and 14). If you frequently dream about your sister, then it becomes more likely that your dream will coincide with her phone call by chance alone. PK refers to apparent mind over matter. For example, a gambler may wish for a particular outcome when throwing dice. He might throw hard for a "six" and soft for a "one" face uppermost. If a hard throw coincides with a six face, in line with the gambler's intentions, an observer might conclude that the gambler used PK to alter the way the dice tumbled. Alternatively, it is possible that the desired outcome came about by chance alone, as this outcome would occur anyway on average in one throw out of every six.

Unlike PK experiences, which are quite rare, ESP experiences are relatively common. A recent representative survey of 1,000 members of the British general public found that almost 50 per cent reported that they had sensed when a friend or family member was in trouble (Pechey & Halligan, 2012). However, as the above examples illustrate, it is difficult to get an accurate understanding of what causes such spontaneous paranormal experiences. Our perception and memory is inaccurate, being shaped by our expectations and beliefs. Therefore, our interpretation of events may be distorted or imprecise. If you have a strong *belief* in ESP you may interpret an ambiguous occurrence such as a coincidence between a dream and a phone call as due to ESP. On the other hand, if you have a strong *disbelief* in ESP you may reject the ESP interpretation as improbable or impossible, and presume an alternative interpretation.

In addition, it is very difficult to estimate the role that chance plays in many spontaneous paranormal experiences. Striking coincidences *will* happen by chance alone, but when such a coincidence happens to you personally, it can be very impressive and meaningful. For these reasons, although spontaneous paranormal experiences are valuable in giving us a picture of how these experiences occur naturally, parapsychologists typically conduct research in laboratory conditions in order to gain a better understanding of psi phenomena. This chapter will focus on ESP phenomena because of their apparent similarity to other more orthodox forms of perception and cognition. So how does laboratory research into ESP proceed?

In the laboratory, parapsychologists are better able to isolate and manipulate variables so as to eliminate alternative normal explanations and focus on paranormal explanations. A great deal of care needs to be taken to avoid experimental pitfalls. For example, a typical ESP experiment might involve three individuals:

1. A sender who will view a randomly selected "target" picture and attempt to concentrate on it and send it psychically to the receiver
2. A receiver who will relax and describe the images that come to mind
3. An experimenter who supervises and conducts the experiment

In order to rule out the possibility that normal sensory channels may allow communication from the sender to the receiver, each one is isolated in a separate sound-shielded non-adjacent room monitored by the experimenter. So, shouting or stamping by the sender will not be heard or felt by the receiver. The target, for example an art print or a short video clip, is randomly chosen by a computer after the sender has been placed in the sending room, therefore only the sender knows the target identity. This eliminates the possibility that the experimenter may deliberately or unconsciously pass on cues to the receiver about the target identity. Also, by randomly choosing the target rather than permitting the sender to choose the target, any knowledge of the personal preferences of the sender gives no clues as to the identity of the target. At the end of the sending period, the receiver looks at the target and three decoy targets, not yet knowing the identity of the actual target. The receiver chooses which of the four target possibilities is closest to their mental impressions. The aim is to see if the receiver can correctly identify the target on the basis of there being a stronger correspondence between that picture and the receiver's impressions, compared to the other three pictures. The decoy targets are important, because correspondences can occur between a person's mental impressions and a single target just by chance.

Because the target is randomly chosen from a larger number of possible targets, we can calculate the likelihood of the receiver correctly identifying the target by chance alone. For example, if the target is chosen from four possibilities, then the chance of correctly identifying the target is one in four – that is, 25 per cent. Standard statistical procedures are then used to estimate the likelihood that the obtained results from a number of sending sessions are due to chance alone. If the results exceed what would normally be expected by chance, and other normal means of knowing about the target have been eliminated, then parapsychologists claim evidence of some additional means of communication, ESP, has been provided. However, a single statistically significant experiment is not enough to provide unarguable evidence for the existence of a genuine ESP effect. Scientists require that the effect can be independently replicated, that is, that it can be found by other scientists in other laboratories.

These are some of the ways in which parapsychologists attempt to use laboratory conditions in order to evaluate the possibility that genuine ESP communication occurs. For a more detailed consideration of how to conduct methodologically sound ESP research, see the guidelines by Milton and Wiseman (1997).

We will start by looking at the line of research that suggests there are similarities between subliminal perception and extrasensory perception. Then, we will explore how parapsychologists have employed altered states of consciousness techniques to study ESP. These two research areas have been selected because they are good examples of the model that paranormal cognition operates like our other normal cognitive processes. This suggests that it is appropriate and useful to consider the cognitive perspective for understanding paranormal phenomena. Finally, we will consider some philosophical and methodological issues raised by research into paranormal cognition.

Subliminal perception and ESP

Subliminal perception refers to the perception and processing of information below the "limen" or threshold of conscious awareness. Nowadays, cognitive psychologists studying this phenomenon use the terms "preconscious processing" or "perception without awareness" because research has shown that there is no such thing as a fixed and easily measured sensory threshold. Also, modern cognitive psychologists perhaps wish to distance themselves from the early subliminal perception studies, many of which had methodological flaws. Some rather extravagant claims can be found, for example that audio tapes containing subliminal suggestions can produce weight loss or influence consumers' buying preferences. There is scant evidence that gross human behaviour can be influenced by such complex subliminal messages. Nevertheless, there is good evidence that individuals can perceive and process simple information, such as a single word or a simple line drawing that is presented at levels too weak for conscious awareness. For example, if a simple drawing of a face showing no emotional expression is preceded by a very brief exposure of the word "happy", then the face is more likely to be interpreted as appearing happy.

Many parapsychologists have noted similarities between subliminal perception and extrasensory perception; for a detailed review of this research, see Nash (1986) and Roney-Dougal (1986). Experimental findings both in parapsychology and subliminal perception research indicate that there are wide individual differences in apparent "sensitivity" to subliminal and extrasensory stimulation. A state of dispersed attention or relaxation is known to facilitate sensitivity to subliminal stimulation. Likewise, ESP seems to be facilitated by an increased awareness of internal processes, feelings, and imagery, by relaxation, and by a passive and non-analytical state of mind. These similarities have led to speculation that, once the extrasensory information has reached an individual, it is processed in ways very similar to subliminal information. That is, both extrasensory and weak sensory information initially arrive at an unconscious or preconscious stage of processing. Then, both sorts of information have the potential to emerge into consciousness, subject to various kinds of distortions and transformations along the way. The area in which most research has been conducted into distortions and transformations of weak sensory material concerns defensiveness.

Defensiveness can be defined in several ways. The concept has its origins in psychoanalytic theory, in which the ego uses defence mechanisms to defend itself against anxiety. In contrast, focusing more on the process of defences than on the goal of defences, the cognitive approach conceptualises defence as the cognitive reappraisal of threatening situations, leading to a reduction of subjective threat. Most conceptualisations of defensiveness do, however, share the general notion of the delayed or distorted perception of potentially threatening information.

Although paper-and-pencil measures of defensiveness exist, the measure that we are most concerned with is the Defence Mechanism Test (DMT). In this test, simple pictures depicting a potentially threatening situation are shown for extremely short durations, and after each exposure the participant is asked to describe what they thought they saw. The rationale behind the test is that, at such short durations, individuals can perceive little if anything of the stimulus picture, so they will project something of their own fears and attitudes into their descriptions, in the form of distortions and transformations. A trained scorer checks the individual's descriptions for signs of various kinds of defensiveness.

Martin Johnson was the first parapsychologist to test the idea that individuals who are defensive to weak sensory information may also be resistant to extrasensory information. As he put it: "people who are prone to draw their preconscious blinds in matters of visual perception might act somehow similarly towards perceptions which are extrasensory" (Carpenter, 1965, pp. 70–71). His expectations were confirmed: individuals who showed defensive reactions on the DMT tended to have lower ESP scores than individuals who were not defensive. This led to a series of studies, conducted in Iceland, USA and Holland, comparing DMT and ESP performance. A meta-analysis of these studies (Haraldsson & Houtkooper, 1992) found positive evidence for a DMT-ESP correlation, suggesting that there was indeed a link between subliminal perception and extrasensory perception. This provided formal confirmation of the speculations and observations of parapsychologists that there seemed to be a similarity between subliminal perception and ESP.

I felt that this was an important finding, as it suggested that ESP information was processed according to normal psychological principles. However, there was a need for independent replication of the DMT-ESP studies, and replication attempts were hindered due to difficulties in administering the DMT. I therefore developed an alternative measure of defensiveness that enabled objective scoring of individuals' reactions to weak sensory stimuli. In two studies, I found that defensive individuals tended to have lower scores on the ESP task than individuals who were not defensive (Watt & Morris, 1995). This finding is a conceptual replication of the DMT-ESP studies, and provides converging evidence of the similarity between subliminal perception and ESP. It underlines the claim that normal cognitive processes may be applied to information that is of extrasensory origin.

Altered states of consciousness and ESP

Probably the strongest evidence for ESP comes from a line of research that uses altered states of consciousness (ASCs) to facilitate ESP performance. The idea underlying his work is that normally we live in very distracting, noisy environments, both externally and internally. The ESP information may be akin to a weak signal – if it were a strong signal then we would know all about ESP already and there would be no debate as to its existence. In order to help the receiver notice the weak ESP signal amongst the distracting noise, parapsychologists use noise reduction techniques such as helping the receiver relax physically and mentally. This is known as the "noise reduction" model of ESP (Braud, 1975; Honorton & Harper, 1974).

Parapsychologists use ASC techniques to study ESP because they noticed several converging lines of evidence suggesting that such states of consciousness facilitated ESP. In the late nineteenth century many "spiritual mediums" claimed to be able to obtain information paranormally by going into a trance. More recently, there have been claims that ESP performance could be enhanced by using hypnosis (Honorton & Krippner, 1969). Also, large-scale surveys of spontaneous psychic experiences have found that about two-thirds of cases occurred while the experient was in the dream state (Rhine, 1969). Throughout history there have been accounts of ESP information occurring in dreams. When parapsychologists tested for ESP using sleep laboratories, they were encouraged by positive results (Ullman, Krippner, & Vaughan, 1973). However, it was expensive, inconvenient and time-consuming to conduct dream-ESP research.

As an alternative, parapsychologists decided to use a mild sensory isolation procedure called the "ganzfeld". In this procedure, the receiver is seated for about 30 minutes in a comfortable reclining chair, wearing headphones that play a relaxation tape followed by white noise (a sound like radio static that becomes quite monotonous). The receiver wears goggles and is bathed in red light (see Figure 2.1). The sensation produced by this procedure is of complete, unpatterned stimulation – indeed the word "ganzfeld" comes from the German for "entire field". Under these conditions, the receiver becomes pleasantly relaxed and may even begin to experience hypnagogic imagery – the kind of vivid imagery that may occur when drifting off to sleep. The ganzfeld stimulation helps to reduce sensory distractions and focus the receiver on their internal impressions. The task is for the receiver to correctly identify the ESP target, on the basis of the similarity between the receiver's mental impressions and the target that the sender is simultaneously viewing while the receiver is relaxing in the ganzfeld. The target is usually visual, such as an art print or a video clip, though other targets such as musical pieces have been used. The target is randomly chosen from a large pool of potential targets. The receiver wears a microphone to record their commentary. At the end of the sending period, these impressions are compared with four target possibilities, and the judging proceeds as described above.

Using this technique, parapsychologists have obtained success rates significantly exceeding the 25 per cent one would expect by chance alone when choosing from four alternatives. Many argue that the ganzfeld research provides evidence for ESP (e.g. Bem & Honorton, 1994; Storm, Tressoldi, & Di Risio, 2010a; Utts, 1991), but not all experiments have produced positive results. This has led to a sometimes heated debate over how to interpret the findings of the ganzfeld ESP studies.

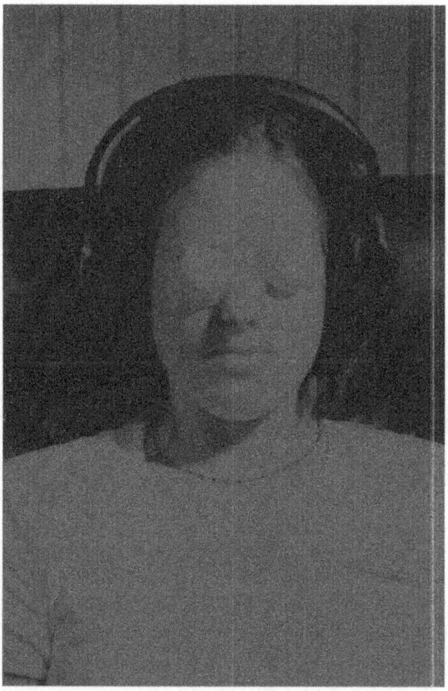

FIGURE 2.1 Participant in a ganzfeld extrasensory perception experiment

Source: Image courtesy of Richard Wiseman.

As we will see, this debate provides a good example of how testing paranormal claims can drive methodological advances, regardless of whether or not paranormal phenomena truly exist.

The ganzfeld debate

The question "Do the ganzfeld ESP studies provide evidence of ESP?" sounds simple. But the answer is rather complicated. To understand why, we first need a brief introduction to the statistical technique called meta-analysis that parapsychologists have employed to assess the combined outcomes of the ganzfeld database. Meta-analysis is an important statistical tool for evaluating the results of groups of studies that seem to demonstrate a weak effect. In meta-analysis, one combines a number of studies using similar methods in order to evaluate the overall size of the effect as well as to detect trends in the combined data that might not be visible in individual studies. The debate over ESP in the ganzfeld began in 1985 when Ray Hyman, a critic of parapsychology, published a meta-analysis of ganzfeld studies that found an overall success rate of 31 per cent, where 25 per cent would be expected by chance. Hyman concluded that this positive effect was due to an "Error Some Place" – that is, to methodological weaknesses rather than extrasensory perception.

In response, Charles Honorton, a successful ganzfeld experimenter, conducted his own meta-analysis of ganzfeld studies and found a 43 per cent success rate. This, he claimed, indicated that the ganzfeld ESP results were a step towards replicability of psi effects. A third meta-analysis was conducted by an independent methodologist, Robert Rosenthal, whose conclusions agreed with Honorton's.

Rather than engaging in further argument over how to interpret past ganzfeld studies, Honorton and Hyman published a joint communiqué in which they agreed upon a set of methodological guidelines to which future ganzfeld studies should adhere (Hyman & Honorton, 1986). Honorton then devised an automated ganzfeld system and a series of 11 experiments with 8 different experimenters was conducted at Honorton's lab, adhering to the methodological guidelines and using the new system. A meta-analysis of these new studies found a 33 per cent success rate overall, a result that would be expected by chance less than one in ten thousand times, which was claimed to provide replicable evidence of psi (Bem & Honorton, 1994).

At this point, it looked as though the debate had been settled. A series of studies had been conducted according to methodological guidelines laid down by a prominent critic, and the analysis of these studies had shown a statistically significant positive effect. However, a further meta-analysis was conducted by Julie Milton (of Edinburgh University's Koestler Parapsychology Unit – KPU) and Richard Wiseman (who had also obtained his PhD at the KPU). Their meta-analysis involved ganzfeld ESP studies conducted after the closure of Honorton's lab and published prior to February 1997 (this date was chosen because the meta-analysis was being submitted in time for the March deadline for a major parapsychology conference). Milton and Wiseman's inclusion criteria yielded 30 studies from 7 independent laboratories, and the results showed only chance success rates. That is, the "new generation" studies appeared to provide no replicable evidence for psi (Milton & Wiseman, 1999). Many parapsychologists reacted angrily to this finding, arguing for instance that Milton and Wiseman had unfairly omitted one very positive study (though that study had not been published at the time Milton and Wiseman were conducting their meta-analysis.)

Other researchers maintained that Milton and Wiseman found chance results because they had included "non-standard" studies (Bem, Palmer, & Broughton, 2001). Milton dealt with this argument constructively by leading a discussion amongst ganzfeld researchers, which revealed little consensus over how one would define the "standard" ganzfeld study (Milton, 1999; Schmeidler & Edge, 1999). Since then, some more positive studies have emerged and claims have again been made that the ganzfeld provides replicable evidence of ESP (Storm, Tressoldi, & di Risio, 2010a). However, Hyman (2010) has again disputed this claim, and the authors have gone on to rebut these criticisms (Storm, Tressoldi, & di Risio, 2010b). Interestingly, Storm and colleagues' meta-analysis also excluded the same study that Milton and Wiseman had omitted, but for different reasons. They eliminated it as a statistical outlier. They were not criticised by parapsychologists for this omission, possibly because their overall results were positive whether or not the study was included. If parapsychologists can move towards prospective meta-analysis (planning a meta-analysis before any data has been collected), progress will be made towards resolving the debate over ESP.

Proof vs. process

Researchers are not simply interested in demonstrating the existence of ESP (known as proof-oriented research); they also need to understand how ESP operates (known as process-oriented research). For example, what kinds of people do particularly well at ESP tasks? What is the mechanism that allows ESP to operate? Is extrasensory information processed in the same way as other kinds of sensory information? Progress in answering these process-oriented questions has been slow, but some patterns are beginning to emerge. For instance, a ganzfeld study in the USA with students from the Juilliard School for the performing arts in New York found remarkably high success rates. 50 per cent of targets were correctly identified, compared to the 25 per cent expected by chance (Schlitz & Honorton, 1992). These results would be found by chance only one in one hundred times. This led to the prediction that creative participants would do well in subsequent studies. Three Koestler Parapsychology Unit ganzfeld studies used creative participants and these confirmed the prediction, with success rates of 41 per cent (Morris, Cunningham, McAlpine, & Taylor, 1993), 33 per cent (Morris, Dalton, Delanoy, & Watt, 1995), and 47 per cent (Dalton, 1997). Other researchers have used meta-analysis to identify which kinds of participants or procedures seem to be associated with positive scoring in ganzfeld studies. Milton and Wiseman (1999), for example, confirmed the observation made by Bem and Honorton (1994) that participants who had practiced some form of mental discipline such as meditation obtained more positive scores in the ganzfeld ESP experiment than other participants. However, they did not confirm the earlier observation that studies using so-called "dynamic" targets (such as film clips) obtained higher scores than those using "static" targets (such as art postcards).

ESP research using the ganzfeld technique illustrates the kinds of methods that parapsychologists are using in order to understand more about extrasensory perception. The noise reduction model has led to a fruitful line of research using altered states of consciousness techniques to facilitate ESP performance. If reasonable levels of ESP performance can be obtained in laboratory conditions, parapsychologists can begin to investigate how ESP works. However, because the ganzfeld procedure requires quite a specialist laboratory setup, relatively few researchers are actively conducting ganzfeld research nowadays. This makes it more difficult to conduct the kind of systematic and programmatic research that is needed to build an understanding of seemingly psi-conducive characteristics.

I have focused here on research with altered states of consciousness techniques and research comparing subliminal with extrasensory perception. There are not the only areas in which parapsychologists are applying psychological principles to the study of paranormal cognition. Indeed, as we saw in Chapter 1, the latest developments in parapsychology, led by Cornell University psychologist Daryl Bem (who has also been influential in ganzfeld ESP research), go further in using variations on established psychological experiments in cognition and memory to test the psi hypothesis (e.g. Bem, 2011).

While the means by which putative extrasensory information reaches an individual are still unknown and may be found to violate currently known physical principles, the evidence just described is consistent with the idea that the processing of ESP information occurs in line with established psychological principles. This should provide some promise that it will in time be possible to reach an understanding of psi with a model that can to some extent integrate psi within existing frameworks. Further discussion of the similarities and differences between psychology and parapsychology can be found in the book by Gertrude Schmeidler (1988).

Learning from parapsychology's challenges

There are a number of complexities in parapsychological research. Some of these concern philosophical issues, others are more methodological in nature. All tend to illustrate how challenging parapsychological research can be. The expertise that parapsychologists develop in responding to these challenges can be usefully applied to other similar fields, for example in behavioural research.

Probably the greatest challenge facing parapsychologists is to find replicable evidence for psi. It is difficult to do this, given that psi seems to be a weak and unreliable effect, and given that parapsychology is a relatively small field with only limited resources to tackle its problems. Like psychology, its studies involve human participants and when humans are involved it is not easy or even realistic to come up with well-established "laws" of behaviour, unlike the physical sciences. This makes replicability difficult, a problem that is faced by behavioural research in general. However, as we have seen, parapsychologists have been among the first to realise the utility of tools such as meta-analysis in dealing with replicability issues. Along with meta-analysis has come an understanding of the importance of related concepts of statistical power and effect size. Parapsychologists have been quick to realise that a measure of effect size is a more accurate indicator of whether or not a study has replicated a claimed effect than the all-or-none indicator of statistical significance.

Another reason why replicability may be difficult in parapsychological research is that the experimental system in parapsychology is an open system. This is true of any research involving human participants: the participant is not an isolated entity that the experimenter impartially observes. Instead, the participant is trying to make sense of the experimental situation and respond in what they think is an appropriate manner. The experimenter can unintentionally affect the participant's behaviour so as to introduce a source of bias into the results. The way researchers deal with this problem is to conduct their research "blind" – that is, keeping both participants and experimenters unaware of the experimental manipulations so that expectations cannot influence behaviour. However, consider the implications of psi research. What if ESP really exists? What if the participant can read the experimenter's mind? What if the experimenter can use PK to directly influence delicate physical instruments? In this case, the experimental environment is even more open than previously thought. If psi is a genuine effect, this has the startling implication that all research is vulnerable to unintended exchange of information and influence. It might be impossible to use completely blind methods because these could be penetrated by ESP. This would mean that all experimental findings could be affected, with perhaps the person having most motivation to find a certain outcome (usually the experimenter) being most likely to influence the experiment.

This scenario does not mean that all experimental research, which attempts to isolate and manipulate variables, is rendered invalid. Instead, it means that researchers have to learn more about how expectancy effects operate, and if psi exists they have to learn more about its limiting conditions. In general, researchers have to become more sophisticated in developing strategies to deal with the study of complex open systems. Parapsychologists are particularly well-placed to develop this expertise, as the question of experimenter influence has a particularly high profile in this field. It is already well-established that certain experimenters consistently achieve positive results, while others consistently achieve null results. The reasons for this "experimenter effect" are yet to be established. One possibility is that it is just a chance pattern. If so, then the pattern would be expected not to appear consistently in future experiments. Some critics have suggested that the successful experimenters are either fraudulent or sloppy so that their positive results are artefacts. However, there seems to be no consistent evidence to support this hypothesis.

Another possibility is that parapsychology's experimenter effect is due to experimenter psi, with some particularly psychic experimenters being able to influence the outcome of the study according to their desires and expectations. There has been some investigation of this possibility, resulting in evidence that successful experimenters do tend to perform well on laboratory psi tasks. Another possibility is that some experimenters are better at eliciting psi from their participants than others – perhaps they are more enthusiastic and more able to help their participants relax and be confident that they can perform well. Also, some experimenters may be more able to recruit the right kind of participants than others. That is, some may be particularly talented in recognising and recruiting participants who are able to perform well under experimental conditions. One ganzfeld experimenter noted that his successful results might have been due to his avoidance of recruiting psychology students as experimental participants, while his less successful co-experimenters did recruit psychology students.

At first glance, it might seem that the ganzfeld debate has generated more heat than light. However, in fact it has helped parapsychologists to make methodological progress. For example, the joint communiqué was used as a blueprint for the design of an influential series of ganzfeld studies. Also, parapsychologists were becoming acquainted with the technique of meta-analysis and associated concepts that are important when assessing study replication way back in 1985, considerably earlier than many psychologists. Also, when we look back at three decades of ganzfeld ESP meta-analyses, we can see that the ganzfeld debate tells us something about the technique of meta-analysis itself. Although meta-analysis at first appears to be an objective tool, because it involves describing and combining experiments quantitatively, in fact there are still many decisions made by the researcher who is conducting the analysis. One key decision is how to set the "inclusion criteria" (the rules about which studies are to be included in the analysis). Each time the meta-analyst makes a decision, there is an opportunity for researcher bias to operate. This is particularly problematic when the researcher already knows the outcome of the studies – and this is nearly always the case in a small field such as parapsychology. If an analyst is motivated to provide evidence for ESP, it is possible for her to shape the meta-analysis so as to maximise the chance of obtaining evidence in support of the ESP hypothesis. On the other hand, the analyst who is sceptical about ESP may make decisions that will lead to the exclusion of positive studies. Parapsychologists are now calling for changes to the way that meta-analysis is conducted (e.g., Kennedy, 2013), and these lessons can be of use to other scientists who are also dependent on meta-analysis to evaluate the outcome of studies with small or unreliable effects.

Parapsychologists have also led the way in minimising questionable research practices (QRPs). QRPs go beyond outright fraud to more subtle ways in which the researcher can nudge his or her study findings towards the desired outcome, including conducting several different analyses and then only reporting the ones that show the "best" results (sometimes known as "data-mining"), and not reporting studies that obtain unwelcome results. This latter QRP is sometimes known as the "file drawer" problem (because researchers decide to leave unwelcome findings in their office file drawer – nowadays probably an electronic rather than a literal drawer). A few psychology journals have recently (since about 2013) started to grapple with QRPs by, for instance, reviewing journal submissions on the basis of the study's planned methodology only, before the study results are known. Nearly four decades before, in 1978, the *European Journal of Parapsychology*, under the combined editorship of Martin Johnson and Sybo Schouten, announced their publication policy was to review papers prior to any data being collected, on the basis of their rationale and methodological quality.

So, perhaps because parapsychology is particularly concerned with replication problems, parapsychologists have been ahead of the game compared to psychologists when devising ways to improve the reliability of research findings. I have been involved in a more recent example of this principle. In 2012, Jim Kennedy and I launched a study registry in parapsychology. Study registration involves placing on public record a plan for how an experiment will be conducted and analysed, crucially before any data is collected. This initiative has two major benefits. First, it helps to identify the file drawer studies, because it will become obvious if a study is registered but later not published. Second, it eliminates data-mining because the analyses are stated in advance of data collection. Furthermore, in running the KPU study registry we have learned many lessons and on the basis of this have published recommendations to improve study registration practices in psychology (Watt & Kennedy, 2015).

We have seen how parapsychologists encounter many challenges when they explore paranormal cognition. In the process they can develop an expertise that can be applied to similar fields with similar problems. Regardless of the reality or otherwise of psi, science has much to gain from investigating paranormal phenomena and experiences.

Suggested further reading

Milton, J., & Wiseman, R. (1997). *Guidelines for Extrasensory Perception Research*. Hatfield: University of Hertfordshire Press.
Schmeidler, G. R. (1988). *Psychology and Parapsychology: Matches and Mismatches*. Jefferson, NC: McFarland.
Watt, C. (2016). *Parapsychology: A Beginner's Guide*. London: Oneworld.

Online educational resources

Koestler Parapsychology Unit website and publication archive: *https://koestlerunit.wordpress.com*
Parapsychological Association website: *www.parapsych.org*
Society for Psychical Research website: *www.spr.ac.uk*
University of Edinburgh online parapsychology course: *https://koestlerunit.wordpress.com/online-course*

3

MEDIUMSHIP AND SURVIVAL

Chris Roe

> *I can call spirits from the vasty deep.*
> *Why, so can I, or so can any man;*
> *But will they come when you do call for them?*
>
> William Shakespeare, Henry IV, Part I

Introduction

Mediums claim to provide evidence for the survival of bodily death. This evidence is usually in the form of physical effects (such as raps, bangs, or movements of objects) that are thought to be caused by discarnate spirits, or in the form of verbal communications that include information that is known only to the deceased person or is characteristic of them when they were alive. Although modern mediumship has its origins in the rise of Spiritualism in the late nineteenth century, it is still very popular today. A recent UK survey (YouGov, 2011) found that 25 per cent of their sample had consulted a psychic or medium, which is similar to the 30 per cent I reported in an earlier survey (Roe, 1998). About half of the YouGov sample had had a reading "for fun", but half regarded it more seriously, and 57 per cent found the information to be accurate. Similarly, when Haraldsson (1985) surveyed people in a number of countries, including the UK, Sweden and Iceland, he found that of those who had attended a séance (a sitting with a medium in order to contact deceased persons), a surprisingly high 83 per cent had found the experience "useful". Over half of respondents (57 per cent) regarded their reading as "quite accurate" or "very accurate", with fewer than 20 per cent describing it as inaccurate. The prevailing scientific world view asserts that human personality is a product of brain activity such that if the brain dies then the personality is annihilated with it, so these kinds of experiences and beliefs present a puzzle to be solved. In this chapter

I will briefly summarise the origins of modern mediumship, consider some of the reasons why a sitting with a medium might seem impressive even if the medium is not able to contact the deceased, and will describe some of the ways in which the claims of mediumship can be tested scientifically, so as to take into account those conventional explanations.

Origins of mediumship

Mediumship has been described by Hunter and Luke (2014, p. 9) as "ancient and ubiquitous across cultures", and they illustrate this by referencing contemporary Shamanistic practices from all continents of the globe. Similarly, communications with the dead are a common feature of human history, from the Biblical account of King Saul's visit to the Witch of Endor to invoke the spirit of the dead prophet Samuel (who foretold his imminent death), to Shakespeare's dramatic use of the three witches to conjure up the spirit of Banquo, to Immanuel Swedenborg's metaphysics that was informed by his many experiences of claimed communications with deceased spirits.

Notwithstanding these references to individuals who were supposed to be able to contact the dead, the beginnings of the Spiritualist movement are usually linked to unusual events that occurred in the home of John Fox in Hydesville, New York, in 1848 (Rush, 1986). Fox shared the house with his wife and two of their daughters who all began to hear raps that seemed to come from chairs, bedsteads, floorboards, and walls. The raps were initially rather random, but became responsive, initially mimicking the number and pattern of hand claps and finger snaps produced by the Fox daughters, Kate and Margaretta, but then occurring in response to instructions or questions. Mrs Fox devised a code (two raps for "yes", silence for "no") that allowed "the ghost" to answer questions. Neighbours were called in who repeated the questioning and added further questions about themselves, receiving correct answers to questions such as the ages of each person present and the number and ages of their children. A neighbour suggested that they call out letters of the alphabet in sequence until the raps responded so that slowly a message could be produced. These communications claimed that the source of the raps was the discarnate spirit of a travelling salesman who had been murdered and whose body had been buried in the cellar of the house. On the second night as many as 300 people were estimated to have been present at the house, organised into "committees" in different parts of the building to question the rapper and to watch for the sources of the phenomena. Eyewitness testimonies were gathered by E. E. Lewis, an attorney from a nearby town, who published his account within weeks of the events (Lewis, 1848). Unsurprisingly, the visitors were particularly interested in the ghost's claim to have been murdered and buried at the house. While one neighbour moved about the cellar, another in the bedroom would ask if this was the location where the body would be found. The raps occurred when the man stood in the middle of the cellar, stopped when he stood anywhere else, but struck up again when he returned to that spot, even though his position would not have been visible to those in the bedroom. Attempts were made to recover the body but these were frustrated by waterlogged ground and it was never found.

Over time it became clear that the phenomena centred not on the house (the supposed site of heinous murder) but on Margaretta and Kate, as the raps followed them when they stayed with relatives. When they were questioned at these times using the alphabet method the responses did not relate to the alleged murder at Hydesville, but seemed to involve communications from deceased persons who were known to the people in attendance, such as their grandparents (Gauld, 1968, p. 8). The girls were quickly inundated with requests from people who were desperate to receive messages from their loved ones who had died. The eldest Fox sister, Leah, spotted a business opportunity, and soon the girls were demonstrating their mediumship all along the Eastern United States.

The cause of the raps had been subject to much speculation. It seems likely that the Fox sisters had been able to produce them by clicking knee or toe joints (Podmore, 1902, p. 184) and many years later Kate and Margaretta confessed to fraud. Although they later recanted those confessions, it is important to note that these confessions included demonstrations of raps that were clearly produced by trickery. However, some commentators have noted that at the time of their confessions the sisters were destitute alcoholics, and this may have been a way to improve their financial situation and satisfy their addiction (Irwin & Watt, 2007, pp. 13–14). Could the original phenomena have been produced by simple joint clicks? The girls do not seem to have been suspected of being responsible – Lewis's original account does not even mention their names, and it seems likely that events were sufficiently disorganised for the girls to be able to move around relatively unnoticed. But even if the girls were responsible for the raps, this still leaves the question of the content of the original messages, which included accurate answers to questions asked spontaneously by members of the crowds who attended. Of course, some answers could have reflected commonly known information, such as how old certain of the neighbours were or how many children they had, but even this might not have been widely known in the community. Other communications are more difficult to explain away. For example, Capron (1855; cited in Gauld, 1968, pp. 8–9) describes tests in which a random number of shells was taken from a basket and held tightly in the hand of one of the investigators, such that no one present knew how many shells there were. Nevertheless the raps were able to provide the correct number. In further tests the girls had to stand barefoot on large feather pillows that might be thought able to muffle any joint clicks, but still raps were heard coming from the floor and wall.

The true source of the Fox sisters' raps is not of crucial concern for this chapter on mediumship because the phenomena were very soon being produced by others. Some of those who had visited Hydesville and witnessed the raps found that the spirits could be encouraged to rap for them at home and answer their questions. By 1854 it was estimated that the Spiritualists' movement had between 1 and 2 million followers across the USA (Stuart, 2005). Very soon interest in mediumship had spread across the Atlantic. As Beloff (1993, p. 40) describes it, "by the mid-1850s, spiritualism had taken Europe by storm so that mediums and 'home circles' were to be found in almost every European country and every stratum of society". The physical phenomena became more elaborate (and perhaps more bizarre), expanding from simple raps and knocks to the movements and even levitations of objects, including heavy furniture, the sudden appearance of objects ostensibly from outside the séance room, and the disappearance of objects from within it, the playing of musical instruments by unseen hands, and even the materialisation of spirit limbs and whole figures.

Early scientific investigations of mediumship

The reported phenomena were remarkable – at times preposterous – but scientifically minded people were drawn to them as a means to establish a scientific basis for matters of faith such as survival of death. Mediumistic phenomena were attractive (in comparison, for example, with accounts of spontaneous experiences such as deathbed visions, or encounters with ghostly apparitions) because they offered the promise that they could be produced on demand in settings that provided some degree of control over the circumstances. In this way, spiritualist phenomena might be amenable to scientific testing and control. Organisations such as the Society for Psychical Research (SPR) were established to examine the phenomena critically and objectively rather than simply dismissing them out of hand. Early investigations took the form of sittings with mediums at which phenomena were carefully observed and details recorded during the session, with later sittings introducing restrictions that would rule out the production of effects by cheating (for example, searching the medium beforehand to ensure that no materials were hidden, and securing the hands and feet to prevent legerdemain). Perhaps the most well-known investigation of a physical medium involved sittings with Eusapia Palladino, an Italian woman who had been orphaned when young and developed mediumistic tendencies soon afterwards (Beloff, 1993, pp. 114–120). Her reputation spread gradually until, in her 30s, she was subjected to a number of investigations by some of the academic elite from the continent (including Cesare Lombroso and Charles Richet). Séances with Palladino usually began in good illumination, but as they progressed conditions deteriorated, so that the only light might come from moonlight or a small lamp used by the note taker. The phenomena grew as the conditions for observation worsened, typically involving noises such as loud bangs on the table, levitations of objects (including the table itself), the appearance of mysterious lights, and sitters reporting being touched or pinched by unseen hands. Although many were impressed, there still seemed to be doubt as to whether all methods of cheating had been prevented, mainly because Palladino was liable to wriggle and squirm during séances in ways that seemed intended to free up an arm or leg that might then cause raps or move objects. When investigators set traps for her by purposely letting go of a hand or foot to see if she would try and take advantage of it, she duly fell into them. Researchers were faced with the dilemma of deciding whether to conclude that because Palladino had been caught cheating on some occasions this therefore rendered suspect all the phenomena she had produced on other occasions ("once a cheat, always a cheat"). Alternatively, it was argued, Palladino's reputation for cheating had in fact ensured that test conditions on many occasions were even more secure and observations even keener than for other investigations; if phenomena still occurred and no cheating was detected then it should be regarded as even more evidential (Feilding, Baggally, & Carrington, 1909). For the most part, sittings with physical mediums were quite unsuccessful and left influential members of the SPR convinced that most, if not all, of the phenomena they had witnessed were fraudulently produced (Gauld, 1968, p. 200); even if on some occasions they had witnessed genuine phenomena, they did not seem amenable to fruitful experimentation.

As the phenomena of physical mediumship became more elaborate and revelations of fraud more scandalous, so researchers turned to the safer and more tractable phenomena of mental mediumship (Beloff, 1993, p. 57). Here, without the distraction of physical effects, the case for survival hinged on the evidentiality of communications that came through the medium. Their evaluation depended on researchers' capacity to determine whether the information was accurate, whether it was specific to the sitter and characteristic of the claimed communicator (rather than being true for most people), and whether it could have been learned of by normal means.

Although, again, some mediums withered under the intense gaze of scientific scrutiny, others were able to produce communications that were difficult to account for by normal means. One celebrated case was that of Mrs Leonora Piper. The eminent psychologist William James, in his Presidential Address to the SPR in 1896, famously asserted:

> a universal proposition can be made untrue by a particular instance. If you wish to upset the law that all crows are black, you mustn't seek to show that no crows are; it is enough if you prove one single crow to be white. My own white crow is Mrs Piper. In the trances of this medium, I cannot resist the conviction that knowledge appears which she has never gained by the ordinary waking use of her eyes, ears and wits.

For James, Piper was the particular instance that disproved the general scientific consensus that survival of bodily death was impossible and that mediums were therefore unable to provide messages from the deceased. Although Piper had had a few parapsychological experiences in childhood, she was quite an unremarkable person until she developed health concerns and visited a medium for healing (Irwin & Watt, 2007). On her second visit she fell into a trance and began to give a message that was apparently from the deceased son of another sitter; thereafter she found that she would enter trance during séances and would communicate messages from the dead, working through a spirit control (a "spirit" that would act as intermediary between the sitters and their deceased relatives) during which time she was apparently oblivious to her surroundings. These controls included famous historical persons such as Longfellow, and also rather anonymous characters who seemed to embody particular qualities, such as a native American girl with the unlikely name of Chlorine, and a French doctor named Phinuit who knew little French and less medicine (though "his" diagnoses of sitters' ailments were often shrewd; Gauld, 1968, pp. 252–268). Nevertheless, the communications produced during James's investigation of Piper were at times very impressive; sitters were previously unknown to her and were introduced under pseudonyms, but 15 of 25 sitters received information that was personal to them. On James's recommendation the British SPR sent Richard Hodgson to America to investigate Piper. He arranged more anonymous sitters, but also employed a private detective to follow her and her family to ensure that she was not gathering intelligence about possible sitters. These produced no evidence of foul play but Hodgson, who had a reputation for exposing fraudulent mediums, was still not satisfied. At his suggestion, Piper was invited to England to participate in further tests. She stayed in the houses of the investigators where her movements could be carefully monitored and her access to information that might be useful when producing messages for sitters was tightly controlled. Nevertheless, many of the sittings were impressive, and Piper's general behaviour was regarded as beyond suspicion, although her spirit controls were notorious for fishing for information when they could get away with it. While some of the spirit controls seemed clearly to be fabrications, others resembled people who had lived and died; one communicator, "GP", was said to resemble the real GP in much the same way that a pen-and-ink sketch can resemble an oil portrait (Gauld, 1968, p. 259). Of 150 sitters to be introduced to GP as spirit control, GP recognised all 30 who were known to him in life and none of the others. Gauld (1982, p. 32) concludes, "Of the mental mediums subject to study . . . she was the first to provide substantial evidence for the possession of some paranormal faculty; the records of her case are still unsurpassed in quantity and detail".

Conventional explanations for mediumistic phenomena

Conventional explanations of impressive physical mediumship demonstrations concentrate on the fallibilities of perception and memory. The séance room provides an environment that is well suited to produce misperceptions that are the result of expectation and suggestion effects – the room is typically only dimly lit so that perceptions of phenomena can be ambiguous, there can be a long delay before anything occurs, by which time concentration might have waned, and because it is difficult to take detailed notes at the time, eyewitnesses' recollections might be susceptible to distortion in ways that make the events seem more impressive than they actually were. These problems were well known to early researchers. For example, Hodgson and Davey (1887) and Besterman (1932) each staged mock séances in which they would know exactly what effects were produced (by trickery) and what methods had been used to achieve them. When they later asked their unsuspecting sitters to write a description of the séance they had just witnessed they found that the accounts were incomplete and failed to mention important events that could indicate how the effects had been produced by normal means. More recently, Wiseman, Smith, and Wiseman (1995) attempted a replication in which participants sat in a large circle in a darkened room, held hands and attempted to psychically move objects marked with luminous paint that had been placed in the centre of the circle. During the sitting two of the objects were made to move via trickery. When asked to recall what they had witnessed, sitters often made errors, including misremembering details that were essential to understanding how the tricks were achieved. Wiseman, Greening, and Smith (2003) went on to look at the effects of verbal suggestion on perception and recall. They used a similar design to their earlier experiment but included objects that did not actually move during the séance; however, the medium leading the séance made statements that suggested that a table had moved while he never gave any indication that a hand bell had moved. When asked two weeks later about what they had witnessed, just over 30 per cent reported that the table had moved but only 10 per cent thought that the hand bell had moved, which suggests that people's perceptions and recall of an event can be distorted by false statements made at the time. Participants with prior belief in the paranormal were more likely to falsely recall that the hand bell had moved, perhaps indicating that suggestions are more likely to be effective where they are consistent with the witness's expectations. If so then we might expect to find that disbelievers are more prone to suggestions that are consistent with their scepticism. Wiseman and colleagues tested this by holding a mock séance in which an object (a slate) did move but the séance leader explicitly stated that it did not, predicting that disbelievers would falsely recall events in line with the suggestion rather than the evidence of their own eyes. In fact there was no difference between believers and disbelievers in their suggestibility. However, the overwhelming majority of participants in this study reported that the slate had not moved, which could mean that the movements that participants were supposed to notice were too subtle – it would be interesting to see if the same effect is achieved with other objects as the target.

The stock explanation for impressive demonstrations of mental mediumship is that they involve the use of *cold reading* (cf. Randi, 1981; Schwartz, 1978). For example, Wiseman (2011, p. 23) claims:

> whether intentionally or unintentionally, most mediums and psychics use a fascinating set of psychological techniques to give the impression that they have a magical insight into the past, present and future. These techniques are referred to as "cold reading".

Hyman (1977) defines cold reading as "a procedure by which a 'reader' is able to persuade a client whom he has never met before that he knows all about the client's personality and problems" (p. 20). It exploits the normal conventions of social interaction to allow the reader to build up a character profile of the client, using shrewd observation, nonverbal and verbal feedback from the client, and the client's natural tendency to try and make sense of the communication in terms that have some personal relevance (Hyman, 1981). In fact, cold reading isn't a single method but rather consists of a set of interchangeable techniques that can vary from case to case depending on opportunity (for a more detailed description, see Roe & Roxburgh, 2013a, 2013b). Some of the more common elements are as follows.

Setting the stage. The success of cold reading often depends on the client's willingness to work hard to interpret or decipher the messages, so it is important to persuade them that the reader is genuine, to engage their active participation in the reading process, and to provide plausible excuses should the reading still not be a success. Thus the reader notes their track record of successful demonstrations, such that any "failures" must inevitably be attributed to the client's muted cooperation. The reader also emphasises that messages that come from the client's loved ones might only make sense to the client, being based on their shared history with the deceased. In this way they are primed to make sense of the ambiguous or cryptic. As Earle (1990, p. 6) notes,

> The best readers always include a statement like, "I only see pieces, as in a jigsaw puzzle. It is up to you to put them together", or, "I may speak of a person being crushed by a house as in The Wizard of Oz, but you recognize it as a friend with overdue mortgage payments".

This opens up the possibilities for the elements to be interpreted in ways that the client regards as accurate. For example, if a reader were to give the statement "I see someone in your family who wore a uniform to work", then this could be interpreted in terms of someone who served in the armed forces, but equally someone who has to wear particular clothing for work such as a chef's shirt or a primary school teacher's tabard. If that symbolic reference does not make immediate sense then this is attributed to the client's faulty memory or failure to recognise the association.

The stock spiel. The staple of the cold reading is a set of prepared phrases that most people are willing to accept as true of them without recognising that they might apply equally well to others. These statements don't require any interaction with the client, so can seem particularly impressive when that lack of contact is a key feature. The stick spiel can include Barnum statements, which have been the subject of study by psychologists for over 60 years. The original Barnum statements were collected by Bertram Forer (1949) from a newsstand astrology book and have been used with great success in psychology studies to show that people tend to readily accept them as true for themselves (Furnham & Schofield, 1987). The original statements are shown in Box 3.1. Their success may be due to their being sufficiently vague to allow the subject to read into them what they want while tending to be positive so as to make acceptance rewarding (Roe, 1995). The Barnum effect is named after the American showman Phineas T. Barnum who is alleged to have attributed the popularity of his circus to it including "a little something for everybody" (cf. Meehl, 1956), a comment which may also apply to Barnum statements themselves.

BOX 3.1 FORER'S ORIGINAL BARNUM STATEMENTS

1. You have a great need for people to like and admire you.
2. You have a tendency to be critical of yourself.
3. You have a great deal of unused capacity which you have not turned to your advantage.
4. While you have some personality weaknesses, you are generally able to compensate for them.
5. Your sexual adjustment has caused some problems for you.
6. Disciplined and self-controlled outside, you tend to be worrisome and insecure inside.
7. At times you have serious doubts as to whether you have made the right decision or done the right thing.
8. You prefer a certain amount of change and variety, and become dissatisfied when hemmed in by restrictions and limitations.
9. You pride yourself as an independent thinker, and don't accept others' statements without satisfactory proof.
10. You have found it unwise to be too frank in revealing yourself to others.
11. At times you are extraverted, affable, sociable, while at other times you are introverted, wary, reserved.
12. Some of your aspirations tend to be pretty unrealistic.
13. Security is one of your major goals in life.

Some people are more accepting of Barnum statements than others, and at times this has been characterised as a "susceptibility" that could be likened to gullibility. However, this would be misleading, and a more accurate characterisation focuses on how people have the capacity and motivation to make sense of communications that are open to interpretation, in particular by "filling in" the semantic gaps without perhaps realising that the gaps have been left there on purpose for us to fill in. To illustrate how good we are at doing this, read the following text (taken from Bransford & Johnson, 1972, p. 719) and see how much sense you can make of it. If you were asked to recall the content, how accurate do you think you would be?

> If the balloons popped, the sound wouldn't be able to carry since everything would be too far away from the correct floor. A closed window would also prevent the sound from carrying, since most buildings tend to be well insulated. Since the whole operation depends on a steady flow of electricity, a break in the middle of the wire would also cause problems. Of course, the fellow could shout, but the human voice is not loud enough to carry that far. An additional problem is that a string could break on the instrument. Then there could be no accompaniment to the message. It is clear that the best situation

> would involve less distance. Then there would be fewer potential problems. With face to face contact, the least number of things could go wrong.

Now read the text again but after taking a look at Figure 3.1, which is included at the end of this chapter. This should illustrate how having an orienting framework (or schema) allow us to imbue material with meaning, shaping our understanding of what is meant and helping us to decide what to encode (commit to memory). With Barnum statements that schema is provided by the expectation that the material will describe ourselves and our circumstances so we make sense of it in relation to the vast amount we already know about those things. Randi (1981) illustrates this when he describes how the psychic Geraldine Smith gave a demonstration on Canadian TV by reporting impressions she received from an object belonging to the host of a Canadian TV show. She said "I'm seeing the month of January here – which is now – but there would have to be something strong with the person with January as well" (p. 107). The host was sceptical of the reading as a whole, but recalled that Smith had correctly determined that his birthday was in January; in fact, no mention had been made of what type of association with January was being referred to – the client was left to fill in the gaps.

Selective recall can also apply at the level of whole statements that can be used as part of a "scatter gun" approach, in which the reader makes a large number of statements in the expectation that at least some will hit the target and so will be memorable to the sitter, while those that miss will be safely forgotten. Stollznow (2011) characterises the performance of medium Rebecca Rosen in terms of this approach:

> To give the illusion of accuracy, Rosen would mention non-specific items that gave the appearance of specificity. She mentioned a number of objects and occurrences that could apply to most people: a ring with a reset stone, a necklace with a broken clasp, a broken zipper, trouble with someone's toilet [. . .] a broken microwave, a broken phone, carrying spare change, and seeing a bear, coyote or deer in someone's backyard or garage (not uncommon in Colorado).

Rowland (2002) similarly offers: a box of unsorted old photographs; old medicines well past their use-by date; at least one toy or book kept as a childhood memento; consecutive issues of a magazine no longer subscribed to; and an item of clothing that was bought new but has never been worn. In keeping with this, there is some (limited) empirical evidence to suggest that clients of psychic readings do tend to recall more of the reading elements which they rated as accurate than those items rated inaccurate (Roe, 1994).

Pigeon-holing. Stock spiel statements are necessarily general, even though interpretation by the client is claimed to make them seem more impressive. To narrow down the number of topic areas that could possibly be relevant, the reader can assign the client to a category and draw on a stereotype for that sub-population that can pick out interests or concerns that are more common among that group. The main distinctions are made according to the sex and age of the client. For example, Webster (1990) describes how for younger sitters, he portrays a very positive, optimistic future (but still within the realms of possibility). From the age of 30 to 35, however, clients "start to realise that the dreams they had will never eventuate", so for an older person he offers the more realistic "money hasn't always been easy. You've had to work pretty hard to get where you have" and he predicts more moderate achievements gained through effort rather than good fortune. For much older sitters, the real concern is with loneliness as much as it is with poverty, so it is always worthwhile to describe how they won't be alone in their old age. Further information can be gleaned from the client's clothing, physical features, carriage and manner of speech which can point more specifically to their past history and future aspirations. If the reading is held in the client's home, then themes found in collections of ornaments, pictures, or books will also indicate some hobbies, interests, and aspirations. These will help the reader to assign the client to a narrower and presumably more accurate category. The reader should not necessarily ignore very obvious sources of intelligence; as Hobrin (1990) notes, "you may be surprised to learn the number of people who forget that they are wearing their birth sign or name around their neck. They say familiarity breeds contempt; I'd say that it breeds forgetfulness [. . .] never overlook the obvious". Simple observation can also provide the reader with titbits which can appear to be remarkably insightful. Selected examples that give a flavour of the kind of information which can be gleaned include: ridges in a belt may indicate fluctuations in weight; a worn left heel (reversed in Britain) indicates a lot of time driving, perhaps with work; tall women tend to dislike their feet (as too big) especially when they were younger; a mole or birthmark on the neck or shoulder is usually accompanied by one on the back, usually lower back (drawn from Martin, 1990).

"True" cold reading and fishing. The stock spiel can be refined by taking advantage of the nonverbal responses that the client gives up as they listen to the medium. For example, if the medium were to declare "I'm getting something about an illness that's affecting one of the younger members of the family; this could be a son or daughter, maybe a nephew or niece" the client need only respond positively to the word "son" or "daughter" or "nephew" or "niece" to confirm that there are such members of their family. If the response is not strong then this can be dismissed as a trivial ailment that will soon clear up (and that member of the family can safely be talked about in relation to other topics), but if the response is strong then the medium knows that the condition is more serious. The decision as to how to proceed depends on an ability to "read" the client's reaction, reflecting the fact that in normal conversation, the speaker looks only intermittently at the listener, especially toward the end of utterances, to see if they are still interested in what is being said, and to gauge whether the listener wishes to take a turn as speaker (Duncan & Fiske, 1977). The listener reacts to this cue by producing "back-channel signals" (Wiener et al., 1972), such as vocalisations (including uh-huh's and similar nonverbal sounds – Argyle, 1988), facially through smiles (Brunner, 1979), and posturally through head nods, forward or sideways lean and drawing the legs back (Bull, 1987). Negative reactions can be signalled through frowning (Argyle, 1988), lowering the

head or turning the head away, as well as adopting characteristics of a closed posture, such as folded arms (Bull, 1987). Pseudopsychics can use these (generally unconscious) responses to gauge the appropriateness of what they are saying and steer the reading accordingly.

Greasley (2000, p. 47) gives the following examples of the effects of positive and negative feedback respectively

medium:	But with the gentleman – he must have gone rather quickly, didn't he?
sitter:	Yes he did – very.
medium:	'Cause he says I was here one minute and gone the next – so you understand it all?
medium:	Did you actually talk about moving at one stage?
sitter:	(pause) Erm.
medium:	Well he says you were a bit unsettled at one stage.
sitter:	(no response)
medium:	You thought about having a change – not particularly moving. . .

However, this haphazard method is unlikely to naturally produce all the information the reader wants to know. Other data will have to be teased out through "fishing", in which the client unwittingly gives up information about themselves without realising they have done so. This can be in the form of direct questions (e.g. "Have you been thinking about a career change?") with the intention of storing away any response to be fed back to the client later in a different form as "new" information. For example, Schwartz (1978) describes a performance by Peter Hurkos in which the efforts made by the client to make sense of a statement are quite explicit:

Hurkos:	One two three four five – I see five in the family.
Caller:	That's right. There are four of us and Uncle Raymond, who often stays with us.

Cold reading can be very impressive to witness, and can lead to very specific readings for which the client can recall only the impressive endpoints in the reading without remembering the quite sophisticated manoeuvring that got them there. Some very interesting analyses have been given of psychic reading transcripts that seem to illustrate its use in practice (e.g. Greasley, 2000; Schwartz, 1978), but these analyses have been conducted after the fact and so haven't set out to test hypotheses. There are surprisingly few experimental tests that have been designed to test the claimed effects of cold reading, and therefore this can only be regarded as a plausible but unproven explanation.

Modern controlled tests

Although these explanations of impressive mediumistic communications in terms of cold reading remain unproven, more formal experimental tests of mediumship have been designed to effectively rule out such factors. To rule out the possibility that the medium is (perhaps unwittingly) pigeon-holing the client, a barrier can be placed between them that prevents the medium from accessing visual cues about the sitter's sex, age, and demeanour. And to preclude readings from being tailored in response to client (usually nonverbal) feedback, the medium and client can be separated visually and auditorily during the reading. It is important that these boundaries are not compromised by the experimenters themselves – if they know the client and their history, then they might also respond nonverbally to the medium's statements in a way that would allow for cold reading. For this reason, most experimental tests of mediumship are *double blind*, which means that not only does the medium have no contact with the client during the test, but neither does the experimenter who interacts with the medium (a second experimenter would interact with the client).

For example, Beischel and Schwartz (2007) recruited eight mediums, each of whom gave readings for participants that they never met (all were students who had experienced the death of a parent or peer with whom they were "very close"). The participants were paired so as to optimise the differences in the characteristics of the deceased person they wished to contact. Each of the eight mediums performed two readings: one for each sitter in a pair. These readings were given to a "proxy sitter", that is someone to take the place of the intended recipient so the medium has a focal person to interact with, but both parties know that the proxy sitter does not know the intended recipient or the deceased person they wish to contact. The medium was only given the deceased person's first name and was asked to report any information they received from them. They were then asked four specific questions about the named discarnate's physical appearance, personality, hobbies, and cause of death. Finally they were asked, "Does the discarnate have any comments, questions, or requests for the sitter?" Each reading was transcribed and a corresponding numbered list of individual items (i.e. separate, stand-alone pieces of information) was created by an experimenter blind to details about the sitters or discarnates. As we have seen, people are very good at interpreting material as personally relevant when they believe that it is intended for them. To control for that bias, as well as scoring the reading intended for him/her each sitter also scored the reading by that medium intended for the other sitter in their pair, without knowing which reading was which. In this way, any tendency to read meaning into the transcript should be as likely for the decoy reading as it is for the reading intended for them. Overall ratings were given using a 0–6 scale (where 0 = No correct information or communication; 3 = Mixture of correct and incorrect information, but enough correct information to indicate that communication with the deceased occurred; and 6 = Excellent reading, including strong aspects of communication, and with essentially no incorrect information). Even under these stringent conditions, which did not allow for direct contact between medium and sitter, the mean rating for the intended readings was 3.56; although this was not extremely accurate, it was still significantly higher than for the control readings of 1.94. When asked to choose which reading was more applicable to them, sitters chose the readings intended for them 81 per cent of the time. Schwartz, Beischel, and colleagues have reported a number of broadly similar studies that also claim above chance performance (e.g. Schwartz, Russek, & Barentsen, 2002; Schwartz, Russek, Nelson, & Barentsen, 2001; see Beischel & Zingrone, 2015, for a review).

In the UK, Robertson and Roy have reported on three studies of mediumship. In the first of these (Robertson & Roy, 2001) they described a double blind procedure in which they could test the sceptical claim that statements made by mediums are so general that they could as readily be accepted by people who were not the intended recipients. Records were made of the statements made by 10 mediums during demonstrations of mediumship, and the acceptance ratings given by 44 intended recipients were compared with applicability ratings given by 407 others who attended the demonstration but did not receive a message intended for them (termed the non-recipients). Whereas the intended recipients accepted 65 per cent of their statements as applicable only 13 per cent of the non-recipients were able to accept them, a difference that was highly significant. However, in this initial study not only did the medium face his or her audience and identify the person for whom the message was meant, so that they might have benefited from verbal feedback from them, but the intended recipient knew that the messages were intended for them and so might have been more motivated to make sense of them. These issues were addressed in a second study (Roy & Robertson, 2001) in which the medium was placed behind a screen so that they could not see any of the participants. The intended recipient of a message was chosen by selecting a number at random with the numbers corresponding to particular participant seats. Once a recipient had been selected, the medium began the reading without knowing for whom it was intended and without being able to see the audience reactions. The reading was given verbally and transcribed by one of the experimenters. The transcript was photocopied and given out to all participants who rated the applicability of the reading statement by statement. This design not only ensures that the medium cannot get feedback from the recipient of the message but also that recipients and non-recipients do not know whether the message was intended for them. Although the weighted analysis is quite dense, it does show that the applicability ratings from intended recipients were significantly higher than for non-recipients (Roy & Robertson, 2004).

Not all experimental tests have been successful. O'Keeffe & Wiseman (2005) recruited five mediums who each gave readings for five sitters drawn from university staff and students who were chosen on the basis that they did not know each other but were relatively similar (in age and gender). Each medium attended for one day during which the five sitters attended sessions in a randomised order. The medium and sitters never met but were located in different rooms in the laboratory. The medium was asked to attempt to contact one or more spirit(s) associated with the sitter and relate any information that they believed appropriate. They were allowed to say as much or as little as they wished during the 60-minute sitting. All of these comments were recorded on videotape. Meanwhile the sitter for that session was provided with headphones and listened to music of their choice for the duration of the reading. Once all five experimental days had been completed, the readings were transcribed from the videotapes and the transcripts were separated into a series of statements. All statements from every sitting were sent to each sitter, who rated them for applicability (from 1 = not applicable, to 7 = very applicable). An overall score could thereby be calculated for each reading by summing the individual ratings assigned to each of the statements making up that reading. Analysis showed that the sitters did not give higher ratings to readings that were intended for them, compared with the ratings given by the other sitters (for whom the reading was not intended).

Although the findings when taken together seem promising, it is difficult to draw any firm conclusions from so few studies. (Beischel and Zingrone [2015] report that just 11 quantitative studies that test the claims of mediumship have been published in the last 15 years.) Given the public's interest in the question of survival of death and the possibility of communicating with loved ones, and the difficulties in differentiating between genuine mediumship (if such is possible) and cold reading techniques, there clearly is a need for more extensive and systematic research into this topic.

FIGURE 3.1 Sketch to help make sense of the text on pages 27–28.

Source: Adapted from Bransford & Johnson (1972).

4

POSSESSION AND EXORCISM

Christopher C. French

> *The only devils in this world are those running around in our own hearts, and that is where all our battles should be fought.*
>
> Mahatma Ghandi

Introduction

A good case can be made that human beings are naturally intuitive dualists. For a number of reasons, we find it hard to believe that our subjective self-awareness is nothing more than complex patterns of neural activity and easy to believe, along with the great mathematician and philosopher René Descartes, that mind-stuff is irreducibly different to matter. This dualist position raises as many philosophical problems – perhaps even more – than it answers but, for my money, no one has yet solved the so-called "hard problem", i.e. explained how it is that consciousness can arise from atoms and molecules in the brain presumably interacting in line with the same laws of nature that govern the atoms and molecules in stones, clouds, stars and pancakes (see e.g. Blackmore, 2004; Chalmers, 1995).

One consequence of such a dualist approach is that we find it easy to believe that each of us has a soul or spirit (Bering, 2011). Indeed, many people believe that this soul or spirit actually survives bodily death in some way, either by transferring to another realm, such as heaven (or the other place), or by hanging about for a while and then entering another human body, usually at the moment of conception (see Chapter 7 on Reincarnation in this volume). Some people believe that souls sometimes hang around on the earthly plane and continue to interact with the living. If any of these beliefs are true, this would provide the ultimate confirmation that mind and brain are indeed separable and dualism is correct. Under normal circumstances, the mind inhabits and controls the physical body in much the same way that a person drives a car but in some circumstances – notably death

(Blackmore, 1993) and out-of-body experiences (Blackmore, 1982) – the mind, it is claimed, can separate from the body.

It is clear to see why such belief systems would be attractive to most people, reassuring us that physical death is not the end, either for us or our loved ones. But there is also a dark side to such belief systems. If we can survive as incorporeal souls, what other spiritual beings might also be out there? What can we know about their intentions towards us? And, perhaps most worryingly of all, is it possible that they might sometimes be able to take over our physical bodies? The idea of possession can be found in many societies around the world, both geographically and historically (Levack, 2013; Spanos, 1996; Spanos & Gottlieb, 1979).

Is it possible that possession, as traditionally understood, is a genuine paranormal phenomenon that defies understanding in conventional scientific terms? Or might it be more plausibly explained in terms of psychological factors?

Before attempting to answer this question it is useful to define our terms a little more precisely and also to provide a broader context for considering possession and exorcism. As we will see, there is a range of phenomena that appear to the casual observer to involve a radical transformation of another's personality and behaviour. Let us start then with a couple of definitions from the late Michael Thalbourne's (2003) *[A] Glossary of Terms Used in Parapsychology*:

> **Possession**: The complete control, by an *ostensible discarnate entity*, of the body of a living person.
> **Discarnate entity**: A disembodied being, as opposed to an incarnate one; the surviving personality of a deceased individual or non-human entity; a *spirit*.

And from the Merriam-Webster online dictionary:

> **Exorcise**: To force (an evil spirit) to leave.

But let us not forget that there are several other phenomena that appear to the casual observer to involve such radical transformation of another's personality and behaviour, including:

> **Channelling**: A phenomenon in which, according to Arthur Hastings (1990, p. 99), "a person purports to transmit information or messages directly from a personality or consciousness other than his or her own, usually through *automatic writing* or *trance* speaking; this other personality usually claims to be a nonphysical *spirit* or being" (Thalbourne, 2003).

Note that the main difference between possession and channelling as usually understood is simply that the latter is believed to be more under the control of the channeller insofar as he or she can retake control of the physical body at any time. In some cultures, benign forms of possession appear to be under similar control by shamans and others who invite possession by spirits through ritual and other means.

And then we have (from Wikipedia):

> **Dissociative Identity Disorder (DID)**, previously known as **Multiple Personality Disorder (MPD)**, is a mental disorder on the dissociative spectrum characterized by at least two distinct and relatively enduring identities or dissociated personality states that alternately control a person's behaviour, and is accompanied by memory impairment for important information not explained by ordinary forgetfulness.

As the Wikipedia entry goes on to point out, "DID is one of the most controversial psychiatric disorders with no clear consensus regarding its diagnosis and treatment". That is certainly true with many commentators convinced that this disorder is purely iatrogenic, i.e. inadvertently produced by the therapy itself (e.g. Spanos, 1996; Nathan, 2011). The point here is that, to the outside observer, the patient appears to have at least two distinct personalities, each of which will have different voices, mannerisms, likes and dislikes, and even (allegedly) memories.

Thalbourne (2003) provides the following definition of so-called past-life regression:

> **Past-life regression**: A process in which a hypnotized person is mentally "taken back" (or "regressed") by the *hypnotist* to one or more apparent previous lifetimes, thus suggesting *reincarnation*.

Again, while in the allegedly regressed state, the subject appears to be a completely different person.

We could also include the phenomenon of stage hypnotists giving subjects the hypnotic suggestion that they are someone or something else including celebrities, animals and even aliens (who might then apparently converse fluently in Venusian) – again, people apparently taking on a completely different personality. Another common example of a dramatic change in personality and behaviour brought about by the use of hypnosis is hypnotic regression back to childhood. Although, to the casual observer, it appears that a grown adult is behaving like a child, with appropriate changes in behaviour, voice, vocabulary and mannerisms, more careful analysis reveals that the hypnotic subject is actually behaving the way that adults *think* a child of that age would behave and not how a child of that age would actually behave (Spanos, 1996).

Thus we can see that possession is by no means the only phenomenon that involves dramatic changes in behaviour implying that a person may have been somehow "taken over" either by an outside entity or else by a different part of themselves. Although I am only going to focus on the phenomenon of possession in this chapter, much of what I have to say will be of relevance to this whole range of phenomena.

Levels of belief in possession in US adults

Belief in possession and related phenomena is not rare even in modern Western societies, as demonstrated by these results from a YouGov survey of 1000 US adults interviewed in September 2013 (https://today.yougov.com/news/2013/09/17/poll-results-exorcism/):

Do you personally believe in the existence of the Devil or not?
Yes 57%
No 28%
Don't know . . . 15%

Do you believe someone can be possessed by the devil or some other evil spirit?
Yes 51%
No 28%
Don't know . . . 20%

How often do you think people are possessed by the devil?
Very Frequently . . . 6%
Frequently 9%
Occasionally 29%
Rarely 45%
Never 11%

Some churches have a ceremony called "exorcism", which is designed to drive the Devil or evil spirits out of a person. Do you believe in the power of exorcism or not?
Yes, I believe in the power of exorcism 46%
No, I don't believe in the power of exorcism . . 19%
Don't know 36%

So, what is the basis for such beliefs? As with many complex allegedly paranormal phenomena, it would be a mistake to expect there to be a "one-size-fits-all" psychological explanation of possession. Instead, a number of different psychological factors can produce behaviour that to the outside observer, and perhaps even to the person themselves, is indicative of possession. We can break these down into two broad categories: neuropathological factors (Beyerstein, 1988, 1996, 2007) and sociocognitive factors (Spanos, 1996). In the past, certain neurological conditions, notably some forms of epilepsy and Tourette's syndrome, would have very naturally been interpreted as possession. Sadly, such interpretations can still be found even in modern times within some communities. There can be little doubt that such conditions would lead observers and perhaps even the sufferers themselves to believe that some outside agency could take control of their actions and make them behave in bizarre and socially unacceptable ways.

Having said that, it is not reasonable to argue that all cases of apparent possession could be explained in neurological terms. In fact, the vast majority are undoubtedly better explained in sociocognitive terms, i.e. in terms of the apparently possessed person taking on a learned role for various reasons. This broad distinction between neuropathological factors and sociocognitive factors should also remind us that in some cases a person can end up being thought of as "possessed" as a result of involuntary behaviour that is completely beyond their control. At the other extreme are those who deliberately take on the role for a variety of reasons. Some of these cases will be deliberate hoaxes such as, in all probability, the case that directly inspired the bestselling book and successful movie *The Exorcist* (Nickell, 2001; Opsasnick, 2000). Finally, there will be many cases that lie somewhere in between these two extremes.

Neuropathological factors

In this section, I am going to mainly concentrate on epilepsy and Tourette's syndrome as examples of medical conditions that in the past would have been seen as evidence of possession, but some commentators would also include a number of other conditions including some forms of schizophrenia, common conditions such as migraine and somnambulism (sleep-walking), and esoteric disorders such as alien hand syndrome.

Let us begin with a quotation from the Bible:

> And one of the multitude . . . said, "Master, I have brought unto Thee my son, which hath a dumb spirit; and wheresoever he taketh him, he teareth him: and he foameth, and gnasheth with his teeth, and pineth away . . . and ofttimes it hath cast him into the fire, and the waters, to destroy him: but if thou canst do any thing, have compassion on us and help us". (Mark 9:17–22)

To modern eyes, this is clearly a description of someone suffering from epilepsy but in Jesus's time, it would be natural to think in terms of possession by demons despite the fact that 400 years earlier Hippocrates himself had argued in *The Sacred Disease* that such symptoms were not indicative of demonic possession but were in fact due to brain disease.

So-called "seizures" can be caused by a variety of genetic, medical, biochemical, and environmental factors but simply having a seizure is not necessarily indicative of epilepsy. For example, a one-off seizure as a result of a fever or a drug overdose would not lead to a diagnosis of epilepsy. Although definitions vary somewhat, the diagnosis of epilepsy is reserved for people who suffer from repeated, unprovoked seizures.

Seizures are typically associated with "a disorderly, paroxysmal neural discharge that produces distinctive 'spiking' in the EEG" (Beyerstein, 1988, p. 250). This abnormal activity may be localised or may spread to engulf the entire brain causing a generalised seizure. Importantly, it should be noted that not all seizures are associated with such abnormal brain activity. In addition to non-epileptic physical causes, such as stroke or migraine, some dramatic convulsions are believed to be intentional simulations engaged in for purely psychological reasons (e.g. secondary gains and/or malingering).

Generalised seizures typically begin with a cry, collapse and unconsciousness. As the abnormal neural activity sweeps across the motor cortex, muscles are activated indiscriminately and uncontrolled thrashing of limbs occurs. Other typical symptoms include oral spasms causing protrusion of the tongue and foaming at the mouth, respiratory paralysis, and incontinence. The convulsions typically subside after a minute or so, often followed by a coma lasting up to half an hour. Not all epileptic seizures are so dramatic. Epileptic discharges in the reticular system that controls arousal levels can cause absence seizures that may result in nothing more than rhythmic eye-blinking and a temporary loss of consciousness. This may well go completely unnoticed to outside observers and even to the victim themselves. Focal seizures remain localised to one area of the brain, most often the temporal lobes or the frontal lobes.

Turning now to Tourette's syndrome, it is worth noting that the first description of Tourette's syndrome is thought to be that given in the book *Malleus Meleficarum* ("Witch's hammer") by Jakob Sprenger and Heinrich Kraemer, published in the late fifteenth century. This book was essentially a guide to assist in the identification and prosecution of witches. The text in question describes a priest whose tics were thought to indicate possession by the devil. In fact, Tourette's syndrome is an inherited neuropsychiatric disorder of unknown cause. It is characterised by numerous physical tics and at least one vocal tic. It is not as rare as was once thought and usually begins in early childhood and often remits with age. It varies in severity from mild to severe but most cases are mild and do not require treatment. Although most people associate Tourette's with obscene vocal outbursts, in fact only a minority (about 10 per cent) of sufferers exhibit that particular symptom. Having said that, it is this particular symptom that is most likely to have been interpreted as an indication of demonic possession in days gone by.

It is easy to see how, in past ages, outside observers may have interpreted such bizarre behaviour in terms of possession of the sufferer's physical body by a spiritual entity. Interestingly, the sufferers themselves typically have a somewhat different perspective. The physical and vocal tics that they exhibit are, in fact, at least partially under their control. They are often preceded by an unwanted premonitory urge, i.e. they feel the need to express the tic in a similar way to the way that you might feel the need to scratch an itch. To some extent they can suppress the urge, but the tension to allow it to be released grows until eventually the tic manifests itself. Suppressing the tics is mentally exhausting for sufferers.

Sociocognitive factors

Now although such neuropsychiatric conditions may have reinforced belief in possession in past ages (and indeed continue to do so in some cultures), it seems highly unlikely that such factors could account for all historical and contemporary cases of alleged possession. To explain the remaining cases, we should consider sociocognitive factors. The sociocognitive perspective is most commonly associated with a particular approach to explaining hypnotic phenomena, an approach which rejects the idea that such phenomena are best explained in terms of the hypnotic trance as a special and unique altered state of consciousness, as different from normal waking consciousness as, say, dreaming is. In contrast, the sociocognitive theorists believe that the whole range of so-called hypnotic phenomena can be explained in much more mundane terms by invoking such psychological factors as attitudes, expectancies, beliefs, compliance, imagination, attention, concentration, distraction, and relaxation (Wagstaff, 1995).

This is how the late Nick Spanos explains hypnosis in sociocognitive terms (1996, pp. 19–20):

> *hypnosis* refers not to a state or condition of the person but to the historically rooted conceptions of hypnosis and hypnotic responding that are held by the participants in the mini-drama that is labelled the hypnotic situation. According to this perspective, hypnotic responding is context dependent; it is determined by the willingness of subjects to adopt the hypnotic role, by their understanding of how role requirements change as the situation unfolds, by how they interpret the complex and sometimes ambiguous communications that constitute hypnotic suggestions, by their willingness and ability to use their imaginal and other cognitive skills to create the subjective experiences called for by suggestions, and by how feedback from the hypnotist and from their own responding influences the definitions they hold of themselves as hypnotic subjects and the interpretations they apply to their hypnotic experiences.

Now, re-read that paragraph but substitute the words "possession" for "hypnosis", "possessed" for "hypnotised", and so on in order to appreciate the relevance of the sociocognitive perspective in explaining the majority of cases of alleged possession that do not involve neuropathology (see also Spanos, 1989, 1996; Spanos & Gottlieb, 1979).

Sadly, Nick Spanos died in a plane crash after submitting his magnum opus, *Multiple Identities & False Memories: A Sociocognitive Perspective*, to the publisher, but before he had the chance to make any revisions in response to editorial review. Fortunately, his colleagues took on that role for him. This book draws together much of his prior theoretical and empirical work into topics such as hypnosis, false memories, alien abduction, past-life regression, possession, and dissociation. This section of this chapter draws heavily on Spanos's book, particularly the third section of the book dealing with *Multiple Identities in Other Cultures and Times*.

The book makes it clear that the full range of phenomena listed at the beginning of this chapter can be explained by adopting the sociocognitive perspective. If we consider possession from a cross-cultural perspective, it is also clear that possession is not always negative and unwanted. In many contexts, the state is brought about deliberately. One relatively common example of this in Western Christian societies is glossolalia, also known as "speaking in tongues". Glossolalia involves the vocalisation of meaningless phonetic combinations that may sometimes be mistaken for a foreign language.

According to Dr William T. Samarin, professor of anthropology and linguistics at the University of Toronto, "glossolalia consists of strings of meaningless syllables made up of sounds taken from those familiar to the speaker and put together more or less haphazardly. . . . Glossolalia is language-like because the speaker unconsciously wants it to be language-like. Yet in spite of superficial similarities, glossolalia fundamentally is not language" (quoted in Nickell, 1993, p. 108; see also Samarin, 1972).

It may be accompanied by convulsions, profuse sweating, eye closure and apparent loss of consciousness but this is not always the case. Whether or not such dramatic displays accompany the glossolalia depends entirely upon the expectations of the glossolalic and their audience. Newberg, Wintering, Morgan, and Waldman (2006) reported the results of a preliminary SPECT study measuring regional cerebral blood flow in a group of five Christian women engaged in glossolalia. As a control condition involving similar movements, the women sang gospel songs. The main finding from the study was reduced blood flow to the frontal lobes associated with glossolalia, consistent with the notion that the glossolalic state is associated with reduced conscious control.

Glossolalia is typically interpreted by Christians as possession by the Holy Spirit, who supposedly speaks his own language through the possessed individual. Glossolalics typically claim that they do not remember what happened during the episode and their utterances often have to be interpreted by a third party, typically a church leader who allegedly has the "gift" of interpretation. In fact, the vocalisations have no linguistic structure whatsoever and are completely meaningless, leaving the interpreter to include whatever they like in their interpretation. It is perhaps not surprising therefore that the interpretations tend to support the central tenets of the particular religious group in question.

Glossolalia is a learned behaviour (Spanos, Cross, Lepage, & Coristine, 1986) and glossolalics do not show heightened levels of hypnotic susceptibility, absorption, or measures of psychopathology (Spanos & Hewitt, 1979). The rate at which glossolalia occurs varies dramatically in line with the expectations of the religious communities concerned as does the form it takes. In religious communities that encourage the practice, there are plenty of opportunities to observe the behaviour in others during religious services and much praise for those who actually perform. The first manifestation of glossolalia is often interpreted as a sign of salvation allowing full acceptance into the religious group. Newly initiated members often reconstruct their biographies to accentuate the differences between their post- and pre-conversion lives, the former being blessed and pure and the latter, full of sin.

Considering possession more generally, Spanos (1996, p. 147) points out, "The characteristics of possession displays in other cultures ... vary greatly both among societies and within societies. Possession is not a unitary phenomenon and differs dramatically depending on the status of the possessed person, the context in which the possession occurs, and the meaning attributed to the possession both by the possessed individual and by his or her audience".

In many societies, possession is deliberately invited as part of healing rituals. The medium becomes possessed and it is then the spirit who actually diagnoses the problem and recommends treatment, along with general advice for dealing with life's problems. The rituals may be one-to-one consultations or public ceremonies.

They clearly illustrate the rule-governed nature of social interactions involving possession. Both the possessed individual and the patient and audience are well aware of their roles and act accordingly.

Different phases of the possession are clearly signalled to the audience who respond accordingly. In Spanos's (1996, p. 148) words:

> the transition from the medium's human personality to that of a spirit is marked by readily identifiable signs (e.g., shaking, eye closure) that the audience has learned to interpret in terms of spirit possession. Similarly, the transition from one spirit identity to another is marked by recognizable changes in behaviour such as changes in voice, personality, and dress. In some cultures, particular spirits dance to some tunes but not others, and in other cultures each change in spirit identity in marked by replacing a scarf of one colour with a scarf of another. When behaving as a warrior spirit, the medium struts to and fro in an aggressive and threatening manner, and the audience responds accordingly by being quiet and respectful. When presenting as a tiger spirit, the medium may walk on all fours and growl while the audience backs away. When presenting as a risqué spirit, the medium jokes with the audience, which responds with relaxation and laughter. The result of these mutually supporting interactions is the construction of spirit possession as a social reality.

Lewis (1987) made a distinction between central and peripheral possession. In central possession, the person possessed is typically a respected member of the community, the possessing spirit is a major deity, and the performance serves to reinforce the central values of the society. In contrast, in peripheral possession the person possessed is a socially marginal and powerless member of society and the possessing spirit is often capricious and amoral. Peripheral possession is typically associated with illness and distress on the part of the possessed and the initial signs that someone is possessed may be physical symptoms such as headaches or stomach ache. Lewis hypothesised that peripheral possession provided a socially acceptable means for the powerless to express their anger and resentment at those above them in the social hierarchy without fear of retribution. After all, they are not held personally responsible for the demands they make during possession or for mocking and insulting their superiors. It is the spirit that is held responsible. Not surprisingly, peripheral possession tends to occur at times of high stress.

In patriarchal societies, it is typically women who are the subjects of peripheral possession. A woman in an unhappy marriage may be possessed by a spirit that demands an expensive public ceremony with lots of new clothes. During the possession, the spirit can insult her husband in ways that she would never normally be allowed to do. As another example, epidemics of spirit possession involving convulsions and bizarre behaviour sometimes occur amongst female Malaysian factory workers engaged in boring repetitive work for very low pay. This provides a way of letting off steam and getting some time off work. This is not to say that such peripheral possession is simply "put on" (although in some instances, it may be). It is a more subtle process than that, in which it seems likely that many of the apparently possessed genuinely believe, through the use of imagination and other cognitive strategies, that they really are under the control of some kind of spirit.

Spanos (1996) also considers historical manifestations of demonic possession. The New Testament provides many examples of possession by demons and exorcism, the most prominent symptoms being "convulsions, sensory and motor deficits, enactment of multiple identities, loss of voluntary control over behaviour, increased strength, and amnesia" (Spanos, 1996, p. 157). In the New Testament, sufferers typically displayed only one or a few of the symptoms but by the medieval period sufferers tended to display most or all of them.

Possession and exorcism were frequently used to proselytise, reinforcing the faith of believers and attempting to convert unbelievers. Thus the rate of occurrence of possession appears to have been high in the early days of Christianity, to have declined once Christianity became the state religion of the Roman Empire, and to have risen again between the fifteenth and seventeenth centuries with the breakup of Western Christianity into competing sects. It was believed in both Protestant and Catholic countries that there was an international Satanic conspiracy bent upon destroying Christianity. It was believed that witches, acting on behalf of Satan, could send demons to possess people. However, the demons possessing their victims could be coerced into naming the witch that had sent them, who could then be arrested and tortured, resulting in the naming of other witches who would then receive similar treatment. Thus, the possessed often served as witch-finders and, as Spanos (1996, p. 158) puts it, "those who controlled the demoniacs had a powerful weapon to use against political, social, or personal rivals".

What were the signs during this period that someone was possessed? Amongst the most dramatic was, as you might expect, convulsions. In the words of the *Compendium Maleficarum*, the most authoritative witch-hunting manual of the seventeenth century, "A man may very surely be known for a demoniac if he is disturbed [i.e. convulses] when the exorcisms are read" (Guazzo, 1608/1970, p. 168).

Demons were also believed to be intelligent and worldly in contrast to the members of the lower social classes whom they possessed. Therefore evidence of intelligence or learning in such folk could also be taken as an indication of possession:

> An even more certain sign is when a sick man speaks in foreign tongues unknown to him or understands in those tongues; or when, being ignorant, the patients argue about high and difficult questions.... It is a manifest sign when an ignorant man speaks literary or grammatical Latin, or if without knowledge of the art he sings musically or says something of which he could never have had any knowledge. (Guazzo, 1608/1970, p. 168)

Demoniacs were also believed to convulse when in the proximity of a witch even if they were not told of her presence:

> but when the witch was brought in again ... although she [the demoniac] could not possibly see her, she would be immediately senseless and like to

> be strangled, and so would continue until the witch were taken out, and then . . . she would come again to her senses. That afterwards Mr. Greatrix, Mr. Blackwell, and some others, who would needs satisfy themselves in the influence of the witch's presence, tried it and found it several times. Although he did it with all possible privacy, and so as none could think it possible that the maid to know either of the witches coming in or going out. (Glanville, 1689, p. 382)

Studying historical cases provides great insight into the process by which someone comes to be labelled as "possessed" and often to adopt that role for themselves. In late medieval and early modern Europe, the idea of possession by demons was taken for granted and the major components of the possessed role were widely known. Possession was one possible explanation for a wide range of physical symptoms as well as for disruptive behaviour. In the early stages, the demoniac's symptoms might be varied and ambiguous but they would gradually learn the more precise and stereotyped behaviour that the role demanded of them. Spanos (1996, p. 161) provides the following example:

> the demonically possessed children who participated in the Salem witch panic initially enacted an array of odd behaviours, such as running about the house, creeping under furniture, and adopting unusual postures. After several weeks of close observation by and interaction with neighbours and clergy who suspected demonic intervention, their symptoms became much more stereotypically diabolical. These symptoms now included convulsions, reports of being bitten and pinched, and "seeing" the spectres of witches attack them and others.

The rule-governed nature of displays of possession is clear in the variations found across religions. Whereas both Protestant and Catholic demoniacs convulsed and displayed sensorimotor deficits, only Catholic demoniacs exhibited direct evidence of indwelling demons. These demons had their own names, personalities, and distinctive voices. During Catholic exorcisms, the exorcist made a clear distinction between the possessed person and their demon(s) and would attempt to talk to the latter directly. This procedure provided strong cues to the possessed regarding what was expected of them. For Protestants, however, direct communication with demons was shunned as being sinful and exorcisms mainly involved prayer and fasting. As a result, demonic self-enactments were much less common amongst Protestants.

Detailed information regarding what was entailed in the demoniac role was available from a variety of sources including direct coaching, imitating others and overhearing others' conversations. But why would the demoniac ever take on such a role? A number of factors are relevant. First, the demoniac shared the same belief system as the rest of their community and would be likely to accept their community's view, and particularly that of the clergy, regarding the cause of their initial symptoms. Second, the demoniac would probably also be dependent upon those around them in terms of social and physical needs. Third, those wishing to apply the label would be sure to isolate the potential demoniac from anyone who did not agree with their interpretation.

Any denials of being possessed were interpreted as the cunning demon attempting to avoid divine punishment and would lead to threats of eternal damnation. Cruel punishments would often be meted out but always, it was claimed, directed at the demon, not the poor soul who was possessed. The only hope for salvation was to accept the clergy's view of the situation. For anyone familiar with certain forms of dubious psychotherapy, the parallels here are striking and very disturbing.

Furthermore, demonic possession, like other forms of peripheral possession, had certain benefits if used strategically. It allowed those with little power to indirectly protest about their lot in life and engage in behaviours which, under normal circumstances, would never be tolerated. It is notable that adult demoniacs were much more likely to be women than men and, in particular, to be cloistered nuns. In those days, becoming a nun was generally not a chosen profession but something imposed upon adolescent girls by their impoverished families. Life for a nun was very tough and extremely dull. Adopting the demoniac role was not necessarily an unattractive option. Furthermore, even a successful exorcism did not guarantee that the demons would not return at a future date, allowing for this option to remain should the need for it arise again.

Exorcism

We can see that both neuropathological and sociocognitive factors can play a role in someone being thought of as being possessed. When it comes to the efficacy of exorcism, it is clear that we would not expect such rituals to work when the apparent possession is, in fact, due to epilepsy, Tourette's syndrome, or some other neurological cause. However, in the majority of cases, where sociocognitive factors provide the best explanation, it is clear that exorcism may well eliminate, at least temporarily, the disruptive behaviour that led to the acquisition of the label in the first place. In just the same way that behaviour is shaped by contextual factors in the acquisition of the role of the possessed, so can the behaviour of the individual during and after the exorcism be shaped.

It should be noted that there are obvious benefits to those involved in enacting their various roles. The exorcist is seen by his fellow believers as a brave hero, doing battle with the most powerful forces of evil based on his faith and compassion for his fellow believers. It is hard to imagine a role with so much kudos. The benefits for the possessed are numerous. First, they are not held responsible for any previous "sinful" behaviour. They were not to blame, their demons were. At the height of their possession and during the exorcism ritual itself, they can display all kinds of socially unacceptable behaviour but, once again, they will not be held responsible for it. Finally, once their demons have been successfully exorcised, they are welcomed back into the community and are seen as being pure and saved. For the religious community concerned, the whole exercise confirms them in their belief that their religion is the one true religion (Spanos, 1996; Cuneo, 2001).

Having said all that, things do not always work out so positively. Exorcisms are sometimes violent in the extreme. In such cases, it does not count for much to the allegedly possessed individual to know that that the violence is directed against the demon possessing them and not against them personally. The following example is given by Barry Beyerstein (1988, p. 249): "In 1978, two West German priests and the parents of an epileptic were convicted of causing her death in a brutal 11-month exorcism. (They received suspended sentences.) The local bishop, citing Jesus' admonition that demons can only be expelled by fasting and prayer (Mark 9:29), authorized starving 23-year-old Anneliese Michel, who weighed only 68 pounds at the time of her death . . . Her epilepsy could have been treated and her life saved as late as a week before her demise".

In the UK today, the authorities are aware of the dangers posed, especially to children, by belief in witchcraft and possession. Examples such as the following, from Louise Hunt (2012), illustrate the problem:

> The link between belief in spirit possession and child abuse came to public attention following the death in 2000 in Haringey, north London, of Victoria Climbié, who was from the Ivory Coast. Research found that her guardians, Marie Therese Kouao and Carl Manning, had tortured the eight-year-old partly through belief that she was possessed by an evil spirit – a belief supported by their church leaders.
>
> In 2005, three adults in east London were convicted of child cruelty to another eight-year-old, from Angola. She had been starved, beaten, cut with a knife and had chilli peppers rubbed in her eyes in the belief that she was possessed.

It is nothing short of a tragedy that such beliefs and practices are still widespread in some communities in the twenty-first century, a situation not helped by Pope Francis's decision in 2014 to officially endorse the International Association of Exorcists, a group of 250 priests who allegedly cast out demons in 30 different countries (French, 2014a).

It is important to emphasise here that these horrifying cases should not be taken as offering support for unfounded claims of widespread ritualised Satanic abuse (French, 2012), contrary to the claims of some (e.g. Committee on Ritual Abuse, 2012). To do so would be to fall into the logical error sometimes referred to as "the argument from spurious similarity" (Radner & Radner, 1982). There is a superficial similarity between cases of child abuse involving attempted exorcisms and alleged cases of ritualised Satanic abuse insofar as both are examples of ritual abuse. But closer examination reveals significant differences between them. The former cases undoubtedly occur and are supported by clear physical forensic evidence up to and including the dead bodies of victims. The latter cases almost certainly do not occur and are instead based upon either false memories resulting from dubious forms of psychotherapy (French, 2014b) or else statements obtained from children subjected to highly inappropriate high-pressure forms of questioning (Nathan & Snedeker, 1995). There is simply no convincing physical forensic evidence to support the claims of sacrifice, cannibalism and sexual perversion that are said to be involved in cases of Satanic abuse (La Fontaine, 1998). It is also worth noting that the proven perpetrators in cases of abuse resulting from exorcisms are typically fundamentalist Christians attempting to expel demons whereas the perpetrators in the alleged cases of Satanic abuse are said to engaging in the practices as acts of worship towards Satan.

Conclusions

As stated at the outset, we seem to be natural dualists insofar as we find it easy to believe that mental stuff is fundamentally different to physical stuff. It is therefore easy to believe that our consciousness is not wholly dependent upon our brains and that it might, under certain circumstances, separate from that underlying neural substrate. If that really is possible, might it not also be possible that external spiritual entities could somehow take control of our physical bodies?

Belief in such states of possession is widespread, both geographically and historically, as is the associated belief that engaging in certain rituals can bring about the expulsion of the possessing spirit. It has been argued in this chapter that such beliefs are best explained in terms of neuropathological and sociocognitive factors. There is no compelling evidence to support the claim that such phenomena involve anything paranormal. Although such beliefs and associated practices may produce psychological benefits for some under particular conditions, they can also result in tragic cases of extreme abuse and even death. Such concepts should have no place in the modern world.

5

ALIEN CONTACT AND ABDUCTION CLAIMS

Christopher C. French

> *Q: Is there intelligent life on Earth?*
> *A: Yes, but I'm only visiting.*
>
> Graffiti, traditional

Introduction

Before reading the rest of this chapter, take a few minutes to write a story in which you are abducted by aliens. Take as much time as you like, and try to include as much detail as you can. Describe both the sequence of events and your reactions to them. Do not read on until you have written your story.

***

For those of you who took the time to write the story, perhaps it went something like this? You are driving along in a car at night on a lonely isolated road when you notice a strange light in the sky. At first you don't pay it much attention, but gradually you begin to suspect that the light is actually following your car – and it does not look like any conventional aircraft! As the craft gets nearer to your car, you can make out that it is definitely circular in shape. You cannot believe your eyes, as your fear turns to terror. You put your foot on the accelerator, in a desperate attempt to outrun the alien craft. A brilliant beam of light engulfs your car and the engine suddenly cuts out completely. You lose consciousness.

The next thing you remember, you are lying on your back on some kind of examination table inside a circular dimly lit room. A number of beings, at least three or four, are standing around you. You try to look closely at their faces, but the whole scene has a strange dream-like quality, as if you had been drugged. The beings appear to be humanoid and around four feet tall. They have hairless grey skin and very large heads. Their piercing eyes are large and black, but they have very small noses and mouths. One of them looks you directly in the eyes and telepathically tells you not to be afraid. You realise that you are naked and that you cannot move. The aliens carry out a detailed examination using strange pieces of equipment which cause you intense, almost unbearable, pain. You cannot scream. They seem to be particularly interested in your genitals and use a probe to extract ova (or, in the case of males, sperm). Finally, they insert some kind of small metallic implant into your brain by forcing a long probe up your nose. Your mind is filled with such intense pain that you again lose consciousness. When you wake up, you are back inside your car beside the road. You look at your watch. Over three hours have passed since you first noticed the strange light in the sky.

Your story is unlikely to have been identical to the one above, but the chances are that there were some strong similarities. In your story, perhaps you were lying in your bed at home when you suddenly became aware that the alien beings had somehow entered despite all doors and windows being locked? And perhaps the aliens somehow transported you back into bed following their unearthly medical interventions? Although there are many variations on the basic theme, alien abduction experiences typically include capture by the aliens and medical examination. These days, the aliens most often correspond to the description provided above. Other common, although not universal, elements in the scenario include tours of the aliens' ship, trips to other planets, and the receipt of messages to humanity, often involving dire warnings of the future destruction of the planet through pollution or nuclear war unless we mend our ways.

It is not difficult to see why most people would come up with a story that is similar to that described above. This standard abduction scenario is now well-known in our culture thanks to widespread media coverage, such as that provided by the popular series *The X-Files* or the films *Communion* and *Fire in the Sky*. Why should psychologists be interested in such flights of fancy? Because thousands of people worldwide are convinced that they really have undergone abduction by aliens and they have clear and vivid memories to back them up. The media have reported many such claims as fact (indeed, the two films referred to are both based on allegedly true stories). Knowledge of the typical alien abduction experience has therefore been provided through books, documentaries, chat shows, and newspaper and magazine articles. Coverage is typically uncritical and sensationalised. It is tempting to say that you would have to have been living on Mars to have escaped exposure to claims of alien abduction, but presumably it might be a hot topic there too.

It is extremely difficult to estimate just how many people believe themselves to be the victims of alien abduction. Thomas E. Bullard (1994) surveyed just 13 UFO investigators and found that between them they had details of around 1,700 cases. Whitley Strieber (1998) claims to have received almost a quarter of a million letters from individuals claiming alien contact. It is often claimed that many more people have experienced alien abduction than actually report it. There are at least two reasons for this. First, people may reasonably conclude that they will not be believed and will be ridiculed if they tell others of their bizarre experience. A second and more sinister reason has also been proposed. It is claimed that the aliens are able to directly erase the memories of the abductees for the events in question. It is further argued that hypnosis is effective in releasing the victims' memories from this alien-induced amnesic block.

In an attempt to circumvent these problems, Budd Hopkins, David Jacobs, and Ron Westrum (1992) took an indirect approach. A random sample of 5,947 American adults was surveyed by the Roper organisation regarding unusual experiences. Included in the items presented were five which Hopkins et al. claimed were often indicative of an alien abduction experience. The respondents were asked "How often has this experience happened to you?" for the following experiences (the percentages in brackets indicate those who said it had happened at least once):

> *Waking up paralysed with a sense of a strange person or presence or something else in the room. [18 per cent]*
> *Experiencing a period of time of an hour or more in which you were apparently lost, but you could not remember why or where you had been. [13 per cent]*
> *Feeling that you were actually flying through the air although you didn't know how or why. [10 per cent]*
> *Seeing unusual lights or balls of light in a room without knowing what was causing them or where they came from. [8 per cent]*
> *Finding puzzling scars on your body and neither you nor anyone else remembering how you received them or where you got them. [8 per cent]*

According to Hopkins et al., if you answered "yes" to four or five of the above items (and "no" to an item allegedly measuring suggestibility), you have probably been abducted by aliens. Of the original sample, 119 people (2 per cent) met these criteria. Extrapolating to the American adult population as a whole, these authors claimed that 3.7 million Americans have probably been abducted by aliens. This figure received wide media coverage. Now, if you are the estimated one out of every fifty readers who has said "yes" to four or five of the above items, don't panic! The Roper poll gives us a lot of valid and interesting data concerning the frequency of unusual experiences, but the interpretation of the data by Hopkins et al. is totally unjustified. As Philip J. Klass (1997a) pointed out, if 3.7 million Americans had been abducted between 1961 (when the first such case is alleged to have occurred) and the time the survey was carried out, the rate of abductions must be about 340 Americans *every single day of the year!* Such a figure must stretch credulity even amongst those who accept that aliens have the amazing ability to abduct individuals from busy cities without any independent witnesses ever seeing them. Furthermore, as Stires (1997) points out, Hopkins et al. made no attempt to validate the claimed association between the unusual experiences and alien abduction. But even if we accept for the sake of argument that alien abductions really do occur and that they do tend to be associated with the experiences reported above, Hopkins et al.'s interpretation is fatally flawed in terms of logic, as pointed out by Devereux and Brookesmith (1997, p. 170). They quote veteran market researcher James R. Adams:

> What [Hopkins et al.] are saying is, if abduction, then all these other symptoms. All these other symptoms (or some of them, even), therefore abduction. This does not follow; the logic has what is known as an "undistributed middle". If it is raining, the pavements are wet. But, the fact that the pavements are wet does not mean that it is raining.

Consider another example: death is associated with a lack of movement, a failure to respond to mild distracting stimuli, and inability to solve simple problems. By Hopkins et al.'s logic, anyone exhibiting these three "symptoms" is probably dead – whereas common sense suggests they may be asleep or just watching TV!

Amazingly, some estimates are even higher. For example Jacobs (1992) has suggested that as many as 15 million Americans may have been abducted. Although the number of people with conscious memories of alien abduction experiences is less than this by many orders of magnitude, it is still the case that many thousands of individuals throughout the world *are* convinced that they have indeed been taken aboard an alien spaceship against their will and have undergone painful medical procedures there. What are we to make of such claims?

Are alien abduction claims deliberate hoaxes?

Uninformed sceptics often assert that those claiming to have been abducted by aliens are simply making the whole thing up. The assumed motivations are financial, in that claimants may make money from books and film rights, and social, in that they may become celebrated cases and appear at conferences and on talk shows. One or two of the most celebrated cases may indeed be deliberate hoaxes. For example, Philip J. Klass (1989) has raised serious doubts regarding the sincerity of Travis Walton, whose alleged abduction was the subject of the feature film *Fire in the Sky*. In general though, even sceptics accept that most claimants are sincere in their beliefs.

Are people really being abducted by aliens?

If the claimants are not deliberately lying, should we then conclude that they really have experienced contact with extraterrestrials? Those who support the "ET hypothesis" would answer affirmatively. Furthermore, they would argue that we need not rely solely upon the testimony from abductees to support the ET hypothesis. However, much of the evidence presented in support of the hypothesis is weaker than uncritical media coverage typically implies. Unfortunately, full discussion of such evidence is beyond the scope of the current chapter. The reader is referred to Bartholomew and Howard (1998); Brookesmith (1996); Clarke (2012);

Clarke and Roberts (1990); Devereux and Brookesmith (1997); Frazier, Karr, and Nickell (1997); Klass (1983); Randles, Roberts, and Clarke (2000); Sheaffer (1998); and Watson (2013) for excellent critical consideration of the ET hypothesis in general. Even such celebrated cases as the alleged crash of a flying saucer and recovery of alien bodies near Roswell, New Mexico, in 1947 are in fact based upon incredibly weak evidence (see Klass 1997b; Korff, 1997).

Much of the general evidence related to the ET hypothesis is not relevant to the specific topic of alien abductions, but some of it is. In particular, it is often claimed that the reason behind the abductions is that the aliens are engaged in a sinister cross-breeding project, the aim of which is to produce hybrid creatures which are half-human, half-alien (e.g. Hopkins, 1987; Jacobs, 1998). In support of this hypothesis, it is claimed that female abductees often report becoming pregnant even though they may have no memory of having engaged in normal sexual activity. For example, Hough and Rogers (2007–2008) found that almost half of their sample of 20 female abductees reported that aliens had impregnated them. After a few months, their pregnancies will mysteriously "disappear". It is claimed that the aliens have abducted the victim initially to artificially inseminate her and have then abducted her again to remove the hybrid embryo or foetus some months later before it has reached full term. Some abductees even claim that they have been briefly reunited with their typically pale and sickly offspring during subsequent abductions. Many researchers claim to have several records of so-called Missing Embryo/Foetus Syndrome in their files. Despite this, not one single convincing documented case has ever been presented to the wider scientific community. There are many reasons why a woman might think she was pregnant when in fact she was not, but the available evidence in no way supports the idea of an alien cross-breeding programme (Randle, Estes, & Cone, 1999).

It is also claimed that the aliens frequently implant small devices into the bodies of their unwilling victims. The exact purpose of these implants is unclear, although it has been suggested that they may enable the aliens to track the abductees in order to facilitate future abductions. If such an implant could be retrieved and subjected to scientific analysis, the results could potentially provide strong support for the ET hypothesis. If it were concluded that the implant was of alien design and construction, the implications would be staggering. Unfortunately, however, this has not been found to be the case. Despite repeated promises from UFO researchers, no such implant has ever been produced. On occasions, items which abductees sincerely believed to have been alien implants have been analysed. They have turned out to have mundane explanations – for example, in one case, an "implant" turned out to be a dental filling (Blackmore, 1999). More often, the implant is mysteriously spirited away (presumably by the aliens?) before proper analysis can take place.

Overall then, there is no strong evidence to support the ET hypothesis. This does not mean that there is no intelligent life elsewhere in the universe. Indeed, many of those who express the gravest doubts regarding the notion that aliens are regularly abducting earthlings are at the forefront of the search for extraterrestrial intelligence by other means (e.g. Sagan, 1997). Many scientists believe that, given the sheer immensity of the universe, it is highly probable that intelligent life does exist elsewhere but the evidence that earth has yet been contacted by aliens is far from convincing. So, if abductees are not deliberately lying and yet they are almost certainly wrong in thinking that they really have had an alien close encounter, how are we to account for their claims?

Psychological approaches to alien abduction

Given that it appears to be extremely unlikely that aliens really are abducting people, a number of commentators have considered whether such claims are best explained in purely psychological terms (e.g. Appelle, 1996; Appelle, Lynn, Newman, & Maktaris, 2014; Baker, 1992; Bartholomew & Howard, 1998; Blackmore, 1994; Brookesmith, 1998; Clancy, 2005; Devereux & Brookesmith, 1997; French, in press; French & Stone, 2014; Holden & French, 2002; Klass, 1989; Newman & Baumeister, 1996a, 1996b; Randle, Estes, & Cone, 1999; Rutkowski, 2000; Showalter, 1997; Spanos, 1996).

Psychopathology

As stated earlier, media coverage of abduction claims is usually uncritical and sensationalised, but when a sceptical approach is taken, there is often an unfortunate tendency to ridicule the claimant. The implication is that "normal" people do not claim to be abducted by aliens. Those that do are therefore "crazy". Does the available evidence support this view?

Although limited, available data suggest psychopathology is no more common amongst those claiming alien contact than among the general population. Spanos, Cross, Dickson, and DuBreuil (1993) compared people who had reported intense UFO-related experiences (e.g. missing time or seeing and communicating with aliens) with those who had reported non-intense experiences (e.g. seeing unidentified lights in the sky) and with control groups not reporting any UFO experiences. The groups were not found to differ on objective measures of psychopathology (but it is unclear how many actual abductees were included in the study). Parnell and Sprinkle (1990) administered the widely used Minnesota Multiphasic Personality Inventory (MMPI) to 225 individuals reporting UFO experiences and concluded that there was no evidence for serious psychopathology in the group as a whole. The conclusion that abductees do not show higher levels of psychopathology was reached by Bloecher, Clamar, and Hopkins (1985) with respect to 9 abductees, Rodeghier, Goodpaster, and Blatterbauer (1991) for 27 abductees, and Mack (1994) for his 76 abduction cases. Bartholomew, Basterfield, and Howard (1991) analysed the biographies of 152 subjects who reported temporary abductions or repeated UFO contact and found them to be "remarkably devoid of a history of mental illness" (p. 215).

Having said that, the data do suggest that abductees are not psychologically representative of the population as a whole. In the study by Parnell and Sprinkle

(1990), those who claimed to have communicated with aliens "had a significantly greater tendency to endorse unusual feelings, thoughts, and attitudes; to be suspicious or distrustful; and to be creative, imaginative, or possibly have schizoid tendencies" (p. 45). Rodeghier et al. (1991) reported relatively higher levels of loneliness, unhappiness, and poorer sleep patterns. Mack (1994) reported high levels of childhood trauma, as did Ring and Rosing (1990). The latter investigators also reported that, as children, abductees were more sensitive to "non-ordinary realities". Stone-Carmen (1994) found that a staggering 57 per cent of her sample of abductees reported suicide attempts. French, Santomauro, Hamilton, Fox, and Thalbourne (2008) reported that a group of 19 "experiencers" claiming to have encountered aliens (though not necessarily classic alien abduction experiences) scored significantly higher than a matched control group on a measure of tendency to hallucinate.

Fantasy-proneness

One personality characteristic in particular has been the focus of much research in this area and that is fantasy-proneness. This construct was first described by Wilson and Barber (1983) in a study investigating hypnotic susceptibility. Fantasy-prone personalities are typically excellent hypnotic subjects, but are also noted for their profound fantasy lives. They spend a great deal of time fantasising and report that when they imagine something, it appears to them "as real as real". The hallucinatory nature of their fantasies leads to frequent confusions between imagination and reality. In line with typical abductees, these individuals often report paranormal experiences of various types and often believe themselves to be psychic. In Wilson and Barber's sample of 22 fantasisers, no less than 13 reported having experienced false pregnancies, an observation that may be highly relevant in explaining so-called Missing Embryo/Foetus Syndrome discussed earlier. Despite the fact that they report having been heavily engaged in fantasy since early childhood, people with fantasy-prone personalities usually lead perfectly ordinary lives and often keep their fantasy lives secret. Interestingly, a much higher incidence of childhood trauma was reported by the fantasy-prone group compared to a control sample. In general, this picture has been supported by subsequent investigations (e.g. Lynn and Rhue, 1988).

Given the overlap between the characteristics of the fantasy-prone personality and the typical abductee, it is often asserted that fantasy-proneness plays an important role in explaining reports of alien abduction (e.g. Bartholomew & Howard, 1998; Nickell, 1997). To the sceptical mind, it is precisely people who cannot easily distinguish between fantasy and reality whom one might expect to report abductions by aliens. The evidence supporting such a link, however, is at best mixed (Appelle, Lynn, Newman, & Malaktaris, 2014; Newman, 1997; Newman & Baumeister, 1996a, 1996b). Studies which present data supporting the link tend to be based upon biographical analysis. For example, Bartholomew et al. (1991) reported that 132 of the 152 cases they analysed show one or more major characteristics of fantasy proneness (see Bartholomew & Howard, 1998, for full details).

The characteristics noted include reports of psychic phenomena, out-of-body experiences, healing, apparitions, hypnotic susceptibility, and physiological effects. A similar analysis by Nickell (1997) of the 13 cases presented in detail by Mack (1994) concludes that all show several major characteristics of fantasy proneness.

However, attempts to test the hypothesis directly by measuring fantasy proneness with questionnaires have generally not offered much support. Spanos et al. (1993) found no significant differences in scores on the Inventory of Childhood Memories and Imaginings (ICMIC; Myers, 1983), the most commonly used measure of fantasy proneness, between those having UFO experiences and control groups. However, amongst those reporting UFO experiences, the intensity of the experience was correlated with scores on the questionnaire. Rodeghier et al. (1991) found no evidence for higher levels of fantasy proneness amongst a group of abductees using the same measure. However, French et al. (2008) did report a small but significant difference between a group with memories of alien contact compared to a matched control group using the ICMIC. Using the Creative Experiences Questionnaire (Merckelbach, Horselenberg, & Muris, 2001) to measure fantasy-proneness, Hough and Rogers (2007–2008) found no significant difference between a group of self-reported alien abductees and a control group.

Ring and Rosing (1990), using a measure which they devised themselves, reported that their UFO experiencers (including abductees) were not, in general, more fantasy-prone than controls. However, as reported above, as children they were more sensitive to "non-ordinary realities". This was assessed by endorsement of such items as those dealing with being "aware of non-physical beings" during wakefulness and seeing "into 'other realities' that others didn't seem to be aware of". In the absence of any objective proof that these "non-physical beings" and "other realities" actually exist, it is obviously a matter of opinion as to whether or not one accepts that these individuals are not fantasy-prone. To many observers, it would appear parsimonious to assume that they may have such high levels of fantasy-proneness that they were simply not aware that they were confusing fantasy with reality. It should also be borne in mind that abductees may well be reluctant to endorse items which indicate that they often confuse reality and imagination given the extraordinary nature of their claims.

Absorption, dissociation and childhood trauma

The fantasy-proneness hypothesis is also indirectly supported by studies which show that some factors known to correlate significantly with fantasy-proneness appear to be associated with abduction claims. One such factor is absorption, defined by Tellegen and Atkinson (1974) as "openness to absorbing and self-altering experiences, a trait related to hypnotic susceptibility". Clancy, McNally, Schacter, Lenzenweger and Pitman (2002) reported that higher levels of absorption were found in a group of self-reported abductees than in a control group and French et al. (2008) found a similar pattern in comparing experiencers with non-experiencers.

Dissociative tendencies (i.e. the tendency for some mental processes to temporarily "split off" from the normal stream of consciousness) have also been shown to be higher in abductees compared to non-abductees by Powers (1994) and in experiencers compared to non-experiencers by French et al. (2008). Tendency to dissociate is known to be associated with histories of childhood trauma (including sexual, physical and emotional abuse) which in turn are correlated with fantasy-proneness. It has been argued (e.g. Lynn, Pintar, & Rhue, 1997) that the tendency to dissociate is a defensive mechanism which allows traumatised children to escape the unbearable reality of their lives by entering a more acceptable fantasy world.

It is therefore of considerable interest that several studies have found the incidence of reported childhood trauma to be higher amongst abductees than amongst the general population. The work of Mack (1994) and Ring and Rosing (1990) has already been referred to in this regard. Research into paranormal belief in general shows that paranormal belief is associated with both fantasy-proneness and reported childhood trauma (e.g. Irwin, 1991; 1993; Lawrence, Edwards, Barraclough, Church, & Hetherington, 1995). There are several possible interpretations of this reported pattern of correlations. The first one, favoured by many parapsychologists and UFOlogists, is that individuals are more likely to experience genuine paranormal events (including being abducted by aliens) if they have a particular type of psychological make-up, corresponding to that found in fantasy-prone individuals. The second interpretation is that described in the previous paragraph, whereby fantasy-proneness and dissociative tendencies develop as a coping mechanism in individuals trying to deal with unbearable childhood trauma. The result is people who find it hard to distinguish fantasy from reality and report imagined paranormal events (including UFO abductions) as objective reality. The third possibility is that certain adults are fantasy-prone for currently unspecified reasons, and that their reports of childhood trauma are as much a product of their imaginations as their reports of paranormal events. At this point in time, it is not possible to offer a definitive verdict in deciding between these possible interpretations. Having said that, a considerable amount of evidence has now accumulated in support of the notion that most reports of alien contact and abduction are probably based upon false memories (French, 2003; French & Stone, 2014; French & Wilson, 2006; Holden & French, 2002).

Hypnotic regression and false memories

One major factor which has been implicated in explaining the formation of false memories of alien abduction is the use of hypnotic regression by investigators such as Budd Hopkins (1987) and John Mack (1994). The public image of hypnotic regression, based upon fictional accounts and pseudo-scientific documentaries, is that it provides an almost magical key to unlock repressed memories. The reality, however, is that hypnotic techniques often encourage the production of fantasy-based narratives which are then believed in as if they were memories for events which actually occurred (e.g. Spanos, 1996). Not surprisingly, then, the widespread use of hypnosis has been condemned by many critics as being responsible for the formation of false memories of alien abduction rather than the retrieval of repressed memories of actual events (Baker, 1992, 1997a, 1997b; Klass, 1989; Newman & Baumeister 1996a, 1996b, 1998; Randle et al., 1999).

Thomas E. Bullard (1989) claimed that hypnosis was employed in about 70 per cent of the "well-investigated, high quality cases" in his sample. He presented an interesting analysis of these accounts, for example comparing abduction accounts produced under hypnosis with those recalled naturally. He claimed that they were very similar, providing evidence, he argued, that hypnosis had not influenced the retrieval of memories. It is unclear, however, why Bullard would expect a great difference between hypnotically and non-hypnotically produced accounts in terms of their actual content. The content of the accounts is likely to reflect a complex mix of culturally derived knowledge, personal idiosyncrasies of the claimant (e.g. the incorporation of dream fragments), and the subtle (or sometimes not so subtle) influence of the hypnotist in question, when hypnotic regression had been employed. The result is likely to be accounts which are generally quite similar, but represent variations on a theme. This is precisely what Bullard's analysis shows. Hypnosis is likely to have the effect of increasing the abductee's conviction that the apparent recollections are memories of real events, but will not necessarily have a huge influence upon the content of the memories.

BOX 5.1 FALSE MEMORIES IN OTHER CONTEXTS

The topic of false memories is one of the most hotly debated within psychology (Lindsay & Read, 1995; Loftus, 1993; Loftus & Ketcham, 1994; Lynn & McConkey, 1998; Ofshe & Watters, 1995; Pendergrast, 1996). Current interest was largely generated by the huge numbers of people apparently recovering repressed memories of childhood sexual abuse upon entering therapy despite having no conscious recollection of such abuse prior to therapy. Alleged abusers were being tried and convicted often purely on the basis of such recovered memories. Needless to say, the validity of these apparent memories is of crucial importance. Following extensive research by experimental psychologists, it is now clear that it is much easier to induce false memories for whole episodes which never actually occurred than anyone would have believed a few decades ago. Hypnosis and other related "memory enhancement" techniques (e.g. guided imagery) have been shown to be risky in this regard. It is unclear what proportion of "recovered" memories of sexual abuse are false, but the potential dangers are now recognised and all major psychological and psychiatric associations have issued guidelines in order to minimise risks.

While recovered memories of apparent childhood sexual abuse appear plausible to therapists, given the appallingly high levels of childhood sexual abuse

(*continued*)

(continued)

within our society, other types of false memories lack such initial plausibility. These include: memories of satanic ritual abuse involving claims of bizarre and extreme abuse including perverted sexual acts, devil worship, human and animal sacrifice, and cannibalism (e.g. Bottoms & Davis, 1997; Loftus, 1993; Ofshe & Watters, 1995; Pendergrast, 1996). No forensic evidence has been presented to support such claims (La Fontaine, 1998). Memories from past-lives: hypnotic regression to "past lives" appears to provide a means whereby subjects produce fantasy-based accounts which they often believe are real memories of prior incarnations (Spanos, 1996; Mills & Tucker, 2014). The content of hypnotically produced past-life memories is strongly influenced by the subject's expectations and beliefs about reincarnation (Spanos, Burgess & Burgess, 1994). On some occasions, hypnotic subjects produce detailed, historically accurate information about their past lives. Further analysis (Baker, 1992; Harris, 1986; Spanos, 1996) however, suggests that such subjects have picked up this information from a variety of sources (books, films, etc.) which they have then forgotten. This phenomenon is known as cryptomnesia (literally, "hidden memories"). Many commentators (e.g. Baker, 1992; Baumeister & Sommer, 1997; Paley, 1997; Showalter, 1997; Spanos, 1996; Spanos, Burgess & Burgess, 1994) have drawn attention to the similarities between these various examples of false memory. In all cases, the use of memory recovery techniques of dubious reliability is prominent. Furthermore, it is claimed that recovery of such memories will explain and possibly eliminate current psychological problems. The "memories" are validated by an authority figure, usually a therapist, who will often encourage the claimant to adopt lax criteria in deciding what constitutes a likely memory of a past event (e.g. fleeting mental images or half-remembered dreams will be taken as memories if they fit the hypothesis). Finally, claimants often join support groups in which they feel under social pressure to recover memories in order to gain the approval of their peers.

Bullard (1989) also compared hypnotically produced accounts produced by four different hypnotists. If the hypnotist is shaping the narrative by, for example, asking leading questions, then the accounts produced by different hypnotists might be expected to reflect such influence. He claimed that the accounts produced by different hypnotists were very similar to each other and did not strongly reflect the influence of the specific hypnotists, but once again this interpretation is open to question. Of typical traits identified in such accounts, only 30 per cent were similar across all four hypnotists, whereas 50 per cent were dissimilar for at least one. In a more recent survey, Bullard (1994) admitted that investigators do influence the content of the accounts produced but insisted that this mainly occurs with respect to peripheral details. Matheson (1998) has argued that the role of the individual hypnotist is much stronger in shaping the final narrative. But in the final analysis, it is unclear how much direct influence from the hypnotist we should expect to see if the core narrative is derived from the generally shared culture in the first place.

Finally, Bullard (1989) compared the accounts of "real" abductees with those produced by eight subjects that Alvin Lawson (e.g. Lawson, 1984) had hypnotised and asked to simply imagine that they had been abducted by aliens. Lawson's subjects were in no way suspected to have had genuine abduction experiences. When Lawson's results were first published they caused great consternation amongst traditional UFO researchers. In Bullard's words (1989, pp. 27–28), "Not only did the subjects readily respond to an initial suggestion with an elaborate and detailed story, with little need for prodding along the way, but the contents bore striking similarities to alleged real abductions, both in more obvious matters and in odd, minute details". However, following more detailed analysis, Bullard concluded that the imaginary abductions did not demonstrate the same coherence as the "real" cases. This difference, he suggests, was most plausibly explained by the assumption that a similar, objectively real, experience lay at the core of the allegedly genuine accounts.

A more obvious explanation appears to have been overlooked. As Bullard (1989, p. 27) himself states, Lawson's subjects were selected on the basis of their "minimal prior UFO knowledge". Is it any surprise then that their imaginative narratives strayed further from the cultural template than the "genuine" abductees who had presented themselves for hypnotic regression to hypnotists specialising in retrieval of alien abduction accounts? It beggars belief to assume that the latter would not have already sought out information on UFO abductions prior to their regression.

It is worth noting here that one factor that often convinces people that claims of alien abduction recounted following hypnotic regression must be true is that the hypnotised subjects do not simply give a matter-of-fact, step-by-step account of the alleged event, they actually appear to be reliving it. The extreme emotions that they experience during such episodes are all too obvious. McNally, Lasko, Clancy, Macklin, Pitman, and Orr (2004) monitored psychophysiological arousal levels in a group of abductees as they listened back to accounts of their own alleged abductions. The measures confirmed that the abductees did indeed experience extreme arousal levels as they listened to such accounts, comparable to those shown by posttraumatic stress disorder patients when they listen to accounts of the traumatic events that they have experienced. Such observations, of course, say nothing about the veracity of the claimed experiences. As McNally et al. point out, they simply demonstrate that as long as the claimants *believe* the events took place, then that is sufficient to provoke such emotional responses.

Other lines of evidence support the notion that alien contact and abduction reports may well be based upon false memories. Experimental psychologists have developed a number of techniques for reliably implanting false memories in a significant proportion of participants. Using such techniques, it has been possible to identify a number of psychological variables that appear to correlate with susceptibility to false memories. These include such factors as fantasy-proneness, dissociativity and absorption, all of which also correlate with paranormal belief and the tendency to report paranormal experiences (French, 2003; French & Wilson, 2006). As already discussed, all of these factors are also significantly higher in those claiming alien contact compared to control groups.

It is also worth noting at this point that those claiming alien contact tend to report a wide range of other ostensibly paranormal experiences and often claim to themselves possess psychic abilities. This observation is supported not only by anecdotal reports (e.g. Basterfield, 2001; Bullard, 1987; Druffel & Rogo, 1980; Evans, 1983, 1998; Mack, 1994) but also by studies using standardised measures (Basterfield & Thalbourne, 2002; French et al., 2008).

In addition to the fact that abductees and contactees tend to have psychological profiles suggesting a susceptibility for false memories, there is also direct experimental evidence for such a susceptibility. Clancy et al. (2002) used the so-called *DRM task* to compare a group reporting conscious memories of being abducted by aliens with a group who believed they had been abducted by aliens but could not (yet) remember the event and a group who did not believe that they had ever been abducted by aliens at all. The DRM task (named after the first psychologists to use it: Deese, 1959; Roediger & McDermott, 1995) involves the presentation of a series of lists of words for memorisation. Within each list, all words are closely related in meaning to a particular word that is not itself presented. For example, the words *pin, thread, sew, thimble, knitting*, and so on might be presented but not the word *needle*. In recall and recognition tasks, many participants incorrectly report that the word *needle* was presented. The total number of such errors across a series of lists is often used as a measure of susceptibility to false memories. Clancy et al. reported that their group reporting conscious memories of alien abduction showed the highest susceptibility while those who did not claim to have been so abducted showed the least. The intriguing question of why anyone would believe that they had been abducted by aliens even though they had no memory of the incident is addressed in the next section. It should be noted that French et al. (2008) failed to find any significant difference between a group of experiencers and a control group in terms of DRM scores despite finding that the former scored higher on dissociativity, fantasy-proneness and absorption.

Hypnosis is by no means the only way in which false memories can be formed. False memories can be induced in many people by getting them to imagine events which never actually took place or simply repeatedly interviewing them, asking them to try to recall details of such events, especially if convincing (but false) information is available to support the notion that the events really had taken place. This approach was used in a study by Otgaar, Candel, Merckelbach, and Wade (2009) in which a considerable number of children aged either 7–8 years or 11–12 years apparently developed false memories of being abducted by aliens at the age of four. The children were told that their mothers had confirmed that such an abduction had indeed taken place. The younger group, but not the older group, was also influenced by being shown false newspaper articles suggesting that such abductions were fairly common.

Sleep paralysis

The question remains of why might someone suspect that they had been abducted in the first place without any clear memory of such an event. For many people the answer would appear to be a phenomenon known as sleep paralysis (Adler, 2011; French & Santomauro, 2007; Santomauro & French, 2009; Sharpless & Doghramji, 2015). The most frequently endorsed item which Hopkins et al. (1992) claim is evidence of an alien abduction is, "Waking up paralysed with a sense of a strange person or presence or something else in the room". This is a concise description of one aspect of the experience of sleep paralysis, which is a common symptom of narcolepsy but can also occur quite commonly in the general population (e.g. Everett, 1963; Dahlitz & Parkes, 1993). It is known that the muscles of the body are paralysed during rapid eye movement (REM) sleep, the phase of sleep typically associated with vivid dreams. This is presumably to prevent one from performing the movements associated with one's actions in the dream. During sleep paralysis, however, one is consciously aware of the fact that one cannot move. Furthermore, there is often a terrifying sense of a malign presence. Fortunately, sleep paralysis is a transient state. It may be an isolated or repeated occurrence and it is now known to be moderately influenced by genetic factors (Denis, French, Rowe, Zavos, Nolen, Parsons, & Gregory, 2015). Estimates of prevalence vary considerably, but according to a systematic review by Sharpless and Barber (2011) approximately 7.6 per cent of the general population report some experience of it with the prevalence rising to around 30 per cent in two groups, students and psychiatric patients, possibly as a consequence of irregular sleep patterns.

Sleep paralysis is likely to be accompanied by hypnagogic and hypnopompic imagery, which consist of anomalous sensory experiences that occur either preceding sleep or upon awakening, respectively. These sensations include both auditory and visual hallucinations (often of lights or strange figures in the bedroom), pressure on the chest, and floating sensations. Cheyne, Rueffer, and Newby-Clark (1999, p. 319) proposed a neurological model of sleep paralysis and associated imagery involving three factors:

> One factor, labelled Intruder, consisting of sensed presence, fear, and auditory and visual hallucinations, is conjectured to originate in a hypervigilant state initiated in the midbrain. Another factor, Incubus, comprising pressure on the chest, breathing difficulties, and pain, is attributed to effects of hyperpolarization of motorneurons on perceptions of respiration. These two factors have in common an implied alien "other" consistent with occult narratives identified in numerous contemporary and historical cultures. A third factor, labelled Unusual Bodily Experiences, consisting of floating/flying sensations, out-of-body experiences, and feelings of bliss, is related to physically impossible experiences generated by conflicts of endogenous and exogenous activation related to body position, orientation, and movement.

The same core experience has been reported throughout history in many different cultures, although the interpretation of the experience may vary (Hufford, 1982). Despite a relatively high incidence in the non-clinical population, the existence of sleep paralysis is not common knowledge amongst the general public. Anyone who has experienced this terrifying (though temporary) ordeal is likely to be keen to explain it. Accounts of alien abduction including the unusual sensations above are common in modern Western society (e.g. Whitley Strieber's [1987] best-selling book, *Communion: A True Story* and the 2009 film *The Fourth Kind*). In the absence of familiarity with scientific accounts of sleep paralysis, many people are likely to believe either that they were going mad or that they genuinely experienced intruders from another world – even if they cannot consciously remember the experience. Not surprisingly, they marginally prefer to believe that they are sane.

As stated previously, the fact that they have no memory of the abduction is explained by UFOlogists as being due to the aliens' remarkable ability to induce amnesia for most of the experience. At this point, sufferers may well present themselves for hypnotic regression with the strong suspicion that they have indeed been abducted by aliens. A full and detailed account of the standard alien abduction scenario is the most likely outcome. Several commentators insist that sleep paralysis is at the heart of many, if not most, alien abduction claims (e.g. Baker, 1997b, Blackmore, 1994; Newman & Baumeister, 1996a; Randle et al., 1999). Given the fact that many UFO experiences are associated with sleep (e.g. 60 per cent of the intense experiences in Spanos et al.'s [1993] study), this is a reasonable assertion. However, there are other unusual experiences that may trigger the suspicion of alien abduction and thus the misguided search to retrieve memories of the event. These include finding unexplained scars of the body and experiencing episodes of so-called "missing time". As French and Stone (2014) discuss, there are many plausible explanations for such mildly unusual experiences, alien abduction being one of the least plausible.

Temporal lobe activity and tectonic strain theory

An interesting hypothesis has been advanced by Michael Persinger to account not only for some UFO abduction experiences, but for a variety of other ostensibly paranormal experiences (e.g. Persinger, 1990; Persinger & Valliant, 1985). In such cases, he believes, the weird experiences may be due to abnormal activity in the temporal lobes. Such activity is thought to be associated with a variety of mystical and unusual perceptual experiences, including out-of-body experiences. At the extreme end of the continuum of temporal lobe activity are temporal lobe epileptics, who sometimes report that a seizure is preceded by odd sensations, deja vu, hallucinations, and mystical feelings. Persinger has developed a technique whereby he claims he can induce bursts of firing in the temporal lobes of volunteer subjects. Reports of weird bodily sensations have resulted (e.g. Blackmore, 1994). Persinger and colleagues have even reported that they were able to induce the subjective appearance of an apparition in a susceptible volunteer using this technique (Persinger, Tiller, & Koren, 2000). If such an effect were to be replicated by independent investigators, it could be of tremendous significance in accounting for a whole range of ostensibly paranormal phenomena. However, at least two studies (Granqvist, Fredrikson, Unge, Hagenfeldt, Valind, Larhammar, & Larsson, 2005;

French, Haque, Bunton-Stasyshyn, & Davis, 2009) have failed to find evidence in support of Persinger's hypothesis.

Even more controversially, Persinger (1990) claims that in susceptible individuals, temporal lobe overactivity can result from magnetic effects produced as a result of the movement of tectonic plates in the earth's crust. Stresses and strains produced preceding earthquakes would be expected to produce a high level of such magnetic effects and Persinger claims that reports of UFO activity correlate with earthquake activity. Furthermore, it is possible that such activity produces strange luminous effects which explain some UFO reports (Devereux, 1989; Devereaux & Brookesmith, 1997). It is too early to assess fully the validity of Persinger's theory, but his claims have been criticised by many commentators (e.g. Braithwaite, 2011; Jacobs, 1990; Long, 1990; Rutkowski, 1984, 1990, 1994, 2000). The final verdict will depend upon the outcome of future studies.

In support of the general claim that abduction experiences result from unusual mental activity rather than reflecting reality, there are several cases recorded of people reporting full-blown abduction experiences whilst other witnesses could see that the individual in question had not physically gone anywhere. Instead, they appeared to have either lost consciousness or to be in a trance state (see Schnabel, 1994, for such cases).

Content of alien abduction narratives

The history of folklore strongly suggests that the alien abduction narrative is simply the latest cultural interpretation of core experiences that can be found in many societies throughout history (e.g. Schnabel, 1994; Nickell, 1995; Evans, 1998; Randle et al., 1999). Tales have always been told of strange nocturnal visitations, of abduction, of transformation, and of return with strange new powers. These tales have always been interpreted within the predominant cultural framework of the particular time and place. Hence, in times past, angels, spirits, fairies and demons were held responsible. In modern Western culture, beings from advanced technological societies are blamed. But is it possible to account more precisely for the actual content of the narratives? Jung (1959) was probably the first commentator to attempt to interpret the UFO phenomenon in symbolic terms. The content of abduction narratives has also been interpreted in various symbolic ways, including:

A. As a memory of birth: Alvin Lawson (1984) argued that much of the imagery of abduction reflects memories of being born. This hypothesis would, however, contradict our current understanding of the development of autobiographical memory as there is no convincing evidence to suggest that people have reliable memories for any events prior to the age of two (DuBreuil, Garry, & Loftus, 1998).

B. As a form of sadomasochism: Leonard S. Newman and Roy F. Baumeister (1996a, 1996b, 1998; Newman, 1997) have drawn attention to numerous parallels between sadomasochistic practices and the contents of abduction narratives (e.g. pain, loss of control, and humiliation).

C. As a reflection of ambivalent attitudes towards technology in modern society. Terry Matheson (1998) has argued that the themes of the abduction "myth" reflect both our fear of being enslaved by technology and bureaucracy and our hope that, in some inscrutable way, technology may be our salvation.

Each of these interpretations offer more or less plausible symbolic interpretations for the abduction narrative. The very fact that three such differing interpretations can be offered (and others could have been provided) highlights the difficulty in providing any kind of definitive interpretation of this multifaceted phenomenon.

Conclusion

The evidence relating to the alien abduction phenomenon does not support claims either that individuals really are being abducted by aliens or that they are, in general, deliberately lying about their experiences. The most plausible explanation in many cases appears to be that accounts of alien abduction are often based upon false memories. These false memories are fantasy-based constructions which the claimant believes reflect actual events and often result from the use of hypnosis or other associated techniques of "memory recovery" (see, e.g. Lindsay & Read, 1995). Shared cultural knowledge of the standard alien abduction scenario and experiences associated with sleep paralysis also appear to be important contributory factors. It is possible that fantasy-proneness and temporal lobe abnormalities are also implicated, but further research is required to clarify the exact role they may play.

Suggested further reading

Appelle, S., Lynn, S. J., Newman, L., & Maktaris, A. (2014). Alien abduction experiences. In E. Cardeña, S. J. Lynn, & S. Krippner (Eds.), *Varieties of anomalous experience: Examining the scientific evidence*. 2nd ed. (pp. 213–240). Washington, DC: American Psychological Association.

Clancy, S. A. (2005). *Abducted: Why people come to believe they were kidnapped by aliens*. Cambridge, MA: Harvard University Press.

French, C. C., & Stone, A. (2014). *Anomalistic psychology: Exploring paranormal belief and experience*. Basingstoke: Palgrave Macmillan. Chapter 9, pp. 201–223.

6

NEAR-DEATH EXPERIENCES

Chris Roe

> *The boundaries which divide Life from Death are at best shadowy and vague. Who shall say where the one ends, and where the other begins?*
>
> "The Premature Burial" by Edgar Allan Poe (1850)

Introduction

Some people who are near death – or believe themselves to be – have found that the dying process is experienced not in terms of a painful and fearful catastrophic loss of function, but rather as a serene, perhaps even blissful, experience that includes coherent and meaningful elements that suggest to them that some aspect of the self continues to exist and to have experiences after the brain is no longer capable of supporting them. Such experiences have been termed *near-death experiences* (or NDEs for short). The contrast between our expectation that the effects of injury or disease upon the brain will include a severely diminished or impaired subjective experience and the reported experiences of NDEs is a puzzle for modern science to solve. In this chapter we will consider what the main features of the near-death experience seem to be, see whether some people may be more prone to have them than others, and assess the adequacy of the theories that have been put forward to account for them, either in natural or supernatural terms.

Raymond Moody (1975, pp. 21–23) describes a "prototypical" near-death experience, compiled from accounts given to him by people who had been clinically dead or come near to death but had survived to tell the tale of the experiences they had had while in this twilight state, as follows:

> A man is dying and, as he reaches the point of greatest physical distress, he hears himself pronounced dead by his doctor. He begins to hear an uncomfortable noise, a loud ringing or buzzing, and at the same time feels himself

> moving very rapidly through a long dark tunnel. After this, he suddenly finds himself outside of his own physical body . . . and sees his own body from a distance, as though he is a spectator. He watches the resuscitation attempt from this unusual vantage point and is in a state of emotional upheaval . . .
>
> Others come to meet and help him. He glimpses the spirits of relatives and friends who have already died, and a loving warm spirit of a kind he has never encountered before – a being of light – appears before him. This being asks him a question, nonverbally, to make him evaluate his life and helps him along by showing him a panoramic instantaneous playback of the major events in his life. At some point he finds himself approaching some sort of barrier or border, apparently representing the limit between earthly life and the next life. Yet, he finds that he must go back to the earth, that the time for his death has not yet come . . . [and] he reunites with his physical body and lives . . . The experience affects his life profoundly, especially his views about death and its relationship to life.

As we shall see, such accounts are given earnestly (indeed many people are loath to recount their experiences for fear that people will think that they are "crazy"), are fairly consistent across different time periods and cultures, and are treated as genuine experiences by theorists who strive to explain them. Particularly challenging is the fact that NDEs have been reported in cases of actual clinical death, where the vital signs are absent for up to (in rare cases) 20 minutes, but also seem to be experienced in situations which are only *potentially* fatal (see Box 6.1).

BOX 6.1 ARE PEOPLE WHO HAVE NDES REALLY "DEAD"?

The *near*-death experience is very carefully named, since the experience isn't restricted to those who have actually "died". NDEs have been reported by individuals who have been pronounced clinically dead but then resuscitated, by individuals who were actually dying but were able to describe their experiences in their final moments, and also by individuals who, in the course of accidents or illnesses, simply feared that they were near death (Greyson, 2014). In all three types it could be claimed that the experience has more to do with the *process* of dying than with the end point of death itself.

Part of the problem lies in the way in which we "diagnose" death. According to Roberts and Owen (1988) there is a long history of misdiagnosis of death. Previously death had been determined by checking for a pulse or respiration and by checking the pupils for a reaction to light. Later, after the invention of the stethoscope, attention concentrated on the heart, but with the advent of cardiopulmonary resuscitation it became clear that people pronounced dead could be brought back to life (Sabom, 1998), and so attention has now switched to brain function. But equally, a lack of cortical activity and even brain stem quiescence may be symptomatic of dying but need not be an indicator of death. In each case there may be a suspicion that there is some vestige of life that is going undetected (at a cellular level perhaps) and that this is capable of maintaining some kind of phenomenological experience.

These shifts in focus demonstrate how difficult it is to identify any single event as defining death. Rather, death is a *process* that takes time and if the appropriate action is taken then the dying process can be reversed. Roberts and Owen (1988) adopt an extreme definition of death which they describe as being "characterised by irreversible loss of organ functions and is a one-way permanent state" (p. 610). According to this definition, no one reporting an NDE has died (since their dying was reversible), and therefore all NDE reports refer to experiences of people who have remained alive.

If the NDE is genuinely an indication of what happens after we die, as many NDErs believe, then we might expect to find differences between those who were *actually* near death and those who only *thought they were*. There are a number of cases of the latter, such as Moody's (1975, pp. 71–72) account of a man who was in a vehicle that was skidding towards a bridge, but wasn't actually involved in any life-threatening collision.

Moody (1975) claims that in such cases the NDE is less complete than when the person is clinically "dead", but Greyson (1983) found little difference in the content or sequence of NDEs occurring in the dying compared with those who only believed themselves about to die. Owens, Cook, and Stevenson (1990) compared NDEs in 28 patients whom they believed would have died without medical intervention with those in 30 patients who believed they were near death but weren't. The only differences in the experiences were in terms of enhanced perception of light and more lucid clear thinking. The fact that virtually identical NDEs can be induced by *perceived* threat needs to be taken into account in developing explanations of what might actually be going on here.

NDEs were originally thought to be very rare (Moody, 1975), but more recent estimates (Klemenc-Ketis, Grmec & Kersnick, 2011; Greyson, 2014; Zingrone & Alvarado, 2009) suggest that up to a third of people who come close to death have them. This figure may be somewhat inflated in retrospective studies, which ask people to recall their experiences, perhaps from decades earlier, in a way that could be susceptible to recall biases. However, prospective studies, in which cases are collected as they occur, also suggest that the experience is quite common: Sartori (2008) found that of 39 patients who had survived a cardiac arrest during the five-year study, seven (17.9 per cent) reported an NDE. Zingrone and Alvarado (2009) restricted their review to studies that adopted designs that were less susceptible to response and memory bias, and found the incidence of NDEs to be 35 per cent for retrospective studies and 17 per cent for prospective studies.

The relatively high incidence could be explained in terms of improvements in resuscitation methods that mean that more people survive the kinds of close brush with death (e.g. heart attack, drowning, road traffic accident) that would previously have been fatal. It could of course simply reflect the fact that the notion of NDEs has entered popular culture and may provide the basis for some fantasised experience produced while unconscious or in crisis.

The person most closely associated with bringing the near-death experience to popular attention, and indeed for coining the phrase, is Raymond Moody. His interest in the phenomenon does not stem from direct experience, since Moody has not had an NDE himself, but while studying philosophy as an undergraduate one of his professors described to him an account of what had happened to him after he had "died" and been resuscitated. Some years later while teaching philosophy, one of his students recounted his grandmother's experience that involved virtually the same series of events. Moody began to take an active interest in such cases from this point and found that many of the classes he took would include at least one student who could describe a personal NDE (his own or a close friend or relative's). After teaching philosophy for three years he went to medical school with the intention of becoming a psychiatrist, and found patients on the wards who had been resuscitated after having "died" for a short time and who were also able to recall experiences from the time when they were "dead". Moody was impressed by the broad similarities in cases even though they involved people from a range of religious, social and educational backgrounds. It is very easy to be blasé about these similarities when thinking about NDEs now, in the twenty-first century, when notions of travelling down tunnels and being met by deceased relatives and so on are part of popular culture (found in movies such as *Flatliners*, TV programmes like *The Simpsons*, and many popular books, for example) to the point where a classic NDE is almost archetypal. But at the time many of the common features were quite unexpected, and certainly didn't conform in many respects to stereotypical views of what might happen after death. As the cases built up, Moody found he had enough material to be able to give public talks on the subject, and members of the audience at these would often volunteer further cases. By the time of his first book in 1975, *Life After Life*, he had amassed over 150 cases.

In this book, Moody identified 15 elements that seemed to recur in NDE reports (see Box 6.2). When considering these we must bear in mind that these have been drawn from a variety of cases, and this sketch isn't representative of any particular case. In fact no single experience included more than 12 of these 15, and no element was ever-present, so we can't claim from this that some elements are more central or more characteristic of the NDE than others. Also, although the features are presented in a particular order, as if they represent successive stages, there is no fixed order to the NDE.

The purpose of Moody's book was to draw public attention to the fact that people were reporting such experiences and to convince serious researchers that the topic was worthy of study. At this level, it was a great success. The book has sold over 31 million copies and has been translated into at least 26 languages

BOX 6.2 MOODY'S (1975) 15 KEY FEATURES

The inherent ineffability of the experience: that people find it difficult to put into words what had happened to them

Overhearing the news of their own death: often some clear statement that others believe them to have died, which may come as a surprise to them

Feelings of peace and quiet: in some cases euphoria, and can be in stark contrast to the intense pain experienced immediately prior to the NDE

The noise: often a rather unpleasant buzzing or rushing sound

The dark tunnel: more often a sensation of being pulled rapidly through a dark space than a vision of an actual tunnel

Out of the body: a sense of being outside one's body looking down at it

Meeting others: awareness of others, perhaps deceased relatives but sometimes not

The being of light: a light that typically begins dimly but becomes intensely bright and enveloping

The review: a panoramic review of major life events

The border or limit: a "point of no return" at which they must "decide" whether to return to the body

Coming back: a sense of making the decision to return

Telling others: reticence in describing their experience to others for fear of seeming insane

Effects on lives: subtle but profound changes in views on life and other people

New views on death: reduced fear of death but greater valuing of life

Corroboration: independent confirmation of elements of the NDE by others

(Holden, Greyson, & James, 2009). A whole new research area of near-death studies has been established, with its own professional body, *The International Association for Near-Death Studies* (IANDS), and peer-reviewed publication the *Journal of Near-Death Studies*. But, as Moody himself freely admits (1975, p. 181), the book wasn't intended to stand as a scientific study – the collection does not allow us to go beyond the purely descriptive, and it isn't possible to derive estimates about which stages are more common or which seem to be precursors of others.

Kenneth Ring (1980) took things a stage further by conducting a more systematic survey using a structured interview and measurement scale that he had devised. This was administered to 102 people who had been near death, of whom 48 per cent reported an NDE of some description. Ring used their accounts to identify a "core experience" which consisted of five stages. Not only did these stages tend to unfold in a particular order, but the earlier stages seemed to be more common than later stages, as one might expect if some people are revived earlier than others. However, we need to be aware that this is still only a trend rather than an invariable sequence – Greyson (1998), for example, reports on some experiences which were out of sequence.

The five stages of the NDE

Feelings of deep peace and well-being

The first and most common stage, reported by 60 per cent of Ring's NDErs, involves a sense of bliss or peace. This feeling is often characterised as an absence of fear and/or pain (which may have been the dominant emotions prior to the NDE, for example during cardiac arrest). Heim's (1892) autobiographical account of his own experience after falling from a mountain to what he believed would be his certain death is a good example:

> No grief was felt nor was there any paralysing fright. There was no anxiety, no trace of despair or pain, but rather calm seriousness, profound acceptance and a dominant mental quickness. The relationship of events and their probable outcomes was viewed with great objective clarity, no confusion entered at all. (cited in Roberts & Owen, 1988, p. 607)

Although for some the feeling is tinged with sadness or loneliness (Irwin & Watt, 2007), for others the experience isn't simply an emotional detachment, but rather one of ineffable euphoria:

> I felt embraced by such feelings of bliss, that there are no words to describe the feeling. The nearest I can come to it in human terms is to recall the rapture of being "in love", the emotion one feels when one's first born is put into one's arms for the first time, the transcendence of spirit that can sometimes occur when one is at a concert of classical music, the peace and grandeur of mountains, forests and lakes or other beauties of nature that can move one to tears of joy. Unite all these together and magnify a thousand times and you get a glimpse of the "state of being" that one is in. (Grey, 1985, cited in Blackmore, 1993, p. 94)

A sense of separation from the body

The next most common experience among Ring's respondents was a sense of being disconnected from the body, often with accompanying sensory experiences. This is often referred to as an out-of-body experience, or OBE. Thirty-seven per cent reported this, with about half of these able to see their own body, usually from a bird's eye view. At times this can allow them an excellent view of the medical staff's attempts to resuscitate them:

> The next thing was I was above myself near the ceiling looking down. One of the nurses was saying in what seemed a frantic voice, "Breathe, Dawn,

> breathe". A doctor was pressing my chest, drips were being disconnected, everyone was rushing around. I couldn't understand the panic. I wasn't in pain. (Fenwick & Fenwick, 1996, p. 35)

Emotional reactions to seeing one's own body can vary from a desperate desire to return to it (but without any idea of how this could be achieved) through to being completely uninterested: "I could see my own body all tangled up in the car amongst all the people who had gathered around, but you know, I had no feelings for it whatsoever. It was like it was a completely different human, or maybe even just an object" (Moody, 1975, pp. 40–41). In some cases the "person" having the out-of-body experience feels as if they don't have any "body" at all, but rather exists as a kind of pure consciousness. Others do describe what could be called a spiritual body which is invisible and inaudible to others, unable to touch and virtually weightless.

Entering darkness/passing through a tunnel

To the general public, the image of travelling along a dark tunnel towards a bright light seems to capture the essence of the NDE. And indeed in about a quarter of Ring's (1980) NDE cases, either before or after the out-of-body experience, the respondent describes how they felt as if they were drifting or even moving very rapidly through a dark space. Although referred to as a tunnel in Moody's prototype, in fact the experience is only sometimes described as being tunnel-like in any literal sense; it is much more commonly thought of as a kind of enveloping space or velvety blackness that gives only a vague sense of being enclosed rather than having perceptible tunnel walls. One NDEr, for example, describes their experience in the following way: "I went through this dark vacuum at super speed . . . I felt like I was riding on a roller coaster train at an amusement park" (Moody, 1975, p. 32).

Seeing the light

For 16 per cent of respondents, as they progressed down the tunnel they became aware of a light at its end, which they seemed to be drawn to. As they moved towards the light it expanded and became brighter until it enveloped them completely. The light is described as brilliant, often golden, but it doesn't seem to dazzle or hurt the eyes in the way that a real bright light might do if viewed normally. There is a very common belief amongst NDErs that the light is actually some kind of being, and is often associated with a religious figure such as Jesus. One's prior religious beliefs do not seem to affect the likelihood or form of such an encounter, although they clearly may affect the interpretation, so that atheists still see the light, but don't associate it with a particular God (Greyson & Stevenson, 1980; Sabom, 1982). Communication with this being does not seem to involve speech, but is more direct and may not even take the form of language as we know it.

NDErs have great difficulty in articulating in their native tongue what was actually communicated, although they can say that it often seems to centre on the life of the person, offering them an opportunity to reflect on what they have done and what they have not done – though this doesn't seem to involve any kind of critical judgement – and to decide whether to return to the body.

There may follow a panoramic life review in which many of the key events in their lives are played out to them. Its exact nature can vary; for some this follows a chronological order, starting with their earliest memories, whereas for others it seems to all come at once. Some view the events as a spectator while others review the scene from the different perspectives of different actors, having an empathic sense of the consequences for others of their actions. The memories themselves are primarily visual, but seem more vivid than normal, and evoke the emotions of the time. The events don't seem to be a random collection but rather seem to have been chosen to illustrate certain lessons, such as when they were particularly unkind to others, or equally were particularly benevolent, or where the course of their life changed, such as with the birth of a child. Some experience the life review in the company of the being of light, whereas others are left to reflect alone. Again the emphasis seems to be on understanding rather than judgement.

Entering the light/beautiful garden

Ten per cent of Ring's (1980) NDErs reported that on entering the light they found themselves in some other world – often so indescribably beautiful that experients didn't want to return from it. This is often classically "heavenly", consisting of a lovely garden with beautiful music and so on, rather than stereotypically "heavenly", with clouds, angels, and Pearly Gates (Irwin & Watt, 2007) although the latter have been reported on occasion (Sabom, 1982). Here they may be greeted by deceased relatives and friends, or by people who are unknown to them but are described as "guardian spirits" or "helpers". These companions are usually present to reassure them or to facilitate the decision to return to the body.

While in this transcendental realm, the NDEr may approach some kind of natural border, such as a river, a wall with an archway, a fence with a gate, or simply a line. This takes on symbolic meaning to them and they become convinced that if they pass across this border they will not be able to return. This typically results in the decision to go back. Most don't recall the "journey" back, but find that they must have lapsed into unconsciousness only to awaken back in their body. However, some do recall being drawn rapidly back into their bodies, and this may be achieved with a jolt.

Correlates of the NDE

If we are to understand the causes of the near-death experience, or at least be able to recognise which explanations are more likely candidates, it could be useful to consider what kind of person reports having them and under what circumstances.

Effects of type of life threat

Surprisingly, physiological details of the close brush with death seem to play only a minor role in the form of the NDE (Greyson, 2014; Holden, Long, & MacLurg, 2009). We have already seen (Box 6.1) that there are only modest differences between those who were actually near death and those who simply thought they were. When looking at different types of threat to life it looks as though those who were chronically ill prior to the NDE were more likely to experience positive emotions and apparitions, whereas those who had a sudden threat to life reported a more typical core NDE (Grosso, 1981). Similarly, Noyes and Kletti (1977) found that features such as hallucinations of beings (guides or relatives) and also panoramic life reviews were more common in cases of drowning or terminal illness than after falls and accidents. Greyson (1985) found that sudden life reviews rarely occurred when the person had *long* been expecting death, presumably because such people had already had the opportunity to take stock and prepare for death. Greyson (2014) reports that the OBE component of the NDE is more likely following cardiac arrest whereas those not suffering a cardiac arrest are more likely to report unreal sensations more typical of depersonalisation.

Demographic and personality factors

The incidence of the NDE does not seem to be related to such demographic factors as age, gender, socioeconomic status, race, marital status, or mental health (Greyson, 2014; Holden, Long, & MacLurg, 2009; Zingrone & Alvarado, 2009), though these factors may be related to the actual content of the NDE (Irwin & Watt, 2007; Roberts & Owen, 1988). But those associations as have been found may be explainable in terms of demographic differences in the type of brush with death that is most likely – males may be more likely than females to have a road accident, for example (Irwin & Watt, 2007; Twemlow & Gabbard, 1984). Young children report NDEs that show the same variety as adult NDEs with only minor deviations – for example, they tended to be greeted by deceased pets rather than relatives (Morse & Moody, 1991) – and don't necessarily conform to religious teachings, nor does the complexity of the experience seem to reflect the child's cognitive or linguistic capabilities, and retrospective recall can seem to exceed the capacities of memory functions in neonates (Sutherland, 2009).

Cultural differences in the content of NDEs

The central features of the NDE have been recorded throughout history and across various cultures and religious groups. Holk (1978) found descriptions in the beliefs of Bolivian, Argentinian, and North American Indians, and accounts from China, Siberia, and Finland that included a sense of joy and peace, being out of the body, being reunited with ancestors, perceiving a light, and reaching a border or dividing line. According to Greyson (2014), accounts similar to Moody's also can be found in the folklore and writings of European, Middle Eastern, African, Indian, East Asian, Pacific, and Native American peoples. But there are also some differences in specific detail. For example, Schorer (1985/6) found Native American NDEs included moccasins, snakes, eagles, and bows and arrows as dominant imagery, whereas Pasricha and Stevenson (1986) found that NDEs from the Indian subcontinent featured Yamraj, the Hindu god of the dead, and his yamdoot messengers who fetched the dead and brought them for reckoning. Experiencers were typically sent back to the living because of an apparent supernatural bureaucratic mistake or because of earthly commitments rather than through their own conscious choice. Osis and Haraldsson (1977) found in their reports of encounters with "God" that no Hindu reported seeing Jesus and no Christian reported seeing a Hindu deity. However, we have already seen that NDErs rarely recognise the entity by their physical appearance, and so this cultural difference in labelling may simply be a consequence of the ineffability of the experience. Despite some cross-cultural variations in specific NDE content, it is worth noting that people do report elements that run counter to their cultural expectations (Holden, Long, & MacLurg, 2009), and that people who have never heard of the NDE (such as most of Moody's original sample) still tend to describe the same features (Sabom, 1982). This may suggest that whereas the process may be universal, the specific imagery and interpretation given to an NDE is determined by the expectations and beliefs of the individual (Roberts & Owen, 1988).

Theories of the NDE

Psychological theories

Depersonalisation

Perhaps the first explanation of the NDE to be put forward was by Pfister (1930, translated by Kletti & Noyes, 1981), who was attempting to account for the experiences of Heim's mountaineers who were falling, they thought, to their deaths. He suggested that when confronted with the terrific prospect of their own imminent demise, they might have attempted to escape from this unpalatable thought by retreating into a more positive fantasy experience in an effort to protect themselves from the emotional shock. Noyes and Kletti (1976, 1977) developed this notion, suggesting that NDEs represent a kind of depersonalisation. Noyes (1972) proposed that where there is any possibility of avoiding death, then physical and mental alertness increase and attention is focused on survival, but where death seems inevitable, fear is replaced by a sense of peace and resignation, with the panoramic life review perhaps reflecting a need for premature grieving for one's own death. This copes very well with some of the features of the NDE, such as the sense of being out of one's body and the general sense of detachment from proceedings, but has a more difficult task in accounting for the greater alertness usually experienced, since depersonalisation is usually rather dreamlike and involves a loss of sense of self (Irwin & Watt, 2007).

Absorption and fantasy proneness

Given that the NDE involves the experient being immersed in an alternate reality, researchers have speculated that it may be related to absorption and fantasy proneness (Greyson, 2014). The former is sometimes regarded as a form of dissociation and represents a capacity to immerse oneself in the focus of awareness (which may be imaginal) to the exclusion of other possible foci. The Tellegen Absorption Scale includes items such as "While watching a movie, TV, or play, I may become so involved that I may forget about myself and my surroundings and experience the movie as if it were real and as if I were taking part in it" and "Sometimes I experience things as if they were doubly real". Fantasy proneness is characterised by a strong interest in fantasy life, vivid hallucinatory ability and intense sensory experience (Greyson, 2014). Wilson and Barber (1983) suggested that high fantasisers may be more likely to report an NDE than others. Although there is some suggestive evidence of a correlation between absorption and fantasy proneness and likelihood of reporting an NDE (Council & Greyson, 1985, cited in Greyson, 2014), the effects are quite weak and have not been replicated by others (e.g. Ring, 1992).

Organic theories

Endorphins

Extreme stress and fear can lead to the release of endorphins. These are naturally produced opiates that seem to reduce pain perception and induce pleasant sensations. It may be that endorphins are also released near death and could therefore be responsible for the positive emotions and calm that are often reported. It is interesting to note that drugs which negate the effects of neurochemicals like endorphins may give rise to NDEs that are more negative in nature (e.g. Judson & Wiltshaw, 1983). Jansen (1997) has similarly argued that the naturally occurring anaesthetic ketamine can trigger experiences of lights, tunnels and so on. However, these neurochemicals have a number of effects that are not characteristic of the NDE: ketamine experiences are often fearful rather than positive (Strassman, 1997) and have an unreal quality that is not found in NDEs (Fenwick, 1997), and the analgesic effects last much longer than the few minutes or even seconds of an NDE (Sabom, 1982).

Cerebral anoxia

Rodin (1980) has noted that the final common pathway to death is cerebral anoxia, or in other words lack of oxygen to the brain. The kinds of effects produced by anoxia, which include a sense of well-being and power, suggests that the NDE might best be explained as the result of an anoxic brain. It is interesting in this context to consider the research by Whinnery (1990, 1997) that looked at the experiences reported by pilots who had briefly fallen unconscious during periods of rapid acceleration that can occur during manoeuvres. Loss of consciousness occurs because the accelerating forces can substantially reduce the blood flow to the head, inducing a kind of anoxia. Whinnery found that a number of the features reminiscent of NDEs are reported, such as tunnel visions, bright lights, floating sensations, OBEs and euphoria, and even the report of "dreams" that can include visions of beautiful gardens and meeting (live) family members. The effects of anoxia have been characterised as involving confused thinking, in contrast to the extreme clarity of the NDE, but in fact the effects of anoxia vary enormously depending upon the type of anoxia, its speed on onset, and the time until oxygen is restored (French, 2005).

Blackmore (1993) explains the tunnel and light phenomena as the result of neuronal disinhibition in the visual cortex. In this area of the brain, the natural state for cells is to fire and they have to be suppressed from firing through inhibition. If the inhibitory cells responsible for this control are more sensitive to oxygen depletion, then the first consequence of anoxia may ironically be an *increase* in cell firing. Given that light receptors in the retina are more densely packed in the middle of the visual field, and more of their impulses survive to be represented in the cortex, then this increasing activity may be experienced as a light at the centre of the visual field which gets brighter and brighter and bigger and bigger (Blackmore & Troscianko, 1988) as more cells start to fire. This expansion may naturally be interpreted in terms of movement towards the circle of light. When very many cortex cells are firing, this could give the impression of a brilliant light, but since the eyes are not involved in perceiving it, it wouldn't hurt. Again, the problem here is in accounting for such experiences among people who are clearly not anoxic.

According to Greyson (2014), the only study to date to actually measure blood levels of oxygen and carbon dioxide during NDEs was by Sabom (1982), and this found no significant differences in the experiences of those with and without anoxia. This finding has been questioned on the grounds that general blood measures (taken, say, from an easily accessible artery) are not good indicators of blood-oxygen levels in particular places (such as certain areas of the brain), so we can't infer from one to the other. This is a convincing argument for cases such as Sabom's (1982), and more accurate measures are clearly needed. However, there are many instances of NDEs where we can be fairly sure that anoxia is unlikely, particularly where there is only a perceived threat to the person's life (such as with Heim's mountain climbers). This does not rule out anoxia as a possible cause of some of these effects, but it does rule it out as the *only* cause.

Temporal lobe seizures

Sabom and Kreutziger (1982) considered the idea that hypoxia (an excess of oxygen) can give rise to temporal lobe epilepsy which has some features that are similar to the NDE, such as the panoramic life review and the changes in affect. However they noted that there were qualitative differences in reports of the two types of experience which led them to conclude that this wasn't an adequate explanation. Seizure-induced perceptions also tend to feature auditory imagery more frequently than visual imagery (Irwin & Watt, 2007) whereas in the NDE it is not uncommon for the person to experience no sound at all, and the memories invoked by temporal lobe stimulation tend to be random and not particularly meaningful, quite unlike the life-review reported by NDErs (Noyes & Kletti, 1977). It has been suggested that OBEs might also reflect triggered disturbances to the brain's temporal lobes (Blanke, 2004). OBEs seem to be consistent across cultures and have been reported to occur more frequently in people who suffer from migraine or epilepsy (Blanke & Arzy, 2005), suggesting a common biological origin. Neurological patients who report OBEs have been described as having damage to the temporal and parietal regions of the brain (Devinsky et al., 1989) which is interesting given that the temporo-parietal junction is thought to be involved in the integration of information from and about the body (Blanke & Arzy, 2005) to generate an internal map of self-perception (De Ridder et al., 2007). Recent transcranial stimulation of this region has been able to induce the perception of disembodiment (De Ridder et al., 2007), and in some cases autoscopy (Blanke et al., 2004). This represents a promising approach to the investigation of NDEs but is sadly under-researched; as Blanke and Dieguez (2009, p. 315) note, "although several authors have speculated on the neurology of NDEs, there is an almost complete absence of neurological data". Further developments in this field are eagerly awaited.

Hallucination

Some medications and some physiological malfunctions can give rise to hallucinations – could these provide the basis for reported NDEs? Although this seems superficially plausible, it seems as though those whom we can be sure have not taken drugs or suffered any injury or malfunction have NDEs that are essentially the same as those whom we are less sure about (Greyson, 2014), suggesting that this isn't the key factor. There is in fact some evidence to suggest that drug- or metabolically induced delirium may actually be an *inhibitor* of NDEs (Osis & Haraldsson, 1977). In any case, hallucinations induced in various other ways typically include confused thinking, disorientation and fear, along with rather bizarre and idiosyncratic visions. This is in stark contrast to the common pattern of events found in NDEs that includes especially lucid thinking and calmness or even euphoria.

Spiritual theories

The final theory that we shall consider here is that NDEs are what they seem to be, since this seems to be the most popular interpretation among members of the general public (Kellehear, Heaven, & Gao, 1990). Roberts and Owen (1988) have claimed that many studies of the NDE are based implicitly on the notion that such experiences can most economically be understood in terms of the existence of an afterlife, and popular interest in the phenomenon is based on the hope that it might provide an empirical basis for what they had previously accepted as an act of faith. Notable subscribers to this view are Ring (1980, 1984) and Sabom (1982, 1998).

But what would stand as evidence for the NDE being a literal experience of an afterlife? It would be extremely difficult to operationalise and test an immaterial interpretation using materialist scientific methods.

One possible strand of support could come from claims that certain early stages are objectively real. If this could be demonstrated then it could indirectly strengthen the case for regarding later stages as similarly real. The autoscopic experience is the most promising stage to concentrate on, since during this experience some people claim to have witnessed resuscitation procedures, or their loved ones being comforted in nearby rooms. Is there any evidence to suggest that these experiences could not have been arrived at through some vestigial sense of hearing and a good imagination? Cook, Greyson, and Stevenson (1998) have bemoaned the lack of interest in testing the survival question and identified three features that might support the spiritual hypothesis

Enhanced mentation: despite diminished physiological functioning, experiences (and even where the experient is not truly "near death" they may still be expected to experience a restriction in mental capacity, for example as a result of a sudden drop in blood pressure) remain coherent and vivid – NDErs typically describe their experience as unusually vivid, equalling or even surpassing those of their normal waking state; state of consciousness isn't wholly dependent on brain state.

Out-of-body experience: may suggest that the mind can function outside of the body.

Paranormal perceptions: perceives events that could not have been acquired normally if consciousness is restricted to the physical brain/body; such confirmations would also provide evidence that NDEs are not entirely subjective.

Cook et al. describe seven published cases and seven cases from their own collection that contain all three features. They argue that "although the evidence for survival from NDEs is far from compelling, it also does not in our opinion deserve the neglect it has received from researchers". In contrast, critics assert that evidence for these features is weak (e.g. French, 2005; Mobbs & Watt, 2011). Counterarguments include that NDErs are not truly near death when they have their experience, that "paranormal" perceptions are simply a result of residual sensory input (particularly hearing) and inference (Woerlee, 2014), and concerns that the NDE might not have been experienced during the window of inactivity but during the period of recovery (French, 2001).

To counter these claims, proponents cite evidence of real-time perceptions. For example, Sabom (1982) collected recollections of CPR (cardio-pulmonary resuscitation) from 32 patients who claimed an NDE after cardiac arrest and then interviewed 25 "seasoned cardiac patients", asking them to describe what they imagined the CPR procedure would consist of given their experiences in acute wards. Sabom found that none of the NDE claimants made errors (including some features that were wholly visual, so were less available as sensory input), while 20 of 23 controls included at least 1 major error. Individual cases that apparently reflect real-time perceptions that seem unlikely to have been shaped by meagre perception and inference are also cited to refute these counterclaims. For example, van Lommel, van Wees, Meyers, and Elfferich (2001, p. 2041) report on the following:

> During a night shift an ambulance brings in a 44 year-old cyanotic comatose man into the coronary care unit. He had been found about an hour before in a meadow by passers-by. After admission, he receives artificial respiration without intubation, while heart massage and defibrillation are also applied. When we want to intubate the patient, he turns out to have dentures in his mouth. I remove these upper dentures and put them onto the "crash car". Meanwhile, we continue extensive CPR. After about an hour and a half the patient has sufficient heart rhythm and blood pressure, but he is still ventilated and intubated, and he is still comatose. He is transferred to the intensive care unit to continue the necessary artificial respiration. Only after more than a week do I meet again with the patient, who is by now back on the cardiac ward. I distribute his medication. The moment he sees me he says: "Oh, that nurse knows where my dentures are". I am very surprised. Then he elucidates: "Yes, you were there when I was brought into hospital and you took my dentures out of my mouth and put them onto that car, it had all these bottles on it and there was this sliding drawer underneath and there you put my teeth". I was especially amazed because I remembered this happening while the man was in deep coma and in the process of CPR. When I asked further, it appeared the man had seen himself lying in bed, that he had perceived from above how nurses and doctors had been busy with CPR. He was also able to describe correctly and in detail the small room in which he had been resuscitated as well as the appearance of those present like myself.

However, in such cases there is always a concern that because the experient is not being physiologically monitored then they might not be in the neurologically incapacitated state that is assumed. In contrast, the case of Pam Reynolds involves very close physiological monitoring during the period of the NDE (Sabom, 1998, pp. 37–47). Reynolds needed a bypass operation to treat a life-threatening aneurysm (a bulge in a blood vessel caused by a weakness in the blood vessel wall) that was at the base of her brain and would have catastrophic consequences if it were to burst. To reduce risk of such a burst occurring during the operation, blood was drained from Reynolds' brain. This in itself is very risky since the brain is likely to suffer irreversible damage within about 4 minutes if deprived of blood oxygen; however, if the body is cooled to 60°F (16°C) to reduce cell activity, then this safe window can be extended, so Reynolds' blood was cooled before her heart was arrested and her brain drained of blood. During the procedure, in which a femoral artery was taken from her groin to replace the defective part of the artery in her brain, Reynolds' condition was continuously monitored, including core temperature, blood oxygen levels, cortical activity, and brain stem activity (in the form of evoked responses to clicks that were played in her ears). All measures indicated clinical death, but nevertheless Reynolds reported a fairly typical NDE involving observation of the procedure (including surprising elements such as that her whole head had not been shaved for the operation, and that the saw for cutting through the skull looked very like an electric toothbrush) and supernatural elements (including encountering a bright light and meeting deceased relatives) during the period when she was brain dead.

Some features of the NDE, particularly the timing of events, have been challenged (e.g. Augustine, 2007, 2008) but this remains a formidable case to explain in conventional terms. Beauregard, St-Pierre, Rayburn, and Demers (2012) have since reviewed 33 patients who had similar hypothermic circulatory arrest procedures, and found three (9 per cent) reported conscious awareness during clinical death, including feelings of peace and observing elements of the operation as if they had left their bodies. However, it is very difficult for proponents of the spiritual hypothesis to explain why there should be cases in which the threat to life was only perceived rather than actual (why should there be Divine or Cosmic mistakes?), although this may simply reflect prejudice about the kind of form that an afterlife should take. Parsimony dictates that the spiritualist interpretation should be set aside until it can be shown that explanations in terms of more mundane mechanisms, with roots in the principles of psychology and psychopharmacology, are inadequate. If these latter theories can account equally well for the data, then they should be preferred because they don't require us to invoke any new or mysterious mechanisms.

Conclusions

We have seen that a number of theories have been put forward to account for the NDE, but none comes very close to providing a comprehensive explanation for all the various features that are typical of the experience. Where these psychological and physiological hypotheses do succeed in explaining elements of the NDE, this is achieved by focusing selectively on some features that can be explained and ignoring or diminishing the importance of those that cannot. But while it may be true that these theories are incomplete at best, they may still be able to provide us with a rich source of speculative predictions that can be tested in future investigations.

We should also bear in mind that inadequate evidence is not the same as absence of evidence, and it is certainly premature to reject the psychological and organic theories in favour of a spiritualistic one. This is particularly so given that we still don't really have an adequate definition of what constitutes an NDE – no single feature seems to be necessary or unique to the experience. Despite the numerous books on the subject of NDEs there is still only limited systematic research available on what is clearly a very complex experience, so it should not be too surprising that we are still some way from developing an understanding of its nature and cause, and further work is clearly necessary. In this vein, it seems likely that the NDE may actually represent a class of more or less related phenomena that are explicable in different ways. As French (2005) notes, "given the heterogenous nature of the NDE . . . [t]here is no reason to assume that a single comprehensive theory will explain the entire phenomenon". Whatever the ultimate resolution, it would be fair to say that the NDE is an intriguing and powerful area of human experience that deserves our continued interest in it.

Suggestions for further reading

Blanke, O., & Dieguez, S. (2009). Leaving body and life behind: Out-of-body and near-death experience. In S. Laureys & G. Tononi (Eds.), *The neurology of consciousness: Cognitive neuroscience and neuropathology* (pp. 303–325). Amsterdam: Elsevier.

Fenwick, P., & Fenwick, E. (1996). *The truth in the light: An investigation of over 300 near-death experiences.* New York: Berkley Books.

French, C. C. (2005). Near-death experiences in cardiac arrest survivors. In S. Laureys (Ed.), *Progress in brain research, Vol. 150: The boundaries of consciousness, neurobiology and neuropathology* (pp. 351–367). Amsterdam: Elsevier.

Greyson, B. (2014). Near-death experiences. In E. Cardeña, S. J. Lynn, & S. Krippner (Eds.), *Varieties of anomalous experience: Examining the scientific evidence*, 2nd ed. (pp. 333–367). Washington, DC: American Psychological Association.

Holden, J., Greyson, B., & James, D. (Eds.) (2009). *The handbook of near-death experiences: Thirty years of investigation.* (pp. 17–40). Santa Barbara, CA: ABC-CLIO.

Kelly, E. F., Kelly, E. W., Crabtree, A., Gauld, A., Grosso, M., & Greyson, B. (2006). *Irreducible mind: toward a psychology for the 21st century.* Plymouth: Rowan & Littlefield.

Moody, R. A. (1975). *Life after life.* New York: Bantam Books.

7

REINCARNATION CLAIMS

Christopher C. French

> *As a man, casting off worn out garments taketh new ones, so the dweller in the body, entereth into ones that are new.*
>
> Epictetus

Introduction

In *The Demon-Haunted World*, one of the last books Carl Sagan wrote before his untimely death, we find these words:

> At the time of writing there are three claims in the ESP field which, in my opinion, deserve serious study: (1) that by thought alone humans can (barely) affect random number generators in computers; (2) that people under mild sensory deprivation can receive thoughts or images "projected" at them; and (3) that young children sometimes report the details of a previous life, which upon checking turn out to be accurate and which they could not have known about in any other way than reincarnation.
>
> (Sagan, 1997, p. 285)

These claims are often presented as being among those providing the strongest evidence in favour of the existence of genuinely paranormal phenomena (i.e. phenomena that defy explanation in terms of currently accepted scientific principles). My own opinion is very much in line with Sagan's. As he went on to write:

> I pick these claims not because I think they're likely to be valid (I don't), but as examples of contentions that *might* be true. [They] have at least some, although still dubious, experimental support. Of course, I could be wrong.
>
> (Sagan, 1997, p. 285)

By one of those spooky little coincidences, the first time I read these words I was lying on a bed in the Commodore Hotel, Beirut. I had been invited to take part in a documentary on reincarnation claims amongst the Druse people of the Lebanon. The programme was produced by Granite Productions for Channel 4 and was broadcast as part of the series, *To the Ends of the Earth*. The basic idea for the programme was that I, a known sceptic, would investigate the claims alongside Roy Stemman, editor of *Reincarnation International*. Our guide was Jad Al Younis, himself a Druse and a believer in reincarnation.

There are obvious advantages and disadvantages with an investigation that is to form the basis of a TV documentary. The main disadvantage is that the top priority of the programme makers is to produce an interesting and visually appealing programme, so you can find yourself spending an entire morning doing shots of a jeep driving up a mountain road. This greatly reduces the time for real investigation. Having said that, this is compensated for by the background research done by the team working on the programme. In particular, Chris Ledger, the producer, and Tima Khalil Majdalani, a journalist acting as one of our translators, deserve special credit in this regard. The background preparation also meant that we did not have to waste our own time setting up interviews and so on. Much of this chapter is devoted to lessons learned during my investigation of Druse reincarnation claims but we will begin with consideration of reincarnation claims in general.

Reincarnation: the general concept

According to Edwards (1996a, p. 11), reincarnation may be defined as follows: "the belief that human beings do not, as most of us assume, live only once, but on the contrary live many, perhaps an infinite number of lives, acquiring a new body for each incarnation". Guiley (1991, p. 500) offers the following definition: "The return of the soul or essence after death to inhabit a new physical form". Although definitions of the term *paranormal* vary greatly, most definitions would include consideration of evidence relating to the possibility of life after death. It is clear, therefore, that the evidence relating to the possibility of reincarnation is well within the remit of parapsychology.

The general arguments put forward by proponents of reincarnation are many and varied, but none of them appear to be particularly compelling (Edwards, 1996a, 1996b). They include:

- It avoids some of the problems associated with other forms of life after death, e.g. where do souls go? But there are, of course, no such problems for those who do not believe in life after death.
- It appears to explain apparent injustice in the world, particularly those versions of reincarnation which involve the so-called "law of Karma". Injustices inflicted upon individuals in this life are said to be punishment for evil acts performed in previous lives, thus ensuring that overall the world is a just place. But there are simply no reasons to assume that the world *is* a just place even though we might like it to be.

- It accounts for allegedly inexplicable empirical facts, e.g. child prodigies (as the reincarnations of adult geniuses – but such "explanations" are unnecessary in the light of modern psychological knowledge), déjà vu (but neuroscience offers more plausible accounts), hypnotic past-life regressions (but fantasy-based role-playing provides a better explanation), and spontaneous memories of past incarnations (as investigated most notably by the late Professor Ian Stevenson, a psychiatrist at the University of Virginia).

Edwards (1996a, 1996b) provides detailed consideration of the general topic of reincarnation from a highly critical and sceptical perspective. For the best treatments of the topic from a point of view that is more sympathetic to the possibility that reincarnation might be a genuine phenomenon, one can still do no better than refer to Stevenson's publications (e.g. 1980, 2001, 2003). For other informative discussions, see Mills and Tucker (2014) and Wilson (1987).

Although all varieties of belief in reincarnation fit the definitions provided, there is a great deal of variation across cultures with respect to the details. For example, there is variation between cultures with respect to:

- Whether one can reincarnate into a body of the opposite sex
- Whether one can reincarnate into a non-human body or even into an inanimate object
- Whether there is a gap between the death of one physical body and reincarnation in another
- Whether the soul enters the new body at the moment of conception or birth

Although there appear to be no compelling arguments in favour of reincarnation, there appear to be several compelling arguments against the most common versions of it. These include:

- The dependence of consciousness on the brain: The fact that all available scientific evidence suggests that consciousness is wholly dependent upon underlying brain states is a strong argument against dualism and any form of life after death.
- Womb invasions: No version of reincarnation even begins to supply a plausible account of how a disembodied soul can retain memories and skills from a previous incarnation or of how the soul can invade a new womb and imprint old memories and skills on a developing embryo.
- The population problem: Many versions of reincarnation assume that human souls always occupy human bodies and that souls can neither be created nor destroyed. This necessarily requires a constant population that obviously contradicts the facts.

Note, however, that not all reincarnationists are committed to a view in which everyone is reincarnated. For some, the existence of a single case in which it could be shown conclusively that an individual possessed true memories of a previous life that could not have come about by normal means would be enough to satisfy them that reincarnation is a reality.

Arguably the strongest evidence in favour of the notion of reincarnation is the fact that some people claim to be able to actually remember their past lives. Such claims fall into two general categories: past-life memories that are apparently retrieved through the use of hypnotic regression procedures and those which occur spontaneously. It is generally accepted that, although occasional hoaxes do occur, most of those who claim to recall memories of previous lives are sincere.

It is possible to argue, in line with Chari (1978), that apparent memories of past lives are in fact based upon the claimant's unwitting use of telepathic and clairvoyant abilities; that is to say, the apparent memories are based upon telepathic retrieval of information about the deceased individual from others who knew him or else clairvoyant retrieval of information about the deceased from other sources. This is, however, very much a minority view. The main debate is between those, such as Stevenson, who argue that past-life memories provide strong evidence for the traditional notion of reincarnation and those, such as the current author, who argue that they are simply based upon false memories. False memories are apparent memories for events that never actually took place at all. Much of this chapter is devoted to one particular example of spontaneous past-life memories, that is, those reported by members of the Druse religion. The next section, however, considers the problematic nature of hypnotic past-life regression.

Hypnotic past-life regression

Many psychotherapists appear to be woefully ill informed about the true nature of the relationship between hypnosis and memory (French & Ost, in press). In the words of Yapko (1994, p. 163), "Survey data regarding hypnosis and suggestibility indicate that while psychotherapists largely view hypnosis favorably, they often do so on the basis of misinformation. A significant number of psychotherapists erroneously believe, for example, that memories obtained through hypnosis are more likely to be accurate than those simply recalled, and that hypnosis can be used to recover accurate memories even from as far back as birth". A minority of psychotherapists go even further, claiming that hypnotic regression can be used to recover genuine memories of past lives. Indeed, they argue that psychological problems experienced in a person's current life may well have their origins in trauma experienced in a past life. For example, an individual may have a phobia of water in this life because they died by drowning in a previous life. The best way to treat such psychological problems, according to these psychotherapists, is by using hypnotic regression to retrieve the traumatic memories from the past life so that they can be worked through during therapy (e.g. Weiss, 1988, 1992).

The available evidence strongly suggests that apparent past-life memories obtained through the use of hypnotic regression are in fact false memories (Baker, 1992; French, 2003; Spanos, 1996). They are products of fantasy, imagination and expectation combined with fragments of real memories of both personal experiences and fictional accounts such as those presented in books and films. Suggestions and leading questions from the hypnotist also play a role. The hypnotic subject may well experience associated imagery that is so vivid that it creates the strong subjective impression that it is based upon actual experiences rather than imagination. It is typically found that the accounts produced reflect the Hollywood version of the era in question rather than the historically accurate version. Furthermore, subjects typically only produce very sketchy accounts and are incapable of answering questions that should be easy if they could genuinely access memories from someone living in the historical society in question (such as "What is the currency in your country?" and "Is your country at war?").

Very occasionally cases arise in which more detailed information is obtained. One such case was that of Colorado housewife Virginia Tighe, the subject of a best-selling book by Morey Bernstein (1956) and subsequently a popular film. In 1952, Virginia Tighe was hypnotised on numerous occasions by Bernstein and encouraged to go back into a past life. Following the hypnotic induction, she would speak with a pronounced Irish accent and claim to be Bridey Murphy living in Cork in the early nineteenth century. She recounted a wealth of detail about her life, told Irish stories and sang Irish songs. Her story caught the public's imagination and it was even featured in a couple of pop songs at the time. It actually generated a brief craze of "come as you were" parties. Sadly, subsequent investigation proved beyond doubt that Bridey had never existed (Gardner, 1957; Harris, 1986). No record of Bridey's life nor that of any of the people she claimed to know was ever found. Instead, it was revealed that Virginia Tighe had been an enthusiastic amateur actress in her youth with a particular liking for Irish roles. Furthermore, she had an Irish aunt and an Irish neighbour during her teenage years. The neighbour just happened to be called Bridey Murphy Corkell.

A few other examples of detailed and largely accurate accounts of apparent past-life memories obtained through the use of hypnotic regression have also attracted interest. Arnall Bloxham, a hypnotherapist living in Cardiff, recorded a series of such accounts. His star subject was a Welsh housewife referred to by the pseudonym of Jane Evans. She produced detailed accounts of no less than six previous incarnations including accurate details that would in many instances only be known to someone with specialist historical knowledge. Bloxham's cases were the subject of a BBC documentary and a book by Jeffrey Iverson (1977). Arguably the most impressive of Evans's accounts was that in which she claimed to be a maidservant in the house of Jacques Couer, a wealthy fifteenth-century French merchant. She could accurately recount much historical detail of Couer's life and his business affairs. Curiously, however, she insisted that Couer was single whereas the historical record showed quite definitely that he was married and had children. This contradiction between the apparent past-life memory and the historical events provided a major clue to Melvin Harris (1986) who ultimately resolved this mystery. Harris tracked down a historical novel based upon Couer's life by Thomas B. Costain called *The Moneyman*. Costain had included many accurate details about Couer's life in his novel but had taken the literary liberty of omitting Couer's wife and children as they kept getting in the way of plot development.

It appears that at least one of Evans's other past-life accounts was also based upon the details in a historical novel. *The Living Wood* by Louis de Wohl, published in 1947, tells the story of Lavonia, wife of Titus, living in York during the Roman occupation of Britain in the third century. We can be fairly certain that the details in Evans's account are based upon the story in the novel as she refers not only to characters who genuinely did exist but also to fictional characters invented by the author.

Although it is conceivable that Tighe, Evans and others are simply deliberately putting on an act to fool others, many commentators believe that these accounts may be examples of the phenomenon of *cryptomnesia* (literally "hidden memories"; Baker, 1992). The idea is that, during the hypnotic regression session, stored information from various sources, such as books, films and TV programmes, as well as personal experiences, is accessed and combined together but the actual source of the original information is not recalled. Thus, as is the case with many apparent memories of alien abduction (see Chapter 5) and ritualised Satanic abuse, the use of hypnotic regression produces false memories and does not retrieve real memories of events that have actually been experienced.

Other evidence undermining the validity of hypnotically retrieved memories of past lives comes from experimental studies. Meyersburg, Bogdan, Gallo, and McNally (2009) used the so-called DRM task (see Chapter 5 for details) to assess susceptibility to false memories in a group claiming to have past-life memories compared to a control group. It should be noted that only 6 of the 15 members of the "past-life" group had actually undergone hypnotic regression in order to "recover" their past-life memory. The rest believed they had past-life memories based on a variety of reasons including déjà vu, "flashbacks", and recurrent dreams. It was found, as predicted, that the "past-life" group were more susceptible to false memories as assessed by the DRM results than the control group. They also scored higher on magical ideation and absorption. Meyersburg and McNally (2011) reported that subjects who had past-life memories showed reduced fear of death and enhanced meaning in life.

Spanos and colleagues (1994, 1996; Spanos, Menary, Gabora, DuBreuil & Dewhirst, 1991) conducted a series of studies that provided great insight into the nature of hypnotically retrieved past-life memories. Volunteers who exhibited past-life identities scored higher than those who did not on both hypnotic susceptibility and fantasy-proneness but not on psychopathology. The studies showed conclusively that the content of the past-life narratives is strongly influenced by suggestions from the hypnotist. For example, in one study some participants were told, prior to being hypnotised, that past-life identities were often of a different gender and race to the current-life identity and often involved living in exotic cultures. In a separate study, some participants were told that child abuse was common in the past. In both cases, the content of the narratives was biased in the direction of the suggestions compared to narratives produced without any such priming. Spanos (1996) concluded that the enactments were goal-directed, rule-governed fantasies that are strongly affected by suggestion and context.

Many investigators who are sympathetic to the possibility of genuine reincarnation have warned against the use of hypnotic regression, acknowledging the inherent risk of producing false memories (e.g. Stevenson, 1994). Instead, they believe that the evidence from cases of spontaneous past-life memories is much stronger. The rest of this chapter deals primarily with such cases within one specific context, that of the Druse in Lebanon. However, many of the points made could also be applied to spontaneous cases reported in other cultures.

Reincarnation: the Druse version

The Druse (also spelt as "Druze") are members of a religious sect which broke away from the Ismaili doctrines of Islam in the eleventh century AD. Since 1042, no new members have been accepted into this closed religion. The Druse live mainly in Lebanon, Syria, Jordan and Israel but there is a considerable diaspora in the USA, South America and Europe. There are said to be some 400,000 Druse in Lebanon. The Druse that we interviewed for this investigation were based in villages in the Chouf mountains, a relatively short drive away from Beirut.

The Druse live in tightly-knit communities and do not intermarry with other religious groups. Their religion is central to their lives and their belief in reincarnation is central to their religion. Their religious leaders, known as sheikhs, wear distinctive black and white clothing and are highly respected members of their local communities. It is often said that the Druse are secretive about their religion and will not discuss it with foreigners but we did not find this to be the case (see also Littlewood, 2001; for more background detail on the Druse, see Abu-Izzeddin, 1984; Betts, 1988; Firro, 1992; Makarem, 1974).

The major distinctive features of the Druse version of reincarnation can be summarised as follows:

- Belief in reincarnation is universal amongst the Druse and treated in a very matter-of-fact manner. This is illustrated by the fact that the Arabic word for reincarnation, *taqamus*, can be translated as "changing one's shirt".
- Not everyone remembers their previous lives. Generally, the previous life is only remembered if it ended violently. The Lebanese civil war unfortunately provided plenty of violent deaths (Fisk, 1992).
- Uniquely amongst all versions of reincarnation, the Druse believe that at the moment of death of one physical body, the soul is immediately reborn in a newborn baby. Other cultures believe that there is a gap between incarnations and/or that the soul enters a new body at the moment of conception.
- Humans reincarnate as humans, not animals or inanimate objects.
- Druse reincarnate as Druse, the number of Druse souls having been fixed since 1042. But don't worry, other religious groups (and even sceptics!) will be reincarnated.

- Reincarnation is always into a body of the same sex.
- There is no relationship between the quality of one's current life and one's actions in the preceding life, i.e. Druse do not believe in Karma. In fact, they believe that all souls will experience the full range of possible lives, from extreme wretchedness, poverty and disease to perfect happiness, luxury and health. Only in this way will the soul be ready to meet God on Judgement Day.

Apart from the general problems to which I alluded earlier, the Druse version of reincarnation faces certain unique problems. The fact that the Druse believe that the last breath in one body is immediately followed by the first breath in the body of a newborn baby avoids what Edwards (1996a, 1996b) refers to as the problem of the *interregnum*, i.e. the problem of how any kind of memories or consciousness can survive between lives without any kind of neural substrate. It does not, of course, explain how memories or consciousness could migrate from one physical brain to another. It does provide an obvious empirical test for Druse reincarnation claims. It would appear that the time of death of the old body should correspond exactly to the time of birth of the new body. The problem is that this is hardly ever found to be the case. The differences between birth and death times typically range from a few months to a few years. Stevenson (1980) argues that the poor correspondence between the two is partly due to poor reliability of Lebanese records, but this argument is unconvincing and presumably would not apply to Druse outside the Lebanon.

The Druse themselves explain away the discrepancy between birth and death times by postulating that one may live an intermediate life between the current life and the past life which is remembered. Thus, a discrepancy of a few months or even years reflects the fact that one lived a short and unmemorable life in between. However, as stated, virtually none of the past-life death dates correspond to the current-life birth dates, implying that for every child who remembers a past life there must be at least one baby or child that died young. The situation is in fact even worse. Only those who die violently remember their past lives but everyone is said to have had them. There is no reason to believe that there would be any better correspondence of dates for those who cannot remember their past lives than for those who can. This implies a child mortality rate of over 50 per cent, i.e. at least one dead child for every living child. I am pleased to say that statistics completely fail to support such a bleak picture.

This shows that the claim of instantaneous death and rebirth, as one may have suspected, is not based upon empirical observation. Instead, it is a culturally transmitted belief. As one might again expect, different beliefs across cultures lead to different manifestations of apparent reincarnation. It is worth noting, therefore, that there is a tendency for the gap between the remembered past-life and the current life to be much shorter amongst the Druse than amongst members of other cultures. According to Stevenson (1980), the median length is about six months, the second shortest interval of all the cultures he investigated. Given that ideally there should be no gap at all, there appears to be cultural pressure for the gap at least not to be very long. Cultural influences presumably also account for the fact that the Druse never report past lives as members of the opposite sex or as animals, although such reports are found in cultures where such accounts are congruent with cultural beliefs. As previously noted, Spanos et al. (1991) showed, in the context of hypnotic past-life regression, that the nature of reported past lives is strongly influenced by the subject's expectations about the likely characteristics of the past life as transmitted by the hypnotist.

The Druse solution to the "population problem" described earlier is worth noting. Although no Lebanese Druse would even try to argue that the number of Druse in the Middle East has remained constant since 1042, it is commonly asserted that the total number of Druse souls, which is unknown, has remained constant since then. It is generally believed amongst the Druse that there are large Druse communities in distant lands, China being a popular choice. If there was an increase in the death rate of Druse during the civil war, this could be compensated by an increase in the birth rate of Druse in China or some other distant country. This is of course a totally non-falsifiable hypothesis, confounded by the fact that the Druse believe that it is possible to be a Druse without realising it! Some Druse even believe that souls may transmigrate between planets. However, the past-life memories which are reported in Lebanese cases are almost always those of individuals in nearby villages, never those in strange distant lands or other galaxies, offering support for the idea that past-life memories are usually fantasy-based constructions founded upon knowledge already available to the claimant.

I hope these arguments are enough to show that the specifically Druse version of reincarnation cannot be universally true. However, many serious investigators of reincarnation claims would not be too concerned about that, arguing instead that if just one case of reincarnation could be shown to be inexplicable by normal means, then that would justify their belief. It is to the investigation of individual cases that we now turn. Upon initial reading, the meticulous cases detailed by Ian Stevenson (e.g. 1980, 2001, 2003) and others (e.g. Haraldsson & Abu-Izzeddin, 2002) of children and adults from around the world spontaneously remembering details of past lives appear to constitute an impressive body of evidence in support of reincarnation. However, I hope to show that the evidence is not as strong as it first appears. I will limit my comments to the Lebanese cases, as these are the only cases of which I have first-hand experience. Clearly, however, my conclusions may well generalise to other similar claims. (For a less critical treatment of these cases, see Stemman, 1998; see also Littlewood, 2001, and Stevenson, 2001.)

The description of a typical Druse case tends to follow a fairly standard format as follows. As the child begins to learn to speak, at around the age of two, he or she will say things that make no sense to the parents. As the child gets older and speech becomes more advanced, it becomes clear the child is referring to past-life memories. From a very young age, the child may make statements of the kind, "My name is not X, it is Y" or "You are not my mother. My mother is Z" and so on. The child may behave in ways that appear very adult to the observer and may demonstrate skills and preferences from the previous life. Eventually, the child will demand to make contact with the past-life family and a meeting will be arranged. The past-life family will not, however, immediately accept the newcomer as the genuine reincarnation of its deceased loved one. They will test the child by showing photographs of family members to be recognised, or by asking about specific incidents in the past life or the location of various objects. They may even try to trick the child by introducing people under false names but the child will see through these attempts and demonstrate clearly that they know the true identities. Often they will find objects which they had hidden in their past life which the family themselves never knew about. Members of the past-life family will be extremely careful not to give any cues as to the correct answers during these tests but eventually, overwhelmed by the sheer weight of evidence, they will accept that the child is the genuine reincarnation of their loved one, to the understandable joy of all concerned. Or at least, that is how they will describe it years later.

When one is trying to evaluate any particular type of paranormal claim, it is important not only to consider the evidence that appears to support a paranormal explanation, but also that which does not – you have to consider the misses as well as the hits. When considering reincarnation claims in the Lebanon, therefore, it is not enough to only consider the apparently impressive cases described in Stevenson's publications but also the wider context. For example, many of the cases we investigated came from a single school in the Chouf mountains. There were around 900 pupils at the school and 21 of them remembered past lives. The 21 children claiming to remember past lives were gathered together for us in one of the school's classrooms. It has to be said that it is a strange experience for a Westerner to be in a room full of children all of whom believe that they can remember having lived before.

Now clearly most of the children in the school did not claim to remember past lives – but over 2 per cent did. In fact, Littlewood (2001) reported that as many as 10 per cent of a group of 12- to 14-year-olds from an assembled class of Druse teenagers reported past-life memories. Systematic surveys of the prevalence of past-life memories are very rare indeed. Barker and Pasricha (1979) reported one such survey, finding that only around one in 500 inhabitants of a community in North India spontaneously reported such memories, but Mills and Tucker (2014) suggest that the incidence may well be higher in other societies (e.g. British Columbia).

Even if we take the fairly conservative 2 per cent figure as representative of Druse schools in general, the total number of Druse children claiming to remember past lives is vast. It is important to bear that in mind when reading those few Druse accounts that Stevenson has chosen to publish as being the best evidence for reincarnation. Considering only the best cases is like only taking account of the hits claimed by a psychic and ignoring the far more numerous misses. As Stevenson himself admits, none of his reported cases, in Lebanon or elsewhere, provide truly conclusive evidence when considered in isolation.

Time limitations meant that we were unable to interview all of the children assembled in the classroom, but the most promising cases were featured in the programme. Others who were not featured in the programme told us something of their memories, but often the memories were so vague that it would have been impossible to attempt to verify them (e.g. "I remember driving along in my jeep and it was hit by a shell. I died and came into this body"). So the initially large number of cases that we found in the school had dwindled down considerably by the time we eliminated cases that were simply too vague to follow up.

The next stage in this filtering process became apparent when we tried to check out those cases that produced sufficient verifiable details. Stevenson claims that the urge to make contact with the past-life family is so strong in the children that such contact is almost always made, but we found plenty of cases in which this had not happened. To Western eyes, it might seem strange that a child's claim that he or she is the reincarnation of a named individual who lived in a nearby village may be accepted by others without any attempt at verification. But as I have already stated, the Druse attitude towards reincarnation is very matter-of-fact. Everyone we spoke to knew personally of several cases.

When we began to check cases out, most failed the test. Rami Abu-Arum claimed to have been Ramiz Haidar in a previous life and to have driven a Pepsi Cola truck to and from the depot in Beirut. No one at the depot had ever heard of Ramiz Haidar, including a supervisor who had worked there for twenty years. Mehdi Hibous claimed that in his past life he was Melhem Melerb and that he had been killed by a shell while digging with a tractor. He gave us the names of his wife and his five children. Upon checking, it turned out that a Melhem Melerb had indeed been killed in the manner described – but the names of his alleged wife and children did not check out at all. It was suggested by Jad Al Younis, our Druse guide, that he was possibly not Mehlem Melerb in his past life as he had claimed but a close friend of Mehlem's who was confused by his past-life memories into *thinking* he was Mehlem. Clearly, if one is determined to find evidence for reincarnation, one can find it in the most unpromising data. But this case is even more problematic for the proponents of reincarnation. Investigation revealed that Melhem Melerb's family had already accepted another boy as being the reincarnation of their dearly departed. Both boys could not be genuine reincarnations, therefore at least one of them had to be basing his claim upon a false memory (see Stemman, 1998, and Littlewood, 2001, for further details of some of these cases).

It is important to consider such cases for several reasons. Firstly, they provide the correct context for assessing those few apparently very impressive cases that find their way into the literature. It is important to know whether the published cases are representative of the quality of all cases and clearly they are not. Secondly, these cases provide evidence of the fact that reincarnation claims are a pervasive aspect of Druse culture. Finally, it shows that at least some Druse reincarnation claims are false. Such cases are likely to range from pure fantasy to a mix of fantasy plus information derived from other sources. There is little reason to suppose that there is any attempt in most cases to engage in deliberate fraud.

Having filtered out most of the original claimants, however, we are left with those few cases that appear to provide a wealth of checkable details, most or all of which have been verified. This is the stuff of published cases and of the main cases featured in our documentary. One thing is immediately striking about such cases. These accounts are always provided a long time, usually many years, after the past-life and the current-life families have made contact and the past-life family have accepted the child as a genuine reincarnation. If one accepts the accounts of what took place all those years previously as generally accurate, as Stevenson did, it is difficult to explain the events without resorting to paranormal explanations. But the lessons of many decades of psychological research would suggest that it would be naïve to do so. Although the claimants involved in these cases may well be sincere, it is extremely likely that their memories are not accurate. As the classic research of Sir Frederic Bartlett showed back in the 1930s, the constant telling and retelling of a story leads to systematic distortion, including the downplaying of elements which are incongruous with the overall plot and the invention of details which sharpen the main points of the story.

One of the two main cases featured in our documentary was that of Rabih Abu-Dyab, an engaging 12-year-old boy, who claimed to have been Saad Halawi in his past life. Saad Halawi was famous as both an international footballer and a successful pop singer. He was killed in an explosion during the civil war. Rabih's mother was a great fan of Halawi. Clearly, she would know a great deal about her hero, who would have been featured in many magazines and newspapers. Rabih did not appear to know much about Halawi's life that was not commonly known. Even when what should have been very strong memory cues were provided, Rabih struggled to come up with any specific memories of Halawi's life. For instance, we took him to the trophy room at the ground where his football team played. Despite the fact that Halawi was one of the star players on the team, being in the trophy room failed to prompt any memories in Rabih.

The following scenario would appear to be a plausible explanation for the events in this and other similar cases (cf. Dwairy, 2006). When the child first begins to speak, many utterances will be unclear and open to various interpretations. In a culture where reincarnation is accepted as the norm, it is likely that some parents will interpret certain utterances as possibly being the child's attempt to talk about a past life. This is especially likely if the child begins to make utterances that in the West would be interpreted as evidence of an imaginary playmate. The parents and others would quite naturally speculate upon the possible past-life identity. In Druse society, deaths are publicly announced in all of the villages around the home area of the deceased. Furthermore, there is a very high level of marriage within the extended family. There are thus many possible routes for transmission of information either directly to the child or indirectly to the child's carers.

Once the parents or others have decided upon a plausible candidate for the past life, they would, again quite naturally, often wish to check their hypothesis. They would be likely to ask the child to recognise photographs and to discuss other details of the past life, giving the child the benefit of any doubts that may arise. After all, the child's recollection of the past life is not expected to be anywhere near perfect. The parents would be likely to help the child by providing reminders of important events in the past life and so on. Unwittingly, they would have provided the perfect social context for the development and embellishment of false memories on the part of the child. All of this could take place before the child ever comes into contact with the past-life family. Once accepted by that family, however, the whole process could continue with even richer information sources. It is worth noting here that over the last couple of decades, controlled research into the topic of false memories has shown beyond all doubt that it is much easier to induce false memories for a whole range of detailed, complex, autobiographical events than anyone had previously suspected (e.g. Lindsay & Read, 1995; Loftus, 1993). French (2003; French & Wilson, 2006; French & Stone, 2014) has reviewed a great deal of evidence showing that susceptibility to false memories tends to correlate with numerous psychological variables, such as tendency to dissociate, which in their turn correlate with the tendency to experience ostensibly paranormal events and to believe in the paranormal.

The scenario outlined above remains speculative but its plausibility is supported by a vast amount of well-controlled psychological research. Furthermore, children reporting past-life memories have been shown to have higher levels of dissociative tendencies in both Sri Lanka (Haraldsson, Fowler, & Periyannanpillai, 2000) and Lebanon (Haraldsson, 2002). The only way to be sure that the explanation outlined is true would be to observe all of the child's interactions with others from the moment of birth – and, even then, proponents of reincarnation would probably argue that it might explain some cases but not others. It would also be useful to observe the child's first contact with the past-life family. Do they really try to stringently test the child's knowledge? Do they really give nothing away?

We were unable to find any case where a child had provided sufficient detail to identify the past-life family, but where contact had not taken place. It is worth noting that Stevenson has also never managed to find such a case. Thus the opportunity to observe such first contact was denied to us. We did, however, manage to arrange for Rabih to meet with his past-life sister for the first time, even though he had already met with other members of his past-life family.

During their initial meeting, it was obvious that his past-life sister provided Rabih with numerous cues to her identity. Given that we had already asked Rabih if he wanted to meet her, he was in fact extremely slow to realise who his "surprise visitor" was. Her acceptance of him as the reincarnation of her dead brother was based purely upon her emotional reaction. No attempt was made to rigorously test Rabih's knowledge.

The evidence does not appear to support the reality of reincarnation claims amongst the Druse. Why then should this belief have persisted so long within Druse society? It seems likely that this is because of the real benefits that belief bestows upon the members of this particular religious sect (Bennett, 2006; Dwairy, 2006; Somer, Klein-Sela, & Or-Chen, 2011). These include:

- Helping the bereaved to cope with loss (Dwairy, 2006; Littlewood, 2001; Somer et al., 2011) – the motivation to be reunited with departed loved ones is very powerful.

- Reducing the fear of death (Littlewood, 2001) – the Druse are famed for their bravery and ferocity in battle, a characteristic that has probably helped them to survive centuries of persecution. It is said that the Druse have a battle-cry of "Tonight my mother's womb", i.e. if they are killed, they will be instantly reborn.
- Increased social cohesion (Bennett, 2006; Littlewood, 2001) – even though the Druse are already a tightly knit community, with many marriages within the extended family, the addition of past-life families increases social connectivity yet further.
- Social support for the poor (Dwairy, 2006; Wilson, 1987) – it has been widely commented upon that in all cultures where reincarnation claims are made, there is a very strong tendency for the past-life family to be wealthier and more powerful than the current-life family. This was certainly true in the cases we looked at. There are obvious advantages to the current family if the past-life family accepts the claimant as a genuine reincarnation. They are likely to provide support in a variety of ways. It goes without saying that this provides a strong motivation for parents to attempt to train their children in attempts at deliberate fraud, documented examples of which do exist. But it is also likely to be an important factor in influencing parents' interpretation of ambiguous behaviour on the part of a child as described earlier, even in cases where there is no deliberate attempt at fraud.

Conclusions

This chapter has reviewed the general concept of reincarnation including both arguments put forward in support of reincarnation and the conceptual problems inherent within it. It has also considered the evidence from cases of apparent past-life memories obtained through the use of hypnotic regression. The available evidence strongly supports the idea that such accounts are based upon false memories.

Much of this chapter focuses upon one specific example of spontaneous past-life memories, those arising amongst the Druse of Lebanon. Most Druse children in Lebanon do not claim to remember past lives. Of those that do, most are unable to provide checkable details. Of those that can, most of the details are untrue. The few cases where it is claimed that a large amount of detail was recalled and verified are all cases in which the past-life family accepted the claimant as a genuine reincarnation many years before. Memory distortions are extremely likely in such cases. Having said all that, it is probably to the Druse advantage that they live their lives *as if* reincarnation really happens.

There is probably still no better way to finish a chapter on a topic such as this than with the famous quotation from Professor C. D. Broad:

> I think I may say that for my part I should be slightly more annoyed than surprised if I should find myself in some sense persisting immediately after the death of my present body. One can only wait and see, or alternately (which is no less likely) wait and not see.

8

DREAMS

Ron Roberts

Introduction

A few months after a close friend of mine passed away, I had a very striking dream in which she appeared to me. The dream was exceptionally lucid. In it I asked my friend, who was dressed in black, if it would be possible for me to talk to her as I knew that for her to stay long might not be possible. She said yes and moved over to me, taking up a relaxed friendly position adjacent to me – this indicating that she wanted to spend this available time with me. We then began a conversation about some of the difficult issues I had once faced in life, before I abruptly woke up with a strong sense of having been in her presence.

Few topics in psychology arouse as much popular interest as dreams, no doubt because these can express intimate and intensely personal aspects of our lives – aspects which nobody else but ourselves are privy to. Since long before Freud appeared on the scene, dreams have been accorded great significance in myriad human cultures. How our cultural and personal relationships to our dreams have changed over time constitute important historical landmarks in the aesthetics of personal transformation (see Harris, 2009, for a review of early Greek and Roman views of dreaming). In the Western world this history arguably begins with the Oracle at Delphi and the temples of Asclepius. Alongside Aristotle's reflections on catharsis in the *Poetics* (Aristotle, 1996), they form a trio of self-purification, self-knowledge, and divine dream interpretation. Catharsis, self-knowledge, and the meaning of dreams constitute the bedrock upon which Freud built psychotherapy and paved the way for humanistic psychology. Yet despite the widespread desire for self-knowledge in Western societies, there are few better examples than the study of dreams to illustrate the gulf that exists between what lay people expect from psychology and what scientific psychology has so far managed to deliver to them.

The reasons for this chasm are plentiful. Freud's theory of dreams (Freud, 1900) was to a large extent the foundation upon which psychoanalysis was constructed. The popularisation of psychoanalytic thinking which followed this led to the widespread dissemination of ideas about dreaming – some of which continue to have little empirical evidence in their favour. To be fair to Freud he was aware of and tried to correct the erroneous belief, attributed to him, that all dreams were derived from sexual conflict – whether infantile or concurrent, although the quote attributed to him to this effect, "sometimes a cigar is just a cigar", was not actually uttered by him. The negative impact of the misunderstanding of psychoanalytic theory was accentuated by the reluctance of other analysts to challenge the Freudian orthodoxy on our night life. Jung maintained that his own ideas in no way constituted a theory of dreams (see also Rycroft, 1981), while Freud himself famously remarked that "The analysts behave as though they had no more to say about dreams, as though there was nothing more to be added to the theory of dreams".

The tempestuous relationship between the psychoanalytic community and the orthodox scientific community – due in no small measure to Freud's initial observations on infantile sexuality and the seemingly widespread nature of sexual trauma in childhood (see Masson, 1992) – coupled with the rise of behaviourism in the 1920s and 30s meant that dreaming largely remained outside the province of scientific enquiry until the advent of the REM (rapid eye movement) monitoring procedures pioneered by Dement and Kleitman (1957). These established a correlation between the reporting of dreams and the presence of rapid eye movement sleep – a phase of sleep characterised by a stage 1 EEG (low voltage mixed frequency; 2–7 cycles per second), bursts of rapid eye movements and suppressed EMG (muscle activity from the neck and chin region achieves its lowest level of activity throughout the night during this phase; see Figure 8.1) (Rechtschaffen & Kales, 1971).

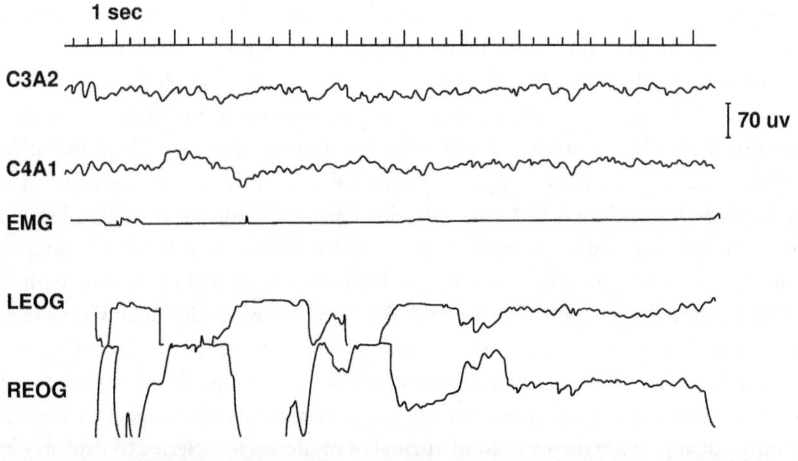

FIGURE 8.1 Electrophysiological characteristics of REM sleep. Key: *C3A2*, EEG left hemisphere; *C4A1*, EEG right hemisphere; *LEOG*, left eye movement; *REOG*, right eye movement; *EMG*, electromyogram.

Shortly afterwards Foulkes (1960) found that dream reporting could also be obtained, though less frequently, from the other so-called non-REM stages of sleep. It is now established that dreaming occurs not only in the lighter levels of non-REM sleep, but also during the hypnagogic period of sleep onset and in "daydreaming" as studied under laboratory conditions (Foulkes, 1993). Dream reports from REM sleep however have maintained their position as the principal focus of empirical investigations of dreaming. So if we wish to enquire into features of dream life, such as lucid dreaming and telepathy, which have attracted the interest of parapsychologists as well as lay people, then we must first become acquainted with what these investigations tell us about the nature of dreaming. In this chapter we will therefore examine contemporary neuropsychological and cognitive theories of dream production as well as evolutionary and developmental perspectives. From there we will proceed to discuss both lucid dreaming and the evidence for the existence of extrasensory perception in dreaming.

Theories of dreaming

The question of what makes a dream a dream is an important place to begin our review. Hobson (2005) sees the cardinal features of dreams as lying in their formal features – the perceptual, cognitive, and emotional qualities which they possess (e.g. loss of self-reflective awareness, absence of logic, and poor memory) – rather than any specific content. Thus, by dreaming, scientists refer to any image, thought, or feeling attributed by the dreamer to a pre-awakening state. The reporting of dreams in terms of quantity, frequency, quality, and type appears to be culturally and historically universal, appearing during ontogeny at about three years of age. The experience of dreaming and its recall vary both between and within individuals as well as across cultures (Von Grunebaum & Callois, 1966). Thus, the emergence, development and transformation of dreams in human life appear to be strongly shaped and constrained by both biology and culture (Foulkes, 1993).

Dream research, both clinical and experimental, is faced with the dual tasks of explaining both the mode of production and the significance of dreams – in short, how our dream life is produced and what importance it carries. Until the advent of more recent technologies (e.g. Magnetic Resonance Imaging), research on the psychophysiology of the REM state, once heralded as the means for testing Freudian dream theory and settling controversies about the relationship between mind and brain, had reached something of a hiatus. Disillusionment had set in and with it a lack of funding for research (Hunt, 1989). While dream research remains a neglected area of psychological enquiry – due in part to the increasing corporate influence in research funding – there are possibilities that this may change. The last two decades have seen a refocusing on consciousness as not merely a viable object of scientific scrutiny but as perhaps the most fundamental of mysteries for science to explain – the conundrum of how to comprehend how self-organised matter can attain subjectivity.

Windt (2015), who defines dreams as "immersive spatiotemporal hallucinations" (p. xxiv), sees in their development an inextricable connection to the phenomenology of selfhood. In approaching the thorny issue of consciousness and dreams, she is aware of an implicit, though often neglected issue. This concerns how we can adequately conceptualise conscious experience in one state (dreaming) by means of the articulation of concepts in another mental state (waking). This is not just how to bridge the gap between private experience and public telling but of how to understand a phenomenon by a process which inexorably begins with a process of translation. This is a philosophical problem as much as it is a scientific one and maybe fundamental to the disjuncture between scientific explanations of psychological phenomenon and public acceptance of these explanations. We live in the world and know that we do only through our conscious experience of it (Laing, 1967). As such, our conscious awareness of our own consciousness is fundamental to any scientific undertaking and thus our understanding of reality. It is also important in quite another sense – the most successful scientific theory to date in human history, quantum mechanics, relies on the presence of conscious observers for a description of the given state of any given physical system to be obtained (Unger & Smolin, 2015). Whilst many of us function as what philosophers describe as naïve realists – taking the world to be what we perceive it to be – the inadequacy of this formulation is more apparent when we consider the nature of consciousness in dreaming. Here the everyday taken-for-granted nature of consciousness disappears and its everyday "strangeness" once more comes to the fore. Dreaming estranges (Boym, 2005) both the world and our own selves and presents them back to us in a form conducive to a different understanding. The significance of this is that as we come to appreciate how this dream consciousness might be produced we may be shedding important light on the nature of reality and the embodiment of selfhood (Windt, 2015). This means that for the first time both scientific and lay interest in dreaming are directed toward a common transpersonal understanding of the world – one that recognises the "strangeness" of our common consciousness of reality.

Neurobiological theories

Our current understanding of dreams, their meaning, and how to analyse them are all intertwined. In this first section we consider dreams as the outcome of physiological processes occurring in the brain. Both Hobson and McCarley's activation-synthesis hypothesis (Hobson & McCarley, 1977; Hobson, 1988; Mamelak & Hobson, 1989; Hobson, 2005) and Crick and Mitchison's neural network model (Crick & Mitchison, 1983, 1986) attempt to derive the phenomenology of dreams from a knowledge of brain functioning, though each arrive at somewhat different conclusions.

Hobson and McCarley followed Freud in spirit by adhering to a belief in the isomorphism of mind and body – that events in the two realms are inextricably linked. However, rather than dreaming being a psychological necessity – a response dealing with occasional neurotic impulses during sleep – they argued that it is the outcome of an automatic, pre-programmed neural process. In their model they describe a functional organisation of the brain that is unique to sleep

(Hobson & McCarley, 1977; Hobson, 1988; Mamelak & Hobson, 1989). REM sleep with its characteristic features of cortical arousal, body muscle paralysis, bursts of eye-movements and other "phasic" phenomena results from activation of the "REM-ON" area located in the pontine reticular formation (a structure at the apex of the spinal column at the base of the brain). This REM-ON area also cuts off most sensory stimuli from the brain. That is to say, in the absence of motor output and sensory input, the brain is virtually isolated during REM sleep.

Although the motor cortex is highly active, generating activity which would normally result in movement, these commands do not reach muscles controlling the limbs, but are "switched off" at a relay station at the top of the spinal column, so that we are effectively paralysed during REM sleep. This explains the loss of tone in the neck muscles under the chin, used as one of the defining characteristics of REM sleep (Empson, 1989). Parts of the brain that control emotions or store memories may also be activated in the REM state. This may occur either directly by the REM-ON system or indirectly via activation of motor or sensory systems. Hobson and McCarley argue that it is through the activation of personal emotionally laden memories that aspects of a person's personality are injected into one's dreams.

When these simultaneously activated motor pattern and sensory systems are synthesised, dreaming is experienced. This process of synthesis is no different from what occurs in the waking brain. Available sensory and motor information is integrated with information on the current affective state – memories of similar experiences and related meanings are then drawn on in order to understand it (Moorcroft, Hoversten, & Foxworthy, 1993). During wakefulness the sensory information is strongly related to our motor information and seems "normal". Our perceptions usually flow smoothly because the sequence of sensory/motor activations follow one another in an orderly fashion. But when asleep, what is activated at one moment may not be related to what is activated next, thus bizarre non-linear shifts in thematic and sensory content may occur in dreams. The difference between dreaming and being awake, then, is not the process of activation and synthesis, but the source of the activation: more external (and sequential) when awake, almost entirely internal (somewhat random) when in REM sleep. It is important to be clear, however, that these processes of activation and synthesis – while they help us to understand why the quality of our mental life may at times be so different under the conditions of waking and sleeping – do not thereby explain the fact of our being conscious in either the waking or dreaming state.

Given that motivational states, memories, emotions, even the movement patterns that are activated in the brain during REM, are products of the individual's experiences and personality, the activation-synthesis model accepts dreams as meaningful productions capable of interpretation. While the synthesis of these elements may be unusual, the elements themselves are not. Further, personal characteristics determine the meaning placed on a specific stimulus regardless of whether its source is external (as in waking) or internal (as in dreaming). Hence, dreams, like waking cognitions, may contain information that is relevant and revealing about the person. Hobson and McCarley caution, however, that care should be exercised in the interpretation of this content. It does not follow that each aspect of a dream has a symbolic meaning (Moorcroft, Hoversten, & Foxworthy, 1993). Meaning is more usually revealed than concealed.

The picture which Hobson and colleagues paint of the activities of the sleeping brain allow a theoretical model of dreaming which is not confined to the REM state but which does provide a broad explanation for the general differences observed between REM and NREM mentation. In addition, it provides the basis for understanding how dreaming may play an important role in the development of self. In our dreams we are effectively self-propelled through a virtual world of our own making. Our sense of agency, Hobson argues, begins with movement and is only later elaborated in thought. Dreaming then provides a means for elaborating both our sense of the external physical world and the nature of our existence through movement in it.

Crick and Mitchison (1983, 1986) (the former, having attempted one of those risky shifts from a Nobel Prize in microbiology to computer simulations of the mind) have developed a theory that relies in part on the activation-synthesis hypothesis. Unfortunately their ideas are not so firmly empirically rooted. Beginning from the observation that memory during sleep and often after awakening is poor, they jump to a startling conclusion – that we dream in order to forget! They reason as follows. REM sleep is almost universal among mammals. The prevention of REM sleep by selective awakenings results in increased amounts of it on recovery, as if what had been missed was then being "made up", suggesting that not only does this sleep stage have its own drive mechanism, but it may have an important function. However, since most dreams go unremembered, this function must either have nothing to do with dreaming, or, if dreaming is essential to the process, the forgetting must be a necessary part of it. Crick and Mitchison contend that the random pontine activity stimulating the cortex during REM sleep has the function of erasing memories, which they believe have become "parasitic". These parasitic memories are beliefs, ideas and interpretations of reality which no longer contribute to our adaptive functioning in the world. Like left over computer programs they persist but are redundant. This accumulation of outdated material is expressed in dreams which are created only in order to be forgotten (Empson, 1989). Recurrent dreams, according to this theory, occur because things (such as the dreamer's name being called or certain meaningful contents of the dream) tend to awaken sleepers. The awakened sleeper then attends to the content of the dream, which reinstalls it in memory. This strengthened memory is more likely to be activated again in the future, thus repeating the process. Thus the theory implies that when we recall our dreams we are defeating their function of weakening associations and therefore, attempts to increase dream remembrance should be avoided (Moorcroft, Hoversten, & Foxworthy, 1993).

These ideas are at odds with much of what we already know about dreaming and memory. Contemporary theories of memory envisage recall as a constructive process which in the very act of recall refashions and reconstructs the stored material (LeDoux, 2012). Consciousness appears to have a significant role in this reconstruction.

To the extent that any experience – and dreaming is one such experience – draws upon our stored knowledge and prior experience, that experience is capable of changing what has been stored about the past. Dreaming then is an important aspect of our individual as well as collective orientation to the past. Because of this it is an important though neglected aspect of the psychology of identity. It may be more accurate to say that we dream – not in order to forget – but in order to work out our place in the world and to know who we are. If we dreamt in order to forget, then some explanation would be required as to why nature has furnished us with a pattern of brain activation that positions the longest period of REM sleep just before we wake up in the morning – the time we are most able and likely to remember the mental activity which has just passed. There are other notable objections. The key assumption of Crick and Mitchison, that dreaming is both meaningless and functionless because there is an inherent random process involved, is incorrect. The fact that neither dream content nor process is entirely random has been well established. Content within any given dream is not arbitrary but is based on associative patterns of spreading activation (e.g. Foulkes, 1982a) – a point accepted by Hobson. Dream content also exhibits cyclical patterns over the course of not just one night but several (e.g. Roberts, 1988) suggesting some functional significance to the repeated processing of the same material.

Cognitive theories

Foulkes (1982a, 1985) developed a cognitive psychological model of REM dream production based on the substantive assumption that speech and dreaming may share some common production routines. Thus, Foulkes sees dreams as originating in the processes of "inner speech", a kind of psycholinguistics which ends not in speech production but in an alternative secondary visual medium. The core of dream formation now becomes its narrative structure. The dream, for Foulkes, is syntax imposed on diffuse memory activations, but without any underlying intentional semantics. The model proposes that, in the absence of specific semantic intentions to convey unitary messages, the momentary organisation and sequential coherence of the dream are attributable largely to syntactic mechanisms whose investment is not so much in saying any particular thing as in insuring that whatever is said is literally and thematically comprehensible. If the model is correct in proposing a verbal syntactic-lexical-phonetic process that supplies inputs to image generation, then a useful focus for recovering the "essence" of the dream would lie in applying linguistic analytic schemes rather than seeking to uncover a single underlying interpretation. For this Foulkes (1978) finds continued value in Freud's method of free association.

Foulkes sees a cognitive account of the dream process as independent of the specific psychophysiology of REM sleep, a position supported by recent brain imaging studies (Solms, 2000) which strongly suggest that dreaming and REM sleep are dissociable states, with dreaming mediated by mechanisms situated in the forebrain. Dreaming can for example be manipulated by dopamine agonists and antagonists without changing the frequency, duration, or density of REM sleep.

In line with Hobson, condensation, sudden displacements and scene changes, and fantastic sensory intrusions and transformations are "peripherally induced aberrations in the central organisation of dreaming" (Foulkes, 1985, p. 328). Again, the most striking "cognitive" feature of dreaming is its narrative cohesion, with the visual surface of the dream only a secondary expression of deeper syntax. Thus, bizarreness in dreams – most REM dreams are in fact relatively mundane – suggests an error that demonstrates the purely formal or deep-structure aspects of cognition and is without semantic significance.

Like Hobson, Foulkes posits a key mechanism for instigating the process. Rather than peripheral brain stem activation, however, Foulkes argues that dreams are formed from a "diffuse mnemic activation" of multiple recent and long-term memory stores that occurs more or less randomly and without any semantic or communicative intent. The organisation imposed on these diffusely and simultaneously activated memories is syntactic, not semantic. The result is the structured storyline of the dream, which includes whatever peripherally induced disorientations it could not fully subordinate. The dream lacks semantics and communicative intentionality because, unlike language, we cannot check the result against a preliminary plan or intention. Unlike language, dreams are simply imposed. We produce them but we also witness their unfolding as if we were not their author. Foulkes describes dream production, the construction of semantic-syntactic structures for the diverse meaning representations active during REM sleep, as highly demanding of attention. This might reduce the attentional allocation to processes that might otherwise be expected to accompany REM dreaming. Hence, during REM sleep we are unable to elaborate the current content by interpreting it within the context of the larger body of one's knowledge. Such elaboration is generally lacking during dreaming, and that absence would lead to poor recall.

The substantial differences in the frameworks adopted in neurophysiological and psychological approaches to dream research stands as an object lesson in the necessary relativity and perspectivism of the human sciences. Indeed, part of the promise of the cognitive era in modern psychology is its potential to address the full extent of human symbolic capacity, as reflected in the multiple "frames of mind" through which human intelligence is manifested – language, imagery, interpersonal relations, mathematics, and aesthetics (Hunt, 1989). It would be tragic for a "cognitive science" to remain focused only on those computational and technical capacities that can be functionally circumscribed and digitally simulated – thereby making psychology the unwitting architect of a science of mind excessively restricted to the artificial and domesticated.

Evolutionary aspects

The assumption that dreaming has an adaptive value is shared by most (though not all) researchers in the field (Montangero, 1993). Indeed, how could biological evolution and ontogenetical development have produced a psychological activity which is so regular and frequent, if it had no adaptive value? One approach to this question has considered whether dreaming contributes to learning and memory consolidation. A coherent picture is slowly emerging, based on both animal (Smith & Lapp, 1986; Smith & Kelly, 1988) and human studies of REM sleep (McGrath & Cohen, 1978; Smith, 1993). It has been observed in studies that if the training task is sufficiently difficult, both animals and humans exhibit post-training increases in REM sleep above normal levels. These increases can occur shortly after the end of the training session, but have also been observed many hours and days after the end of training as well. Further, if REM deprivation is applied at times after training that coincide with these expected REM sleep increases, learning-memory deficits occur. However, in humans, not all learning seems to be sensitive to REM deprivation. Material that is relatively simple and with which the subject is already familiar does not appear to be affected. It rather seems that it is material that requires learning and understanding of new previously unfamiliar concepts that is vulnerable to REM deprivation (Smith, 1993). The suggestion that REM sleep is crucial to memory consolidation is strengthened by the observation that one of the major physiological features of the REM state is the presence of activated hippocampal theta rhythms, which are also characteristically present in wakefulness during exposure to emotionally arousing stimuli (Winson, 1985). The hippocampus itself has already been implicated in the establishment of long-term memories. The question of course remains as to whether it is the non-conscious processes of REM sleep or the conscious experiencing of dreaming during REM sleep that is crucial.

The possibility that dreams provide material for the solution of problems is a fascinating one. Smith (1993) notes that the success of the dream incubation process is markedly enhanced by choosing only those subjects that have already had a dream about the problem they wish to dream more about. The timing of the more valuable dreams is several days later when often a much more helpful, comprehensive dream is experienced. It is of interest that incorporation of what Freud noted as the "day residue" more commonly occurs not the day after the lived events but 5 or 7 days later – suggesting a good deal of processing of the events has already occurred prior to their insertion into the dream (Nielsen & Powell, 1992; Hobson, 2005).

Consistent with the idea that processing/problem solving is in progress, the first dream might indicate that a problem has been taken seriously and occupied enough of the individual's time to become a major learning experience. The processing of this experience continues and of course could be enhanced by further thought and related daytime activity. Dreams of events that have been in process for some time would be expected to contain more complete solutions or perspectives than the initial dreams of newly considered problems (Smith, 1993). This idea has already been suggested by Cartwright (1977). In a series of studies she found that the first dreams of the night appeared to be directly related to present anxieties, whereas later dreams incorporated emotionally associated experiences from the past and final dreams of the night appeared to involve contemplation of possible problem solutions. Thus, within a single night and over a period of days, there would appear to be continual processing. This process would take place whether the individual remembers her or his dreams or not, though it does not refute the notion that the conscious experience of the processes during sleep is an aid to their effectiveness in problem solving. Griffin's (1997) evolutionary account of the function of dreaming unites these twin strands of learning and problem solving. In this he proposes REM sleep first evolved to program instinctive behaviour – which he describes as genetically anticipated patterns of stimulation. This mechanism for processing anticipated stimulation is then used in later life to deactivate emotionally arousing schemata arising from unresolved problems by representing them as sensory analogues. This accords with the increased autonomic arousal and drive expression which follows REM deprivation.

Children's dreams

Our understanding of children's dreams owes a considerable amount to the pioneering work of David Foulkes at the Georgia Mental Health Institute in Atlanta. This began in the late 1960s and continued into the mid-1980s comprising major longitudinal and cross-sectional studies. The first longitudinal study utilised sampling of dream reports in both laboratory and home settings (Foulkes, 1982b). Over a five-year period (1968–1973) a younger group of 7 boys and 7 girls (initially aged 2–4 years) and an older group of 8 boys and 8 girls (initially aged 8–11 years) each spent 9 nights per year in a sleep laboratory. In addition, new groups of 7- to 9-year-olds were brought in for comparison with the younger group in the fifth year of the study. A subsequent cross-sectional study involved a total of 80 children, with equal numbers of boys and girls aged 5, 6, 7 and 8 years. Each child spent a total of 3 non-consecutive nights in the laboratory. The main aim of these studies was to describe changes in the nature of children's dreams over time, which with the sampling procedure used enabled comparisons of dreams from children aged from 2–15 years. As well as recording dream reports, a range of additional information was sought. This included the results of objective and projective personality tests, behavioural ratings collected from teachers, parent's attitudes to child rearing, IQ, and a variety of cognitive skill tests. During the first three summers observational data was also collected from younger children's play groups. What then were the principal findings to emerge from this?

First of all, in a comparison of home and laboratory collected dreams – which controlled for the method of dream sampling – Foulkes found no evidence of bias in the content of laboratory dreams (Foulkes, 1999). Because of their much greater frequency, these laboratory dreams can therefore be said to constitute a more representative sample of children's dream life than those collected at home. In fact the lab dreams of the young children, like adults, were found to be mundane and realistic – strikingly at odds with the predictions of Freudian theory, which would lead one to expect the unrestrained expression of instinctual wants and needs, due to the poorly developed egos of children being unable to hold at bay the strivings of the id (Foulkes, 1979).

Secondly, and perhaps more importantly, the dreams unfolding over the course of childhood revealed a clear developmental pattern. This is summarised in Table 8.1. Initially children's REM periods appear to be, in Foulkes' words, "largely empty of those organised experiences we call dreams". Between the ages of 3 and 5 years they reported REM dreams on average only about 15 per cent of the time – increasing to an average of 31 per cent between the ages of 5 and 7 (Foulkes, 1999). As children do report dreams between 3 and 9 years of age they became progressively longer and more complex. For example, whereas at ages 3–5 the reported imagery is generally static (movement verbs are rarely expressed in the reports), by the ages of 5–7 there is a more "movie-like" quality to the reports, although movement is usually employed by non-self characters. At ages 7–9, REM reports contained movie-like sequences with the dreamers themselves as actively participating characters. Average recall was now in the region of 43 per cent. By ages 9–11, report rates approximating to adult levels (79 per cent cf. 85 to 90 per cent in adults) were found. Of great significance was that neither the rates of dream recall nor the formal properties of the dreams were predicted by personality, behavioural or observational variables nor were they by verbal skills such as vocabulary or the ability to describe static and moving pictures from memory. They were, however, relatively well predicted by visuo-spatial skills – particularly the block design sub-test of the Wechsler IQ test and other tests involving mental rotation.

One inescapable conclusion from these studies is that the ability to dream in a form which we as adults recognise as dreaming is a cognitive accomplishment which takes years for us to master and it is one which is linked with our capacity for conscious self-representation – the ability to form, in consciousness, a representation of our own self. As such, it must depend on the evolution and prior development of other cognitive systems (Foulkes, 1993) and is unlikely to exist in all but the higher mammals in any form which we would recognise as dreaming. The issue of conscious self-representation leads to a consideration of a special class of dreams in which the ability to be consciously aware of oneself is not merely a cognitive prerequisite to dream construction, but is actively expressed in real time within it; I am referring of course to the lucid dream.

TABLE 8.1 Stages in REM dream development (adapted from Foulkes, 1999)

	0	*1*	*2*	*3*
Approximate ages	*0–3*	*3–5*	*5–7*	*7–9*
Dream frequency	*none*	*rare*	*rare, but increasing*	*relatively frequent*
Dream form		*isolated event*	*simple event sequence*	*complex narrative*
Dream imagery		*static*	*kinematic*	*kinematic*
Active self-participation		*absent*	*absent*	*present*

Lucid dreaming

Lucid dreaming occurs relatively infrequently – only around one person in five reports lucidly dreaming at least once a month (LaBerge & Gackenbach, 2000), a period when on average one would expect between 120 and 150 dreams to have occurred. Estimates of lifetime prevalence are however much higher; varying from 47 per cent to 100 per cent of the population (Snyder & Gackenbach, 1988). When compared to non-lucid dreams, lucid dreams have been found to have higher levels of control and more positive emotions, to contain more physical activity, to be more vivid and to have more scene changes (Levitan & LaBerge, 1993). The pivotal role of self-consciousness in lucid dreaming has led some researchers to argue that it should be considered a state distinct to ordinary REM sleep – principally because the main characteristics used to define sleep have been the absence of self-consciousness and a lack of awareness and communication with the external world. On the basis of extensive electrophysiological monitoring, Voss et al. (2009) have suggested that lucidity during dreaming is in fact a hybrid state of consciousness, distinguishable from both REM sleep and waking, with large-scale neuronal synchronisation patterns (coherence) particularly evident in frontal regions of the brain.

Lucidity is often triggered by an awareness of some anomaly in the setting or content of the dream – something more likely to be appreciated by people who are familiar with what their dreams are like. Unsurprisingly then lucid dreams are more often reported by high dream recallers. In addition a number of demographic factors have been associated with lucid dreaming: younger rather than older people, single rather than married, and first-born offspring have all been found to report them more often. No consistent differences have been found with respect to gender, occupation, or educational level. There is some evidence that risk taking, an androgynous sex-role identity, and field independence (the extent to which one's perceptions are independent of environmental cues) are associated with the frequency of lucid dreaming, with some, albeit inconsistent, results pointing toward a relationship with introversion (Snyder & Gackenbach, 1988). As yet no simple theoretical framework can adequately account for these individual differences.

Laboratory studies have found that lucid dreams are more likely to occur late in the sleep cycle – perhaps because as the night progresses REM dreams become longer, thus affording the sleeper more time to become aware of cues in the dream which might trigger lucidity. Laboratory-based studies have enabled a unique perspective to be gained on dreaming by searching for correspondences between events and actions in the dream world and observable events in the real world (Schatzman, Worsley, & Fenwick, 1988). This has been possible through subjects who are able to signal lucidity in the REM state by making a prearranged sequence of volitional eye movements and forearm muscle contractions (Hearne, 1978).

In a series of experiments, Alan Worsley, an experienced lucid dreamer, having signalled lucidity, proceeded to carry out a variety of pre-planned action sequences in his dreams. These included counting while writing the numbers on a suitable surface, moving his finger from side to side and following it with his eyes, drawing large triangles on a wall while watching his hand move, and picking up and putting down a shoulder bag. The majority of these attempts showed clear EMG (muscle) or EOG (eye movement) activity in the region of the body corresponding to that moved in the dream. These correspondences strongly suggest that enacted events in the dream world unfold not in some transcendental realm but in the workings of the brain and central nervous system. Whether the context in which the dreams unfold can be similarly correlated with specific neural events in the brain is less clear.

In these experiments Worsley (1988) set out to perform a range of activities to assess their impact on the dreamed world. These included reading (the longer the material the more difficult it is to achieve), flicking a light switch in a darkened room (it invariably fails; gradually increasing brightness is much easier) and firing a gun (a click rather than a bang ensues). The outcomes of these experiments provide clues as to how and why the dream process operates as it does. Worsley in fact noted the lack of conscious control he had over kick-starting the generation of dream imagery (in any sensory modality) as opposed to modifying it. This is consistent with what we know about the construction of waking perception. If for example we consider vision, it has long been known that optically stabilising an image by attaching a small mirror to a contact lens on the eye leads to progressive degradation of the image, eventually leading to a blank homogenous visual field (Gregory, 1977). During wakefulness a continuous stream of new visual information via saccadic movements of the eyes ensures that this degradation does not occur. In the absence of continuous visual input from the environment during sleep, the dreaming brain similarly seems to require a compensatory mechanism to inhibit adaptation to the internally generated images. The continuous generation of new imagery fulfils this function and ensures adaptation to existing visual scenarios cannot take place. Difficulty in reading occurs then because images cannot persist for a sufficient length of time before new ones are automatically generated. Sudden effects in other sensory modalities (the gun firing) similarly require an ongoing prior stream of activity to be present. The inability to instantly generate complete fully formed scenarios informs us that constructing dreams – like all forms of thinking – takes time and that there is an upper limit to the processing power on hand to do this.

Lucid dreaming is considered to be related to other kinds of unusual experiences: out of body experiences (OBEs) (see Green, 1968), near-death experiences (NDEs), and UFO abduction experiences. Three dimensions have been suggested which enable these states to be distinguished – a recognition that one's current state of consciousness is different from the usual waking state, a particular belief system to make sense of the experience and a set of goals which are concerned with either inducing the experience or which delineate the actions/exercises which can be pursued from within the experience. LaBerge and Gackenbach (2000) note that lucid dreams and OBEs, for example, share a recognition of the divergent nature of the current state of consciousness but differ with respect to the other two dimensions. As unusual and striking as lucid dreams are, the available evidence provides no grounds for believing there is anything intrinsically mystical about them. To be sure, there are applications of lucid dreaming to psychotherapeutic practice and in enhancing general psychological well-being – notably with respect to mindfulness (Morley, 2013) – but we have no reason to doubt that the phenomenon cannot eventually be fully accommodated within existing scientific frameworks. If, on the other hand, the presence of ESP during dreaming can be reliably demonstrated, our current assumptions about the world would face a serious challenge.

Paranormal cognition and dreaming

For parapsychologists the chief interest in our dream life concerns the validity of long-held claims – held in many cultures – that dreams may connect us to the realms of the supernatural and the sacred. Many esoteric notions have survived from earlier times – chief amongst them the belief that dreaming permits the boundaries of space and time to be transcended – the future to be divined and the experiences of others to be shared through telepathy (see Box 8.1). Certainly the internal logic of remembered dreams often seems to defy common sense – entertaining possibilities beyond the bounds of rational thought. Indeed, lucid dreams aside, ordinary reflective self-consciousness, on which much of our everyday rationality and understanding of the world is predicated, appears to be suspended in dreams (Roberts, 1981). This provides fertile ground for the imagination. The big question is whether there is an evidential basis for believing the mind to be capable of paranormal feats during sleep.

BOX 8.1 BELIEF IN PARANORMAL DREAMS

Psychologists have considered ways in which belief in the paranormal ability of dreams can be realised in the absence of real telepathic or precognitive dreams. In one scenario increased tolerance of ambiguity, coupled with a prior belief in the paranormal can lead people to believe accidental hits – meaningful coincidences between dreamed and real life events – are in fact precognitive dreams (Houran & Lange 1998). How can this actually occur? Suppose that the chance of a meaningful coincidence in the absence of ESP is quite rare, let us say for argument the probability for this is 1 in every 40,000 dreams. Given that on average we produce around 4-5 dreams per night, then we should expect such a meaningful coincidence to occur once every 8-10,000 nights – or roughly once every 22 to 28 years. In a dreaming lifespan of roughly 65 years we might expect 2 or 3 such dreams – rare indeed. Given the population of the UK (the adult working population is approximately 31 million [ONS, 2015]) however we might expect by chance some 775 people each night to be dreaming such meaningful coincidences. Given the personal impact such an event might have we could expect word of it to quickly spread. In a culture where belief in paranormal phenomenon is already established this would receive continuous support from misattributing coincident dreams to the paranormal.

Instances of spontaneous telepathic dreams have been reported for many years including by many psychotherapists impressed by the material revealed to them by their patients. In fact a large proportion of all spontaneous cases of ESP have been reported during dreams (Van de Castle, 1977). Foremost in these accounts are themes of death or danger, which seem to provide a rationale for the existence of a primitive extrasensory system sensitive to threat. But impressive as these reports sometimes appear to be, they lack the firm foundation that can be provided by a rigorous repeatable demonstration of the phenomenon under properly controlled conditions, one moreover in which the chances of the phenomenon being explained away on the basis of coincidence can be precisely estimated. Fortunately, during the 1960s a group of researchers at the Maimonides Medical Center in New York undertook a series of experiments which directly sought to establish whether paranormal cognition could occur in dreaming (Ullmann, Krippner, & Vaughan, 1989). These have been the subject of continuing debate. In all, fifteen separate investigations (including two pilot studies) were undertaken. The basic experimental paradigm followed by the researchers in eight of the studies is described in Box 8.2 below and results from the studies which utilised this protocol are summarised in Table 8.2. For details of the other studies conducted in the series, readers are advised to consult the book by Ullman et al. (1989).

A relatively simple way for statisticians to analyse this data is to use the theory of probability to decide if the number of hits exceed what would be expected by chance. If results from all 8 studies are combined together we see that the judges scored 92 hits and 38 misses (a success rate of 67.6 per cent) and the dreamers 86 hits and 33 misses (a success rate of 72.3 per cent), both higher than the chance

BOX 8.2 A TYPICAL TELEPATHIC DREAM EXPERIMENT

A percipient is first of all prepared for physiological monitoring of sleep. At the beginning of each period of REM sleep an experimenter in an adjacent room signals to an agent situated at a different nearby location. The agent then concentrates on a randomly chosen picture target (selected only when the agent was physically alone in the room) and attempts to communicate this to the dreamer. Near the end of each REM period the dreamer is awakened in order to report any dream material. (This procedure itself is not straightforward: astute questioning may be needed to elicit the dream material; see Winget & Kramer, 1979.) Following awakening in the morning the dreamer is asked for their impressions as to what the target might have been. This is conducted by an interviewer blind to the identity of the target. Subsequently several judges independently attempt to match the dream reports to the targets. In the Maimonides studies this was done by ranking the possible targets from most to least correspondence with the dreams. A hit would be designated where the correct target received a mean rank from the judges which fell in the upper half (e.g. with 12 possible targets a hit would require a mean rank of 6 or less).

TABLE 8.2 Pooled results from eight ESP dream studies (Ullman et al., 1989, Child, 1985)

	Judges		*Dreamer*	
Study no.	*Hits*	*Misses*	*Hits*	*Misses*
1	*7*	*5*	***10***	*2*
2	***5***	*2*	***6***	*1*
3	***4***	*8*	***9***	*3*
4	***6***	*2*	***6***	*2*
5	***3***	*5*	***5***	*3*
6	***8***	*0*		
7	***6***	*2*	***8***	*0*
8	***53***	*14*	***42***	*22*

rate of 50 per cent. The probability of such a result occurring by chance is less than 1 in 7,000 for the judges and for the dreamers less than 1 in 100,000. These are way beyond what is normally required to convince scientists that something of interest is going on.

Child (1985) raised the question of why the Maimonides results received so little attention from the wider psychological community. One plausible reason is the failure by researchers in two other studies to replicate the findings, although the procedures followed in one of these may have prevented significant results being obtained (Van de Castle, 1989). It must be said, however, that Child's view that the research community is biased is difficult to take issue with. It really isn't plausible to attempt to explain these results away on the basis of either chance, sensory leakage or fraud. While there have been no direct replications, there have however been a number of conceptual replications. Sherwood and Roe (2003) provide a detailed review of over 20 dream ESP studies which were published between 1977 and 2002. Though these are procedurally different than the original studies, they nevertheless provide results which are broadly comparable. The effort in running a sleep lab has (perhaps unfortunately) meant that parapsychologists now resort to more accessible (and inexpensive) procedures such as the ganzfeld to investigate psi. However the strength of effects reported in the Maimonides research presents a strong case for the continuation of work on psi and dreaming and for this work to be undertaken with rigour. As Holt, Simonds-Moore, Luke, and French (2012) note, the data from dream ESP studies have not been explained away by sceptics. As such, they constitute serious evidence for the existence of psi, perhaps the best there is. Given the challenges this poses for the view of reality enshrined within the dominant scientific paradigm, one ought to expect a serious large scale and well-funded series of studies to settle the matter. If such research were to finally settle the question and confirm the existence of extrasensory perception, then we may be entitled to ask questions about how and why such a "weak" and barely detectable communication system has arisen and why it has found the dream state to be a particularly conducive state for it. It has been argued that "psi" is a primitive communication system but dreams as we have seen are not primitive – they are contingent on higher cognitive processes and connected to the ability to form conscious self-representations. They are an ability which in evolutionary terms has arisen relatively recently.

The study of the putative link between dreaming and ESP covers only one aspect of the possible relationship between the dream world and the paranormal. What then are we to say of other ostensible connections between dreams and the supernatural? For example, how should one make sense of the dream report with which I initially opened this chapter? A number of possibilities present themselves, only one of which is tied to the question of another person's conscious survival beyond the boundaries of death. Our sense of the presence of others in life is of course a regular cognitive occurrence – and hence that sense is stored in our memories and capable of being activated under the conditions of sleep. Why on any one occasion they are activated is no doubt tied to each individual's complex psychology and the circumstances of their lives. But this more mundane explanation does not thereby reduce the significance of such dreams. On the contrary. We live in a society which places a premium on youth and which fears and denies the realities and inevitabilities of ageing and death. In the Western world these remain a source of anguish and are to be packaged and kept out of sight. Dreaming of those we once knew is a part of the grieving process but also perhaps an attempt to restore the balance – to keep the dead in our lives, to develop a more healthy ongoing relationship with them and with our own mortality. Such dreams may not tell us much about another ethereal and magical world beyond this one – but they may tell us much about life in this extraordinary one.

Suggestions for further reading

Foulkes, D. (1999). *Children's dreaming and the development of consciousness.* Cambridge, MA: Harvard University Press.

Gackenbach, J., & LaBerge, S. (Eds.) (1988). *Conscious mind, sleeping brain: Perspectives on lucid dreaming.* London: Plenum Press.

Hobson, J. A. (2005). *Dreaming: A very short introduction.* Oxford: Oxford University Press.

Ullman, M., Krippner, S., & Vaughan, A. (1989). *Dream telepathy: Experiments in nocturnal ESP (2nd Edition).* London: McFarland and Company.

9

ASTROLOGY

David Groome

Men at some time are masters of their fates:
The fault, dear Brutus, is not in our stars,
But in ourselves that we are underlings.

William Shakespeare, *Julius Caesar*

Astrology and its significance today

Did you read your horoscope in the paper this morning? Recent surveys have revealed that 20 per cent of British people (Theos, 2009) and 29 per cent of Americans (Harris, 2013) believe that astrology is true, and that the stars can tell us something useful about people. But many more read their stars in the newspaper, and about 70 per cent of a UK sample reported that they read their horoscope regularly (Blackmore & Seebold, 2000). In many other countries the acceptance of astrology is far more prevalent. For example, in India belief in astrology is almost universal (Narlikar, 2013), and more than 60 per cent of the population consult astrologers, whilst many Indian employers make use of astrologers to help them in making business decisions or the selection of staff. Many of those who believe in astrology are likely to make real decisions about their lives on the basis of astrological advice, such as whether to get married or when to make a journey. So for many people astrology is a serious matter, which has a very real impact on their lives and on the decisions they make. Even if you are not one of those people, you could still find your life being affected by it, since other people may make decisions about you on the basis of your birth date.

Astrology is accepted by many people as a method of classifying people, and astrologers do therefore have a very real influence over some people's lives. Consequently psychologists have become interested in finding out whether there is any truth in astrology, because it has real-life implications for us all. If astrologers are genuinely able to provide us with accurate and predictive information about the character and behaviour of individuals simply from a consideration of the time and place of their birth, then psychologists would obviously want to make use of this approach. On the other hand, if astrology does not offer any valid information, then its use in real-life applications such as employee selection or decision making should obviously be discouraged. It is for this reason that psychologists have seen a need to investigate the validity of astrologers' claims.

The origins and rationale of astrology

Astrology has been in existence for several thousand years, and it was practised in the ancient Egyptian, Greek, and Roman civilisations. The people of those early times were greatly preoccupied with cyclic events such as the passing of the seasons, because they had a profound effect on people's lives, on their crops, and indeed on their very survival. Since the stars and planets were found to move in regular and predictable cycles, they too were assumed to control events on earth. In those early times most things were assumed to be under the control of the gods, and since the stars and planets were assumed to be some sort of manifestation of the gods it seemed reasonable to suppose that they might influence a person's destiny, especially those stars which were overhead at the moment of birth.

Over the last few centuries astronomers have discovered the true physical nature of the stars and their movements, and as a result we no longer regard the stars and constellations as representing the gods. Astrologers responded to these new findings by suggesting other theories, for example that the stars might exert their influence by their gravitational pull, citing the moon's influence on the tides as a fairly convincing example of such a mechanism. However, this theory also lacks plausibility since it has been shown that the gravitational forces exerted by the stars and planets are incredibly small, so that a newborn baby would actually be subjected to greater magnetic forces from nearby objects such as their cot or the midwife.

One of the biggest problems for astrological theory is trying to explain why the moment of birth should hold such crucial significance. Thousands of years ago the moment of birth may have seemed to be a defining moment, because it is observable and appears to be the moment when life actually begins. Today we know that it is merely a point in the gestation period, whose timing is made all the more arbitrary by the possibility of premature or even induced birth.

It is probably fair to say that nobody has been able to provide any plausible explanation for the theory that the position of the stars at the moment of birth should influence our character or our destiny (Kelly, 1998). Even so, this does not mean that astrology has been disproved. There are many valid phenomena for which we do not yet have an explanation, and it would be unwise and even unscientific to dismiss them all on that basis. Whilst astrology lacks a plausible scientific rationale, astrologers claim that it has been found to work for thousands of years and there remains a possibility that they could be right.

The rest of this chapter will be concerned with reviewing the research carried out by psychologists to test out the claims made for astrology. First, however, it would be helpful to consider what astrologers do actually claim.

The claims made for astrology

Astrologers believe that a person's character and destiny is affected by the stars, and in particular by the position of the stars at the moment of birth. Moreover, this influence is believed to be both powerful and lasting. In other words, the position of the stars at the moment you are born is considered to shape the kind of personality you will have for the rest of your life.

The best-known form of astrology, and the one that will be most familiar for those who read their horoscope in the newspaper, divides people's birth dates into the twelve signs of the zodiac, which are twelve bands (or "houses") through which the sun passes during the course of a year. A person's zodiac sign therefore indicates the position of the sun at the moment when they were born, for which reason these twelve signs are also known as "sun signs". This means, for example, that if you are born when the sun is in the house of Pisces, then astrology would predict that your personality will always tend to show Piscean qualities. You probably already know your own sun sign, but if not (or if you want to look up someone else's sign), the generally accepted birth dates for each sun sign are given in Figure 9.1.

1. ARIES	21 March – 20 April
2. TAURUS	21 April – 21 May
3. GEMINI	23 May – 21 June
4. CANCER	22 June – 23 July
5. LEO	24 July – 23 Aug
6. VIRGO	24 Aug – 23 Sept
7. LIBRA	24 Sept – 23 Oct
8. SCORPIO	24 Oct – 22 Nov
9. SAGITTARIUS	23 Nov – 21 Dec
10. CAPRICORN	22 Dec – 20 Jan
11. AQUARIUS	21 Jan – 19 Feb
12. PISCES	20 Feb – 20 March

FIGURE 9.1 The twelve sun signs and their associated birth dates

The twelve sun signs can be divided into four main groups, which are as follows:

Fire signs (Aries, Leo, Sagittarius)
Earth signs (Taurus, Virgo, Capricorn)
Air signs (Gemini, Libra, Aquarius)
Water signs (Cancer, Scorpio, Pisces)

People born under fire signs are considered by astrologers to be fiery by nature, tending to be energetic, optimistic, enthusiastic, and aggressive. Those born under earth signs are said to be down-to-earth types, being practical, dependable, logical, and cautious. People born under air signs are considered to be lighthearted, friendly, open-minded, and very changeable. Finally those born under water signs are thought to be imaginative, artistic, sensitive, and emotional.

At a more fundamental level these twelve sun signs are divided into two basic groups, known as the "active" signs (fire and air signs) and the "passive" signs (earth and water signs). The active signs (also known as "positive" or "masculine" signs) are characterised by energetic, impulsive, and outgoing tendencies, whereas the passive signs (also known as "negative" or "feminine" signs) denote a more restrained, cautious, and withdrawn character. In some ways this distinction reflects the contrast between people who are ruled "by their heart" or "by their head". It could also be said to mirror the more scientifically based distinction between "extravert" and "introvert" personality types, a dichotomy which is of some interest to psychologists because it is measurable and thus open to scientific testing (see the next section for the findings). It will be noted that the positive and negative signs alternate with one another when the signs are listed in their chronological sequence.

The broad groupings of positive/negative signs and earth/water/fire/air signs are regarded as offering only a very general indication of personality, and for a more detailed analysis of the individual it is necessary to consider each sun sign separately, as they are each considered to have their own more specific qualities. The characteristics usually attributed by astrologers to the twelve sun signs are summarised in Figure 9.2.

The sun sign descriptions listed in Figure 9.2 represent a combination of the views of a number of different astrologers in an attempt to achieve a rough consensus, bearing in mind that different astrologers are not always in complete agreement about the exact qualities associated with each sun sign. The main sources of these descriptions were Harvey and Harvey (1999) and Huntley (2000), and readers who seek a more detailed account of astrology should refer to such books.

Some astrologers are rather scornful of the sun sign approach, and insist that precise details of not only the date of birth but also the exact time and place of birth are essential for the construction of an accurate astrological chart which includes all planetary influences. However, whilst it may be argued that a precise horoscope requires precise birth details, there is still general agreement among astrologers that the broad characteristics associated with the twelve sun signs are fundamental to any astrological reading. More importantly, it is the twelve sun signs which provide the basis for astrological prediction by most members of the public.

ARIES	Assertive, extravert, energetic, determined, ambitious, courageous, impulsive, impatient
TAURUS	Reliable, practical, materialistic, persistent, open, honest, generous, sensitive, easily upset
GEMINI	Versatile, lively, witty, sparkling, articulate, communicative, changeable, moody, highly strung
CANCER	Sensitive, sentimental, emotional, affectionate, nurturing, shy, timid, hesitant, easily upset
LEO	Confident, proud, warm, friendly, extravert, loud, courageous, strong-willed, egocentric, bossy
VIRGO	Analytical, conscientious, discerning, fussy, perfectionist, critical, quiet, secretive
LIBRA	Fair-minded, indecisive, imaginative, intuitive, self-indulgent, charming, agreeable, outgoing
SCORPIO	Emotional, strong-willed, forceful, courageous, aggressive, reserved, secretive, possessive
SAGITTARIUS	Optimistic, impulsive, outspoken, inquisitive, restless, freedom-seeking, unreliable
CAPRICORN	Cautious, practical, logical, reliable, honest, fair-minded, loyal, capable, reserved, insecure
AQUARIUS	Open-minded, imaginative, creative, inquisitive, opinionated, idealistic, outgoing, likes change
PISCES	Creative, artistic, intuitive, romantic, unworldly, vague, sensitive, shy, emotional, easily hurt

FIGURE 9.2 The main characteristics associated with the twelve sun signs

The outline of sun sign astrology given above is essentially no more than a brief summary of the main points. This chapter is not intended to be a complete manual of astrology, and the brief list of sun sign character descriptions given in Figure 9.2 is intended merely as a rough guide to basic astrological concepts, sufficient to allow an evaluation of the scientific studies discussed below.

Scientific studies of astrology

Astrology is essentially an art rather than a science, based on theories and beliefs put forward centuries ago. Modern astrologers claim that these theories have been supported by observations over many years, that they have stood the test of time. They also claim that their experience confirms that most people do seem to fit the characteristics attributed to their sun sign. But this is not scientific evidence. In recent years psychologists have introduced a more objective approach to astrology, by devising experiments which enable them to test the claims and predictions of astrology scientifically.

From the psychologist's viewpoint the most interesting claim made for astrology is that it enables us to predict someone's personality and abilities simply from the time and date of their birth. If this is true then we might reasonably expect to find measurable differences between people born under different signs, using an objective test of personality such as a questionnaire. Another claim made by astrologers is that birth sign can be useful in guiding an individual towards the type of career they might be best suited to. This too can be put to the test by finding out whether people born under certain signs really are more successful in a particular profession. Finally, some astrologers claim that they can predict future events. Once again, it should be possible to find out whether their predictions actually come true.

Can astrologers really live up to their claims? You will find the answer below.

Astrology and personality questionnaires

There are a number of ways we can test personality, many of which rely on one person making a subjective judgement about another person, as for example in the case of a job interview, or a rating given by a friend or a previous employer. Because these subjective judgements are prone to all kinds of errors and biases, psychologists have come to regard questionnaires as a more dependable way of assessing personality, because questionnaires are objective. Each individual answers the same set of questions, and there is a standardised scoring system, so that they will get the same score regardless of who administers the test.

A questionnaire essentially provides a means of obtaining a self-rating from the person being tested, but it does so in a very controlled and standardised way. Questionnaires are by no means infallible, but they are the best method of measuring personality that is currently available. For this reason personality questionnaires have been widely used to test out the claims of astrology.

In one early study carried out by Mayo, White, and Eysenck (1978), a total of 2,324 participants all completed the Eysenck Personality Inventory (EPI), which is a widely used questionnaire measuring both extraversion and emotionality. The birth dates of the subjects were then used to sort them into the twelve signs of the zodiac, in order to find out if there were any differences in personality scores between one sun sign and another. The hypothesis put forward by astrologer Jeff Mayo (who was one of the authors) was that the "active" signs (i.e. fire and air) would be more extravert than the "passive" signs (i.e. earth and water). Remarkably, this is exactly what was found in this study, though the differences between adjacent signs were actually very small. Since the active and passive signs alternate as one works through the calendar, the average E-score (extraversion) for each of the twelve signs of the zodiac showed an alternating pattern as shown in Figure 9.3.

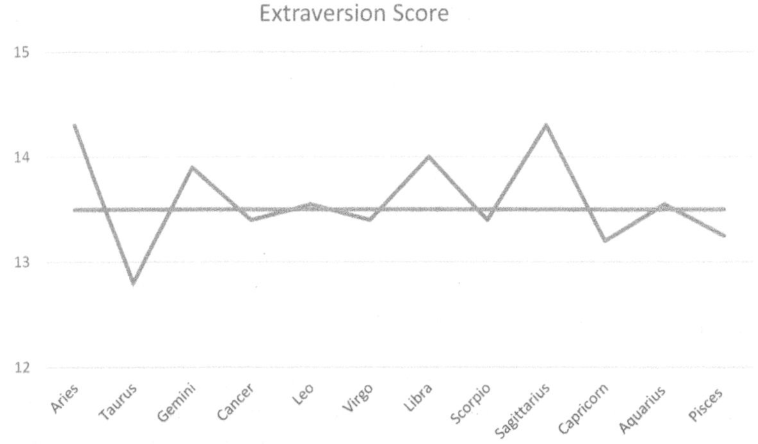

FIGURE 9.3 Mean extraversion scores for the twelve sun signs

Source: Mayo, White & Eysenck (1978)

At first glance these findings appeared to offer some support for astrology. However, a different explanation was subsequently found for the findings of the Mayo et al. study. The participants in their experiment were found to have mostly been very knowledgeable about astrology, and they were all well aware of what characteristics were supposed by astrologers to be associated with their sun sign. A person who knows that their personal sun sign is characterised by extraversion may come to believe that they are more extravert than they really are, because that would fit in with their expectations and beliefs. In other words they make a "self-attribution" based on their knowledge of astrology, and this will affect the answers they give on a questionnaire. Evidence that this was indeed the correct explanation was soon obtained. Eysenck and Nias (1982) were able to demonstrate that the small E-score differences between adjacent sun signs completely disappeared when the study was repeated on children, or on adults who had no knowledge of astrology. Clearly then, the effect was associated with the knowledge and expectations of the people tested.

Subsequent studies have failed to find any significant personality differences between groups with different sun signs (Jackson & Fiebert, 1980; Saklofske, Kelly, & McKerracher, 1981; Shaughnessy et al., 1990; Dahlstrom et al., 1996; Van Rooj, 1999). Van Rooj (1999) selected 12 sets of traits which fitted the 12 sun signs. Each set comprised 8 traits, thus giving a total of 96 trait words. A sample of 422 participants were asked to select which of those 96 traits best applied to them. Those participants who had some knowledge of astrology were found to be more likely to pick out trait words which fit their sun sign, but those with no knowledge of astrology did not. Indeed, for the latter group there were no significant differences between the trait selections made by individuals representing the different sun signs. Once again, the findings offered no support for astrology, but again there was evidence for a self-attribution effect. This phenomenon in itself has considerable significance to the psychologist, providing a cautionary note for all who study the paranormal. Specifically, we can learn that experimental results can be significantly influenced by the knowledge and expectations of the subjects tested. At a more general level, we should be wary of accepting a "paranormal" explanation of our experimental findings without first eliminating all of the possible "normal" explanations.

Matching birth charts with test scores

Carlson (1985) took a different approach to evaluating astrology, by testing the ability of astrologers to match up questionnaire data with astrological data for the same person. Carlson tested 116 subjects who knew the precise time, date, and location of their birth, which were used to construct their astrological birth chart. The same 116 subjects then completed the California Personality Inventory (CPI), a widely used personality questionnaire which yields a profile of 18 scores. A team of professional astrologers were then presented with the birth chart of one participant together with three CPI profiles, one belonging to that participant and the other two being chosen at random. The astrologers' task was to decide which one of the three CPI profiles matched up with the birth chart. This same procedure was repeated for all 116 participants.

The results showed clearly that the astrologers were unable to match up the charts with their corresponding questionnaire scores beyond chance level. Moreover, in a further experiment it was found that the participants themselves were unable to recognise their own astrological personality profile based on their birth charts, again from a choice of three, where the two other choices represented different people but of the same sun sign. Incidentally, the same participants were equally bad at recognising their own CPI scores, so if the results offer little comfort to astrologers they offer little to psychologists either.

Carlson's study is worth this detailed consideration because it was one of the most carefully designed astrology trials ever performed, and there is much to be learned from it. In the first place Carlson used a "double-blind" design, which means that neither the astrologers nor the experimenters were told which test profile was correct, and the identities of the participants were kept secret until the experiment had been completed. Carlson also chose to involve professional astrologers in the design and planning of the study, thus overcoming a criticism directed at most previous studies. One further criticism made of previous astrological studies was that participants had usually been grouped under the twelve sun signs, which the astrologers felt was not sufficiently precise or discriminating. To overcome this criticism Carlson used the team of professional astrologers to produce individual birth charts for each of the 116 participants, based on their exact time, date, and place of birth. This study was designed and carried out to exacting scientific standards, and its failure to find any support for astrology was consequently all the more convincing.

Astrology, success, and fame

Many astrologers offer guidance about the sort of job or career that an individual is suited to, and in some countries astrologers are actually employed to help with personnel selection. The claim that astrology can predict career success is therefore a matter of real practical importance, and it is a claim which should be open to scientific testing.

One criterion of career success is the achievement of fame in one's chosen occupation. This was the criterion chosen by Michel Gauquelin (1972), who looked up the birth dates of 16,000 famous people, to find out whether fame and success in a particular field was associated with any particular sun sign. Astrologers have suggested for example that Scorpios and Leos tend to make good soldiers, Sagittareans make good lawyers, and Capricorns make good politicians. In fact Gauquelin found no support for any of these predictions, nor was there any significant link between sun sign and fame in any particular profession.

However, when Gauquelin looked at the actual time of day when famous people tended to be born, he discovered that there were apparently some variations from a random distribution. Famous sportsmen and soldiers were more likely to have been born at two particular periods of the day, which roughly corresponded to the times when the planet Mars was either on the rise or at its highest point. There were similar, albeit smaller, effects for a few other professions.

Gauquelin's findings were seized upon by astrologers as proof of their skills, but this was hardly justified. Although Gauquelin had found some apparent variations from the expected random distribution of birth times, his findings offered no support whatsoever for conventional sun sign astrology, as Gauquelin himself admitted. Furthermore the discrepancies were fairly small, and they are probably either chance variations or a consequence of some social influence unrelated to astrology. For example, Dean (2002) suggested that birth times may have been incorrectly reported, possibly in an attempt to fit in with astrological assumptions which were widely accepted at the time. Dean points out that the Mars effect has not been found in more recent studies, where birth time was recorded by a doctor or midwife.

Astrology and choice of profession

Alan Smithers (1984) investigated the birth signs of individuals who had chosen a particular profession, but this time using a far larger population sample. Smithers obtained his data from the 1971 British population census, which provided him with birth dates and occupations of no less than 2.3 million British adults, representing roughly 10 per cent of the British working population. For each occupational group Smithers calculated the total number of people born under each sun sign. Examples of his findings for two of the occupational groups (Coalminers and Secretaries) are shown in Figure 9.4.

(a)

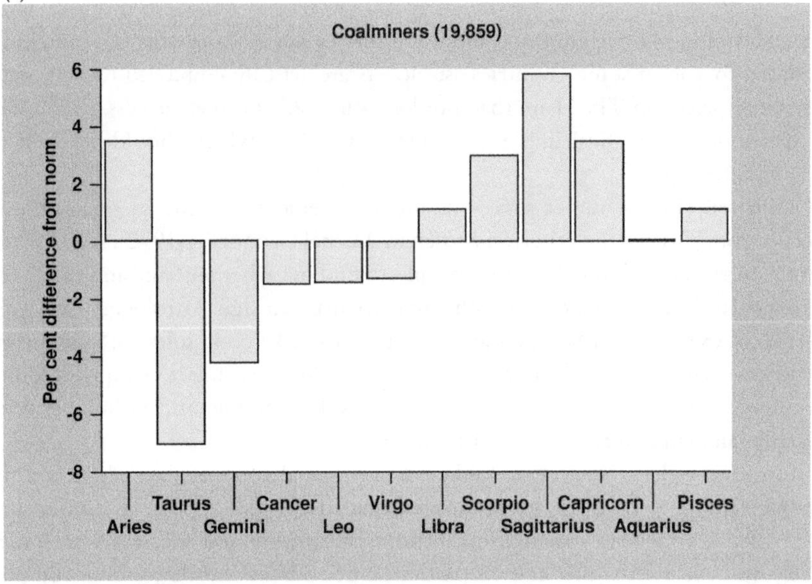

(b)

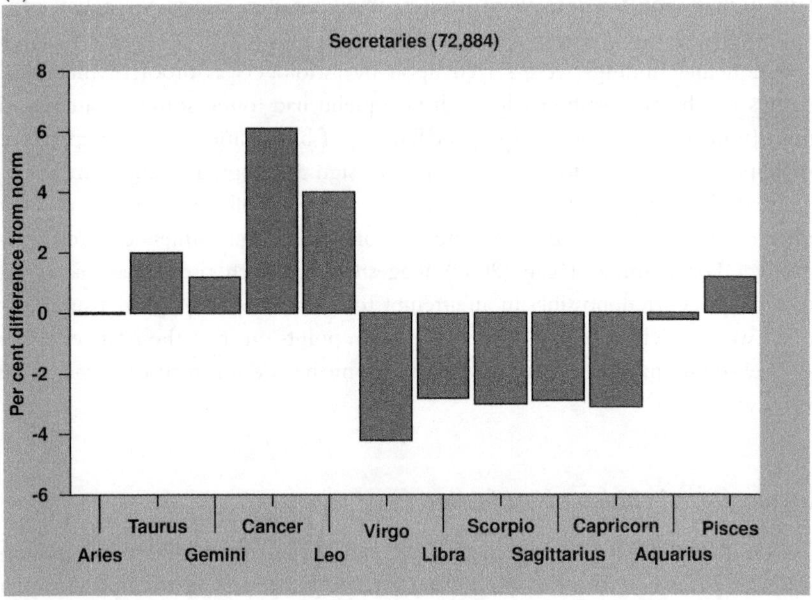

FIGURE 9.4 Frequency of sun signs for (a) coalminers and (b) secretaries

Source: Smithers (1984)

The distribution of sun signs for the various professional groups caused considerable surprise, since there were some signs which occurred far more frequently than others for a given profession. The peak sun sign varied from one profession to another, and in some cases these differences reached statistical significance.

These intriguing results raised the question of whether or not the varying sun sign peaks might be the result of astrological influence. In order to answer this question, Smithers recruited a team of 15 professional astrologers, who were asked to predict (without seeing the data of course) the sun sign which they felt was most likely to predominate in each of the 27 main professions represented in the survey. Unfortunately the astrologers were unable to agree on their predicted sun sign for most of these professions. In fact there were only 10 of the 27 professions for which a consensus could be reached. Their choices for these 10 professions are shown in Figure 9.5.

When Smithers examined the actual distribution of sun signs in members of these ten professions, he found that the astrologers had only guessed the correct sun sign in one case out of ten. For the profession "Authors and Journalists" the astrologers had predicted that Geminis would predominate, and this was indeed the most frequently occurring sign. However, for the other nine professions the most frequently occurring sun sign was not the one suggested by the team of astrologers. A success rate of one "hit" out of ten guesses was roughly what would be expected by chance, so there was no evidence that the astrologers had achieved anything better than a random guess.

The sun sign distributions of the two professions shown in Figure 9.4 are fairly typical of Smithers' data. For coalminers the most frequently occurring sign was found to be Sagittarius, but the team of astrologers had predicted that Scorpios would be most likely to take up this occupation. For secretaries the most frequently occurring sign was Cancer, whereas the astrologers had predicted a predominance of Virgos, which in this case actually turned out to be the least frequently occurring sign. Smithers concluded that his data offered no support

1. Author/journalist	**Gemini**
2. Baker	**Taurus**
3. Car mechanic	**Aries**
4. Civil engineer	**Capricorn**
5. Clerk/cashier	**Virgo**
6. Coal miner	**Scorpio**
7. Hairdresser	**Libra**
8. Optician	**Virgo**
9. Secretary/typist	**Virgo**
10. Tailor/dressmaker	**Libra**

FIGURE 9.5 Sun signs predicted by astrologers as being appropriate for 10 occupations

Source: Smithers (1984)

whatsoever for sun sign astrology. One argument made against this conclusion (Harvey, 1984) was that those employed in a particular profession are not necessarily the people most suited to it, since many people do not actually choose the occupation they enter. However, if astrological forces really did exert significant control over people's aptitudes then we would expect some effect to show through in their choice of occupation.

Although Smithers' data offered no support for conventional astrology, an explanation was still needed for the non-random distribution of sun signs in many of the occupational samples.

As noted above, certain sun signs occurred more frequently than others, often to an extent that reached statistical significance. Moreover, different sun signs predominated in different professions. This was a phenomenon that had been noticed in several previous studies, and it had often been cited as evidence of astrological influences, albeit influences which differed from the accepted tenets of astrology.

In fact there proved to be a far simpler explanation. When Smithers examined seasonal birth trends in the UK population, some quite large variations were found between different social/occupational groups which fitted in remarkably well with the occupational data. For manual workers there was a pronounced peak in the birth rate in late autumn, whereas for non-manual workers the peak birth rate occurred in the spring (Smithers, 1984). If we return to the data in Figure 9.4, it is now possible to see these two trends clearly, with an autumn peak for coalminers and a spring peak for secretaries. In fact these seasonal class trends provide a complete explanation for all of the apparently non-random variations in Smithers' data. This is an important finding, because it illustrates how easily a variation from the norm could be attributed to the stars when in reality it merely follows a social trend. This general principle not only applies to Smithers' data, but probably to that of many other studies too. The moral of all this is that we should never attribute a discrepancy in the data to astrological influences without first considering all of the other possible causes.

Time twins

"Time twins" are people who are born at the same time on the same day. They are not literally "twins" in the normal sense, in that they are not closely related and therefore have no genetic similarity. This makes time twins a very suitable target for study, since astrology would predict that they would grow up to be very similar people with a similar destiny. However, Roberts and Greengrass (1994) found that there was actually no correlation whatsoever between the personality scores, interests, profession, or significant life events of time twins. In a subsequent study, Dean and Kelly (2003) tested no less than 1,400 time twins, measuring over 100 variables relating to personality, abilities, and behaviour, but again no correlations were found. Since all of their pairs of time twins were born within 5 minutes of one another in the same location (London), astrology would predict strong similarities, but none were found.

Marriage compatibility

Astrologers claim that some sun signs are particularly compatible with one another, and that choosing a partner from the right sun sign will increase the chances of a long and happy marriage. However, this is another claim that has not stood up to scientific testing. Voas (2007) used data from the 2001 UK census to examine the marriages of no less than 10 million married couples, the largest sample ever tested in a study of astrology. From a survey of the birth dates of the 20 million individuals involved, Voas concluded that marriages involving a "favourable" sun sign pairing (for example, Virgos and Capricorns are said to be a good combination) did not occur more frequently than those involving "unfavourable" sun signs, nor were they more likely to enjoy a lasting marriage than those with an unfavourable pairing. So it can be concluded that sun sign combinations do not predict whether people will be attracted to one another or whether they will make successful marriage partners.

Predicting future events

Some astrologers claim that they can predict future events from the stars. This certainly does not seem very likely, but a slightly more plausible version of this claim is that although the predicted event may not be absolutely inevitable, the stars could still determine the basic conditions which make it more likely. On a similar basis, you could predict that there will be more people wearing overcoats next winter than there were in mid-summer. This prediction is not certain to come true, but if it doesn't then a lot of people will be shivering.

One of the reasons why astrologers so often seem to get their predictions right is that observed confirmations tends to be selective. The predictions that come true tend to be widely publicised, whereas the predictions that fail tend to be forgotten. The famous American astrologer Jean Dixon made three major predictions in the 1950s. The first was that President Kennedy would die young (he did). The second was that the Russians would reach the moon before the Americans (they didn't). The third was that World War III would begin in 1958 (again, not as far as I recall). Many people were impressed that she had predicted John Kennedy's death, but her less successful predictions went largely unnoticed.

In an effort to obtain more scientific evidence about the accuracy of such predictions, Culver and Ianna (1979) examined the predictions made by a number of professional astrologers for the coming year. Altogether 3,000 separate predictions were made, but less than 2 per cent of them actually came true. Furthermore, the few that did come true were mostly the ones that were the vaguest and the most obvious, for example "Tension will continue in the Middle East" and "There will be a tragedy in the Eastern USA next spring". It would be a reckless person indeed who chose to bet money against either of these events occurring, that year or any other year.

Conclusions

From the studies reviewed above, it must be concluded that no evidence has been found in support of astrology. This is not quite the same as saying that astrology has been disproved, since the existence of astrology is essentially non-falsifiable. It is impossible to prove that something does not exist or that it is never true, and this applies to astrology just as it does to Santa Claus or the unicorn. There will always remain a faint possibility that there are some valid astrological effects, but what we can say is that any such effects are so small that they cannot be detected by any known method of study, so they can probably be safely ignored for all practical purposes.

It has been clearly shown that astrologers are unable to predict personality, career aptitude, or future events with anything beyond a chance level of accuracy. It would therefore be unwise to base any major decisions on astrological predictions. It can also be said quite clearly and unequivocally that astrology should never be used in personnel selection, as it has no proven validity as a measure of personality or aptitude. It would also be a bad idea to pick a marriage partner on the basis of astrological compatibility.

In reply to these findings astrologers have argued that the methods employed by psychologists are not suitable for testing astrological claims. They argue that personality questionnaires only measure very broad traits and lack the sensitivity to detect the more subtle aspects of human character described by astrology. Astrologers have also protested that one's choice of profession does not imply suitability, since many people do not have much choice in what they do for a living (Harvey, 1984). But psychologists point out that astrology is formulated in such a way that it can never be subjected to any completely acceptable scientific test, so it can never be completely refuted (Kelly, 1998). For example, astrologers tend to make statements and predictions which are vague and unspecific, so that there will always be some way of reconciling their predictions with actual events.

Given that there is no scientific evidence for astrology, it seems strange that so many people are prepared to believe in it. This apparently irrational belief is of interest to psychologists in its own right, and several studies have been carried out which help shed some light on the phenomenon. Snyder and Schenkel (1975) asked a large number of people for their time and date of birth, and then presented each of them with a personality description allegedly based on their horoscope. In reality all of the participants had been given exactly the same personality description, despite which most of them agreed that it described them quite accurately. In a similar experiment French et al. (1991) found that most people accepted a description of their personality as being "good" or even "excellent", despite the fact that it contained both extremes of each personality dimension (e.g. "at times you are extraverted . . . while at other times you are introverted").

These experiments illustrate the so-called "Barnum Effect", named after the famous showman who claimed that people will believe anything about themselves so long as it includes "a little something for everybody". The trick is to say things that are fairly positive and which virtually anyone could identify with (e.g. "you feel at times that some people do not appreciate your good qualities enough . . ."), and to keep the content as vague and nonspecific as possible. Astrologers tend to make rather vague and general predictions, and they focus on the more flattering aspects of the readers' personality so that people are being told what they want to hear. If you are not convinced that these tactics really work, you might like to try reading through the star columns of your daily newspaper. If you try hard enough you will find some snippets in all twelve of the zodiac signs which you can recognise in yourself.

One possible motive for accepting the tenets of astrology so uncritically is that most people seek an understanding of their lives, and an insight into the minds of other people. The rather limited knowledge offered by psychologists is not enough for many people, who find it frustrating to have no satisfactory framework which enables them to understand other people. Those who simply cannot accept our incomplete knowledge of people and the universe will readily grasp at a system such as astrology which promises to give them the insights they require.

The available scientific evidence offers no support for astrology. This being the case, it would be unwise and in many cases unacceptable to make use of astrology in making real decisions about people's lives, as for example in personnel selection or career guidance. On the other hand, there is probably no harm in reading your stars in the newspaper if you want to, and you may even find that it sometimes comes true.

Suggested further reading

Dean, G., Heukelom, W., Smit, R., Terpstra, B., Nias, D., & Mather, A. (2013). *Astrology under scrutiny: Close encounters with science*. Amsterdam: Wout Heukelom and Cygnea van der Hooning.

This is a very thorough summary of the research which has been carried out on astrology over the years. Some of the information it contains can also be found on this website: www.astrology-and-science.com.

10

RELIGION, BELIEF AND SCIENCE

Michael W. Eysenck

The easy confidence with which I know another man's religion is folly teaches me to suspect that my own is also.

Mark Twain

Introduction

One of the few incontrovertible facts about religion is that it is of enormous importance worldwide. There are various ways of assessing religiosity. Two very common ones are by asking people to indicate whether religion is an important part of their daily lives and whether they attended a religious service or worship in the past week. Diener, Tay, and Myers (2011) found in a study covering 154 countries that 78 per cent of people reported religion was important in their lives. However, their data did not include China – adding data about China from a previous study, they estimated that 68 per cent of humans (approximately 4.6 billion people) regard religion as an important part of their daily lives.

The above may imply there are relatively few atheists in the world. However, that is not the case. Zuckerman (2007) reported evidence that there are over half a billion atheists worldwide. Of all the thousands of religions, that number is exceeded only by the numbers of Christians, Muslims, and Hindus. Atheists are 58 times more numerous than Mormons and 41 times more numerous than Jews.

For the purpose of this chapter, I will rarely distinguish among different religions. Religions differ in several major ways, but many of the world's leading religions (including Christianity, Islam, Judaism, and Mormonism) are all monotheistic (believing in one God or the oneness of God). In addition, there are major commonalities in terms of the psychological processes responsible for adherence to the world's religions. It is easy to see the attractions of religion such as social support, purpose and meaning in life, and the prospect of life after death. In spite of those attractions, there has been a fairly rapid decline in religious belief in most Western societies in recent times (Barber, 2011).

Religion vs. science

At the risk of oversimplification, there are two major ways we can try to understand religion. First, there is the position espoused by many (probably most) religious believers: religion is entirely a matter of faith and the scientific approach is totally irrelevant to an understanding of religion. According to this viewpoint, the religious approach is based on revelation, faith, and sacredness, whereas the scientific approach is based on reason, evidence, and empiricism.

Adherents to the above position often claim that religion addresses different issues to science. More specifically, religion considers *why* there are humans and *why* the universe exists based on the assumption that there is some underlying purpose behind everything. In contrast, science considers *how* the human race and the universe have developed over time.

In sum, it follows from the religious position that trying to understand religion from a scientific perspective is an entirely fruitless enterprise. As a liberal thinker, I totally respect that position (even though it would render this entire chapter supererogatory!).

Second, there is the scientific approach, according to which our understanding of religion and individuals' religious beliefs can potentially be enhanced through research. That is the approach forming the basis for this chapter. I must warn anyone who thinks there is an unbridgeable chasm between religion and science that the rest of this chapter is likely to increase their blood pressure. I would respectfully suggest they focus on the other chapters in this book.

Some incompatibilities

One obvious way the religious and scientific perspectives differ most profoundly is in terms of their accounts of the place of the human species. Most (but not all) religions regard the human species as uniquely important because we are of unique significance to God, possess souls, and can potentially go to heaven. This uniqueness or specialness is missing from the scientific account.

Which approach is more correct? We will briefly consider four kinds of evidence more consistent with the scientific approach. First, scientists have discovered the universe is approximately 13.8 billion years old but humans have existed for only an almost infinitesimal part of that time. If God created the universe, why did He wait almost 14 billion years before humans made an appearance?

Second, the universe is approximately 91 billion light-years in diameter (and will be larger by the time I have finished this sentence!) and our Earth occupies a vanishingly small amount of that space. As the American theoretical physicist Richard Feynman argued, "It doesn't seem to me that this fantastically marvellous universe, this tremendous range of time and space and different kinds of animals, and all the different planets, and all these atoms with all their motions, and so on, all this complicated thing can merely be a stage so that God can watch human beings struggle for good and evil – which is the view that religion has. The stage is too big for the drama" (cited in Gleick, 1992, p. 372).

Third, the notion that the human species is totally unique and qualitatively different from any other species received strong disconfirmation from Darwin's (1859) theory of evolution, according to which the human species evolved out of other species. Subsequent research on the fossil record, genes and DNA has provided compelling support for Darwin's theory. For example, we share over 98 per cent of our DNA with chimpanzees. More surprisingly, we share 70 per cent of our DNA with sponges (Srivastava, Simakov, Chapman, Fahey, Gauthier, Mitros, et al., 2010) so perhaps we should treat them with more respect!

Fourth, the evidence strongly implies it is entirely fortuitous that the human species exists at all. The Earth was dominated by dinosaurs for far longer than it has been dominated by humans and their extinction approximately 65 million years ago was due in large measure to an enormous meteor striking the Yucatan peninsula in Mexico. It is very likely that there would be no human species on Earth if it had not been struck by this meteor.

It could be argued that the scientific approach has significant limitations and so we should not attach undue weight to scientific evidence. This is indisputable. Scientific findings can be difficult to replicate. Scientists can refuse to accept evidence that disproves their favoured theoretical ideas (Okasha, 2002). Feyerabend (1975) went further and claimed that science progresses by a sort of "who-shouts-the-loudest" strategy in which publicity and visibility count for more than research quality. However, Feyerabend's notion that anarchy prevails in science is a gross exaggeration of what actually happens even though (sadly) it contains a grain of truth.

The great majority of improvements in people's lives over the centuries are due to science. Examples include electricity, the dramatic increase in longevity, faster and more comfortable travel, increased availability of food, instant communication, and so on. One of the greatest advantages of the scientific approach is that it is typically self-correcting. Numerous erroneous theories have been put forward but their deficiencies have been uncovered leading to their replacement by superior theories.

Chapter content

This chapter addresses five major theoretical issues:

1. **Religion, the paranormal and superstition**: There is the issue of the extent to which there are important commonalities between the possession of religious beliefs and other irrational beliefs.

2. **Motivational forces, religious beliefs and irrational beliefs**: There is the issue of the motivational forces leading individuals to have religious beliefs. The discussion will include consideration of whether the motivational forces responsible for other irrational beliefs are similar in nature.
3. **Cognitive mechanisms underlying religious belief**: There is the issue of the underlying cognitive (and other) mechanisms associated with the development and maintenance of religious beliefs. As we will see, various cognitive biases play an important role.
4. **Religion and evolutionary psychology**: There is the issue of the role of evolution in the development of religious beliefs. Evolutionary psychologists have argued that religious beliefs have adaptive value and their claims are evaluated.
5. **Content of religious beliefs**: There is the issue of the *content* of individuals' religious beliefs – why do most people's religious beliefs take certain forms? To anticipate, conceptualisations of God often contain human and quasi-human features. They sometimes also have an egocentric quality about them.

Religion, the paranormal and superstition

What is the relationship among religious, paranormal, and superstitious beliefs? As Lindeman and Svedholm (2012) pointed out, the use of terminology with respect to irrational beliefs (including religious beliefs) has often been incoherent and inconsistent. For example, belief in an afterlife or reincarnation has often been categorised as a paranormal belief, but has also been categorised as a supernatural belief and occasionally as a superstition or a magical belief. In similar fashion, belief in extrasensory perception has typically been categorised as a belief in the paranormal but has sometimes been categorised as superstitious or supernatural belief.

Lindeman and Svedholm (2012, p. 241) carried out a thorough analysis of the ways different concepts relating to irrational beliefs have been used and concluded as follows: "The concepts paranormal, superstitious, magical, and supernatural denote the same thing . . . [all these beliefs are] category mistakes that confuse the distinctive attributes of mental phenomena, material objects, living and animate organisms, and the processes they engage in". I accept that there are important commonalities among these four concepts, but would contend that religious beliefs often have a richness and complexity lacking in many other kinds of irrational beliefs.

Research evidence indicates there are important overlaps between religious and paranormal beliefs. For example, Banerjee and Bloom (2014) obtained a moderately strong correlation of +.53 between belief in God and paranormal beliefs. They hypothesised that both kinds of belief might reflect an exaggerated tendency to perceive the world as being governed by agency and purpose (i.e. teleological reasoning).

Banerjee and Bloom (2014) tested the above hypothesis by presenting participants with six fictional scenarios concerning important life events and asking them to imagine themselves experiencing each event. One scenario was as follows: "Imagine that you are planning on travelling across the country for a very important business meeting. On the morning of your trip, you accidentally sleep through your alarm clock and miss your flight. Later that day, you learn that the plane you were scheduled to be on crashed just after take-off and left no survivors" (p. 294). Teleological reasoning was assessed by asking the participants to indicate the extent to which they believed fate was responsible for causing each event. Religious beliefs correlated +.54 with teleological reasoning and the correlation between paranormal beliefs and teleological reasoning was precisely the same.

Conclusions

In sum, the findings of Banerjee and Bloom (2014) suggest there are important commonalities between religious and paranormal beliefs. More specifically, both types of beliefs are moderately strongly associated with a given cognitive bias (i.e. teleological reasoning) suggesting that they depend in part on similar cognitive distortions. This issue is discussed further later in the chapter and the extent to which religious and other irrational beliefs depend on similar motivational forces is discussed in the next section. Before we proceed, note that many people have religious beliefs but not paranormal ones (and vice versa). That means there are important differences between the two types of beliefs (mostly unexplored so far).

Motivational forces, religious belief and irrational beliefs

It is a commonplace notion that religion thrives among people living in very difficult circumstances. This notion was perhaps most vividly encapsulated in the saying (often attributed to the U.S. military chaplain William Cummings), "There are no atheists in foxholes" (a foxhole is a hole in the ground providing limited protection from enemy gunfire).

Findings relating to the above notion were reported by Barber (2012) in a study of 114 countries. He used two measures of economic security: (1) the Gini coefficient (a measure of income inequality); and (2) personal taxation as a percentage of GDP. As predicted, religiosity correlated strongly with the Gini coefficient (+.44) and with taxation (%GDP) (–.63).

Further support for the hypothesis that difficult life circumstances are associated with religious belief was reported by Diener et al. (2011). As predicted, religiosity and difficult circumstances correlated positively at the country and individual levels (+.29 and +.65, respectively). In general, there was a small positive association between religiosity and subjective well-being and this association was mediated by social support, purpose or meaning in life, and feeling respected.

However, the above effects depended on whether any given country experienced relatively difficult or easy living conditions – the effects were fairly strong among countries with difficult conditions but were very small among countries with relatively easy conditions. Within the latter countries, "the benefits of religiosity for

SWB [subjective well-being] are attenuated because even nonreligious individuals have high levels of social support and respect, as well as SWB" (p. 1,289).

There is a negative relationship between intelligence and adherence to religious beliefs (Zuckerman, Silberman, & Hall, 2013; discussed in more detail later). How can we explain this negative relationship? In general terms, a plausible answer is that, "High-IQ people are able to curb magical, supernatural thinking and tend to deal with the uncertainties of life on a rational-critical-empirical basis" (Nyborg, 2009, p. 91). More specifically, Zuckerman et al. (2013) argued that several benefits of religion (e.g. compensatory control, self-regulation, self-enhancement, and secure attachment) are also associated with high intelligence. As a consequence, intelligent individuals have less need for religious beliefs. Of particular relevance here is compensatory control. Zuckerman et al. reviewed several studies showing that intelligence is positively associated with a belief in personal control and self-efficacy.

An important limitation with the research discussed so far is that it is correlational. It is possible, for example, that some of the negative relationship between religiosity and material comforts occurs because religious people are more inclined than non-religious ones to reject materialism. As a consequence, it is hazardous on the basis of such research to try to identify the mechanisms underlying religious beliefs.

Anxiety and perceived control

Lerner (1980) argued that most humans are highly motivated to perceive the world as orderly even when that is not objectively the case. Indeed, he claimed (with supporting evidence) that our strong belief in a non-random world is our "fundamental delusion".

The above notion serves as our starting point for explaining several phenomena in addition to religious belief including perceiving illusory patterns in the world, being superstitious, and believing in the paranormal. Why do most people find it so important to perceive the world as being non-random? One major reason is that anxiety is very often caused by (or at least strongly associated with) a lack of perceived control and/or perceived unpredictability.

There has been a certain amount of controversy concerning the strength of the relationship between control and predictability (Barlow, 2002). There is some evidence that being able to exert control reduces the emotional impact of stressful events even when predictability is held constant (Miller, 1979). However, perceived control and perceived predictability are typically closely linked: being able to control one's environment implies being able to predict what will happen in the future. We will assume there is substantial overlap between perceived control and perceived predictability even though the concepts are not synonymous.

There is a wealth of empirical support for the assumption that a lack of perceived control is of central importance to anxiety (Barlow, 2002). For example, Sanderson, Rapee, and Barlow (1989) exposed panic disorder patients to carbon dioxide in air. Some were given potential control over the concentration of carbon dioxide whereas others had no control. Even though none of the patients with potential control exerted it, they had lower levels of self-reported anxiety and fewer symptoms than those without control. Most strikingly, patients with perceived control were far less likely to experience a panic attack than those without perceived control (20 per cent vs. 80 per cent, respectively).

Gallagher, Bentley, and Barlow (2014) used meta-analysis to assess the relationship between perceived control and anxiety. In one meta-analysis, they reported a large effect size (k = 29) between perceived control and trait anxiety (anxiety as a personality dimension). In a second meta-analysis, the overall effect size between perceived control and disorder-specific anxiety measures was also large (k = 37). Perceived control was significantly associated with all five anxiety disorders considered (generalised anxiety disorder, obsessive-compulsive disorder, social phobia, panic disorder, and posttraumatic stress disorder).

Perceived lack of control, compensatory control and religious beliefs

Kay, Whitson, Gaucher, and Galinsky (2009) put forward an interesting theoretical approach to understanding religious beliefs (as well as other irrational beliefs). The essence of this approach (entirely consistent with what has been said so far), was expressed as follows by Kay et al. (p. 264):

> To insulate themselves from the disabling anxiety that perceptions of randomness incite, individuals psychologically imbue their social, physical, and metaphysical environments with order and structure.

Of key importance is the notion that an important reason why individuals lacking perceived control over their lives have religious beliefs is because such beliefs provide them with compensatory control.

Kay, Gaucher, McGregor, and Nash (2010) argued that compensatory control to reduce the anxiety associated with a random world can be achieved in two ways. First, some individuals have the resources or motivation to achieve perceived personal control. Second, individuals can focus on external sources of control. Believing in the existence of a controlling God can convince individuals the world is not random or chaotic.

Whitson and Galinsky (2008) carried out six experiments using various methods to produce a perceived lack of control in their participants. Perceived lack of control increased the tendency to perceive illusory patterns and conspiracies. Of most relevance was an experiment on superstitious beliefs in which participants were presented with scenarios in which an outcome was preceded by a potentially unrelated behaviour (e.g. knocking on wood before an important meeting at which one's idea was approved). Perceived lack of control increased the tendency to see a connection with the behaviour and the outcome and made participants more worried about performing that behaviour in future.

An interesting real-world demonstration of the effects of loss of perceived control was reported by Sibley and Bulbulia (2012). There was a major earthquake in Christchurch, New Zealand in 2011 which led to extensive loss of life. Those directly affected by the earthquake showed a significant increase in religious commitment.

Why do huge numbers of people prefer to explain the origins of life in terms of intelligent design rather than Darwin's theory of evolution? It seems almost inexplicable since there is no empirical support for intelligent design but possibly more support for Darwin's theory than any other within the realm of science. According to Rutjens, van der Pligt, and van Harrveld (2010), Darwin's theory emphasises a quasi-random process based on unpredictable environmental changes whereas intelligent design postulates a controlling designer. As a consequence, individuals' perceived control is greater with the latter explanation.

Rutjens et al. (2010) tested the above notions. Some participants' perceived control over the future was experimentally reduced whereas there was no experimental manipulation for the others. They used short summaries of three explanations for the origins of life: (1) intelligent design; (2) Darwin's theory of evolution; and (3) Conway-Morris's (2005) version of the theory of evolution. Conway-Morris's version differs from Darwin's mainly in claiming that evolution is regarded as somewhat orderly and predictable rather than random.

What did Rutjens et al. (2010) find? Participants' substantial preference for Darwin's theory of evolution over intelligent design was less among those with reduced perceived control. In addition, a preference for Conway-Morris's (2005) theory over that of Darwin was much greater among participants whose perceived control had been reduced than among controls. Finally, reduced perceived control did not lead participants to prefer intelligent design over Conway-Morris's theory. The take-home message is that individuals lacking perceived control are motivated to regard the world as orderly and such orderliness can be achieved via religious or non-religious means.

There is strong evidence that a perceived lack of control is seen as aversive in part because perceived uncontrollability can create a state of high anxiety. A perceived lack of control increases individuals' tendency to adhere to religious beliefs because such beliefs increase perceived control.

Note, however, that numerous factors influence religious beliefs. Norenzayan and Gervais (2013) identified nine such factors. Perceived lack of control is one of these factors but others include inferring the mental state of others, the notion that there is a purpose for events in the world, awareness of mortality, social isolation, and conforming to the beliefs of high-status others. Some of these factors are discussed in detail later.

Superstition and precognition

As discussed earlier, Kay et al. (2009) argued that many irrational beliefs (e.g. superstitions, precognition) occur in part as a response to a lack of perceived control. Superstition plays an important role in professional sport. For example, Schippers and van Lange (2005) found among leading sportspersons that 80 per cent reported rituals before a game. Many sportspersons use religious rituals as well as superstitious behaviours to enhance their performance (Maranise, 2013).

When are superstitious rituals used in sport? Schippers and van Lange (2005) argued perceived uncertainty of the outcome is important – uncertainty is relatively high if the opposing team is comparably good to one's own team (or better) but low if the opposing team is clearly inferior. Outcome uncertainty reduces perceived control and so should increase the use of superstitious rituals.

Schippers and van Lange (2005) also argued that individual differences in locus of control (Rotter, 1966) are important: perceived control is less in sportspersons with an external locus of control and so their use of superstitious rituals should be greater than that of sportspersons with internal locus of control. As predicted, more superstitious rituals were reported when the outcome was uncertain than when it was predictable. In addition, sportspersons with external locus of control used more rituals than those with internal locus of control.

Many sportspersons claim to use superstitious rituals because they lead to enhanced performance. Damisch, Stoberock, and Mussweiler (2010) carried out several studies in which they observed the effects on performance of various good-luck superstitions (e.g. keep your fingers crossed). In a further study on putting, participants in one condition were informed the ball they were using had proved to be a lucky ball so far. Performance on tasks including motor dexterity, memory, and anagram games was enhanced by the good-luck superstitions and the success rate for putting with the "lucky ball" was much higher than in the control condition (65 per cent vs. 48 per cent). Superstitions enhanced performance because they increased participants' perceived self-efficacy.

Further support for the notion that superstitions enhance performance was obtained by Lee, Linkenauger, Bakdach, Joy-Graba, and Parfitt (2011). Golfers informed they were using a famous golfer's putter performed much better than controls on a putting task.

Research has not invariably discovered that superstitious rituals enhance performance. Calin-Jageman and Caldwell (2014) tried to replicate Damisch et al.'s (2010) finding that putting performance was greatly enhanced when participants used a "lucky ball". However, there was no difference in putting performance between those who did or did not use the lucky ball. The reasons for the discrepant findings are unclear.

Greenaway, Louis, and Harvey (2013) extended research in this area to beliefs in precognition (i.e. the ability to predict the future). Approximately 25 per cent of Americans believe in precognition, agreeing with statements such as, "Astrology is a way to accurately predict the future". We might expect the findings for beliefs in precognition would resemble those for beliefs in superstition given that the two types of belief are highly correlated (Rudski, 2004).

Greenaway et al. (2013) manipulated people's perceived control by instructing them to recall and write about a time they felt in control or had no control. The key finding was that perceived loss of control enhanced precognition beliefs. In another study, they manipulated beliefs in precognition. Participants whose belief in precognition was increased by reading a text indicating that precognition exists reported higher perceived control. In a third study, they obtained evidence that when people lacked control, believing in precognition assisted them to regain a sense of control.

Conclusions

Much light has been shed on the motivational forces associated with the possession of religious beliefs. People in countries with difficult life circumstances are much more likely than those living in more affluent countries to be religious. Religious belief is only associated with enhanced subjective well-being in countries with difficult life circumstances. One explanation of this finding is that religious belief provides perceived compensatory control (and serves to reduce anxiety) in individuals living in conditions permitting very limited control.

Research on superstitious behaviour and precognition has shown that similar processes are involved. More specifically, perceived lack of control typically increases individuals' superstitious behaviour and belief in precognition.

Cognitive mechanisms underlying religious belief

This section is concerned with the cognitive (and other) mechanisms that are associated with religious belief. Several such mechanisms have been identified but our focus will be on those that appear to be of most relevance and importance. First, we discuss the extent to which religious belief depends on mentalising (the ability to infer others' mental states). Second, we consider various cognitive biases that are stronger in religious believers than non-religious individuals.

Mentalising

An extremely significant difference between humans and members of other species is that we have the ability to engage in mentalising or theory of mind. Mentalising or theory of mind can be defined as "the tendency to infer and think about the mental states of others" (Willard & Norenzayan, 2013, p. 381).

An increasingly influential notion is that religious believers use mentalising to think about (and to interact with) God. For example, Gervais (2013, p. 380) argued that, "Gods and minds are perceived in predictably similar ways and processed by the same neural mechanisms". Indeed, it is probable that individuals could not conceptualise supernatural agencies such as God in the absence of theory of mind or mentalising ability.

Why have billions of individuals extrapolated from their ability to infer the intentions of other people to believe in a purposeful God possessing agency and intentions? A plausible answer to that question is that it depends on an asymmetrical relationship – it can be much more dangerous to fail to detect an agent with aggressive intentions (e.g. a large wild creature) than to detect an agent that is not actually there (this is discussed further later in the chapter).

Brain-imaging studies

Neuroimaging studies on theory of mind or mentalising have discovered it is associated with activation in three main brain areas: the anterior medial prefrontal cortex, the temporo-polar region, and the temporo-parietal junction (Eysenck & Keane, 2015). Schjoedt, Stødkilde-Jørgensen, Geertz, and Roepstorff (2009) found when religious individuals conversed with a personal God that these three brain areas were all strongly activated, suggesting that praying to God involves very similar processes to interpersonal interaction.

In similar fashion, Kapogiannis, Barbey, Su, Zamboni, Krueger, and Grafman (2009) found the brain regions associated with mentalising were activated when religious believers thought about God's mental states (especially anger). In another study, Neubauer (2013) found that religious believers' praying was associated with the activation of large-scale brain networks including those involved in mentalising or theory of mind.

Riekki, Lindeman, and Raij (2014) compared brain activation in believers in the supernatural and in sceptics who viewed 2D animations of geometrical objects moving randomly and rated the intentionality of the objects' movements. There were two main findings. First, supernatural believers rated the random movements as more intentional than did sceptics. Second, there was a positive correlation between activation in brain regions associated with mentalising and the intentionality ratings.

Most research in this area is essentially correlational and so reveals only an association between mentalising or theory of mind and religious and/or other supernatural beliefs. As a consequence, it is difficult to decide on the direction of causality: do mentalising biases predict supernatural beliefs or do supernatural beliefs predict mentalising biases? There is no conclusive evidence on this point. However, model testing (e.g. Riekki et al., 2014) suggests the former direction of causality is more likely than the latter.

Mentalising ability

One way of assessing the role played by mentalising in religious belief is to consider individual differences in mentalising ability. For example, there is compelling evidence that a major difficulty experienced by individuals with autism is that they have very impaired (or absent) theory of mind or mentalising. Norenzayan, Gervais, and Trzesniewski (2012) found that autistic adolescents in Florida were only 11 per cent as likely as controls to endorse strongly belief in God. The inverse association between the autistic spectrum and belief in God was fully mediated by measures of mentalising but not other measures covarying with the autistic spectrum or religious belief.

Gervais (2013) argued that another relevant type of individual difference is gender. On average, women have superior mentalising ability or theory of mind than men and are also more likely to have religious beliefs. However, there are clearly various ways of explaining the gender difference in religiosity other than in terms of differences in mentalising ability.

Mentalising and loneliness

When people are lonely or socially excluded, they typically seek out other minds in the world by forming new social contacts (Maner, De Wall, Baumeister, & Schaller, 2007). If the same mentalising ability involved in seeking new acquaintances and friends is also involved in religious belief, we might expect loneliness or social exclusion would increase individuals' religious beliefs. Evidence supporting that expectation was reviewed by Gervais (2013). For example, Gebauer and Maio (2012) found that individuals having a high need to belong reported stronger belief in God than did those whose need to belong was lower.

Epley, Akalis, Waytz, and Cacioppo (2008) argued that loneliness motivates individuals to create social connections. Individuals who were chronically lonely (or who had been induced to feel lonely) had stronger belief in God than those who were not lonely. They were also more likely to attribute human-like attributes (e.g. considerate, thoughtful, sympathetic) to pets and to create human-like gadgets and pets.

Mentalising, prosocial behaviour and self-awareness

The assumption that mentalising plays an important role in believers' interactions with God leads to various additional predictions. For example, it has been found repeatedly (e.g. Bateson, Nettle, & Roberts, 2006) that individuals are more likely to engage in prosocial behaviour when they believe other people are monitoring or observing their behaviour. A similar effect has been reported among religious believers. Randolph-Seng and Nielsen (2007) found religious believers showed greater honesty when primed with thoughts of Gods and religion. In another study (Shariff & Norenzayan, 2007), religious priming increased believers' anonymous generosity and fairness.

The findings discussed so far suggest that mentalising about God increases prosocial behaviour because people feel their behaviour is being monitored. Would similar findings be obtained if individuals engaged in mentalising about some other supernatural agent? A positive answer to that question was reported by Bering, McLeod, and Shackelford (2005). Adults were less likely to cheat when they heard about the ghost of a deceased graduate student.

The feeling of being watched by other people typically increases prosocial behaviour. More generally, it leads individuals to present themselves in a social desirable way but it does *not* necessarily make them more honest (Sproull, Subramani, Kiesler, Walker, & Waters, 1996). Is the same the case when religious believers are primed with God concepts? Gervais and Norenzayan (2012b) asked participants questions to which the socially desirable answer was unlikely to be the honest one (e.g. "No matter who I'm talking to, I'm always a good listener"). The responses of religious believers primed with God concepts were more socially desirable (and hence less honest) than those of believers who were not primed.

Gervais and Norenzayan (2012b) argued that the effect on believers of thinking about God is similar to a "camera in the sky". Previous research had shown that individuals with a video camera pointing at them experience increased public self-awareness (i.e. they focus their attention on themselves). Thinking about God increased the public self-awareness of Christians with strong religious beliefs to the same extent as thinking about being judged by other people.

Cognitive biases: mind-body dualism and teleological reasoning

Individual differences in mentalising ability provide no more than a partial explanation of individual differences in religious beliefs. Some researchers (e.g. Lindeman, Svedholm-Häkkinen, & Lipsanen, 2015) have gone further and claimed that religious and paranormal beliefs do *not* depend on mentalising abilities. Of importance, very large numbers of atheists have good mentalising ability. This suggests that the ability to mentalise may be necessary but is certainly not sufficient to produce religious beliefs. The general religiosity of an individual's cultural context is also important (Norenzayan & Gervais, 2013) as are factors discussed earlier in the chapter (e.g. poverty, perceived lack of controllability, difficult life circumstances).

What factors in addition to mentalising ability do we need to consider to account for religious beliefs? Willard and Norenzayan (2013) and Norenzayan and Gervais (2013) argued persuasively that religious belief does not depend on cognitive processes unique or specific to religion. Rather, religious belief depends on various cognitive biases that are *byproducts* of everyday cognitive processing. Two of the most important of such cognitive biases are mind-body dualism (the notion that minds can operate independently of physical bodies) and teleological beliefs (the notion that animals, natural objects, and artefacts exist for a purpose, discussed earlier). Bloom (2004) argued that religion is in part a by-product of such cognitive beliefs. It is certainly true (as Piaget and other developmental psychologists discovered a long time ago) that young children are virtually all dualists and teleologists.

There are various reasons why mind-body dualism and teleological beliefs might be associated with religious belief. Mind-body dualism can lead to a belief in disembodied intentional agents such as God or spirits. Teleological beliefs are consistent with the belief that the universe and the creatures within it have been created by a God through purposeful design. Note that a belief in mind-body dualism and teleological beliefs probably depend on a pre-existing mentalising ability.

What is less obvious is the adaptive value of these irrational beliefs. According to Dennett (1987), there are three "stances" we can adopt when trying to understand the behaviour of other people, animals, machines, and so on. First, there is the physical stance based on working out how an object works based on the laws of physics. Second, there is the design stance based on an object's design (e.g. we can see that an alarm clock is designed to make a noise at a given time).

Third, and most importantly, there is the intentional stance which involves predicting what another person or animal will do based on assessing their intentions. The crucial point is that using the intentional stance has adaptive or survival value in dangerous situations because it permits rapid decision-making. For example, instead of wondering how a tiger is designed, you decide that its intentions are aggressive and immediately run away. The cognitive belief in teleology is of direct relevance to the intentional stance. It is also plausible (although less obvious) that mind-body dualism (distinguishing between the other person's body and their mind's intentions) is also involved in the intentional stance.

Cognitive biases

Willard and Norenzayan (2013) found mind-body dualism was a strong predictor of religious belief. Religious belief was also predicted (although to a less extent) by teleological beliefs. Banerjee and Bloom (2014) obtained further support for an association between teleological and religious beliefs in a study discussed in detail earlier in the chapter. Individuals having religious beliefs were more likely than non-believers to explain events in their lives in teleological terms.

Willard and Norenzayan (2013) considered inter-relationships among religious beliefs, mentalising ability, mind-body dualism, and teleological beliefs in more detail. Modelling indicated that the relationship between individuals' mentalising ability and their supernational beliefs (including religious beliefs) was mediated fully by their belief in mind-body dualism and their teleological beliefs. However, this modelling was limited in that it was based only on correlational evidence.

If there are close links between mentalising ability and teleological beliefs, we might expect individuals with deficient mentalising ability to be less likely than others to have teleological beliefs. This prediction was tested by Heywood (2010), who asked religious believers, atheists, and individuals with Asperger's syndrome (characterised by mentalising deficits) to discuss the causes of two significant life events. Those with Asperger's syndrome provided fewer teleological explanations of these life events than members of the other two groups.

The research discussed so far suggests that cognitive biases such as mind-body dualism and teleological beliefs depend on mentalising ability. However, cultural factors may also be important: we might expect that individuals living in more religious cultures would be more likely to have these biases than those living in less religious cultures.

In fact, the available evidence disconfirms the above expectation. Willard and Norenzayan (2013) found the extent of cultural exposure to religion (defined as the proportion of religious adherents in the local community) was unrelated to mind-body dualism and teleological beliefs. Heywood and Bering (2013) compared teleological beliefs in the United States and the United Kingdom. In spite of compelling evidence that there is a more pervasive religious culture in the United States, there was no difference in teleological beliefs among atheists in the two countries.

Intuitive or heuristic vs. analytic processing

We can gain additional insights into cognitive biases such as mind-body dualism and teleological beliefs by considering them in the context of prominent dual-process theories of thinking and reasoning (see Eysenck & Keane, 2015, for a review). It has frequently been claimed (e.g. Kahneman, 2003) that there is an important distinction between rapid, "automatic" heuristic or intuitive processes and slower, deliberate, analytic processes. It could be argued that the various cognitive biases associated with religious belief are typically associated with rapid, heuristic processing. Two predictions follow from that hypothesis. First, people's use of such cognitive biases should increase when their available cognitive resources are reduced experimentally. Second, the use of these cognitive biases (and perhaps religious beliefs) should be reduced when people are persuaded to make increased use of analytic processes.

Bègue, Bushman, Giancola, Subra, and Rosset (2010) compared intentionality bias in individuals who had consumed a high dose of alcohol or no alcohol. They were presented with ambiguous sentences (e.g. "She cut him off in traffic", "He deleted the email") referring to actions that might have occurred intentionally or accidentally. The intoxicated participants were more likely than the sober ones to interpret the actions as intentional.

Rosset (2008) also presented her participants with sentences (e.g. "He set the house on fire") that could be interpreted as referring to accidental or intentional actions. Participants who had to decide rapidly whether the actions were accidental or intentional were more likely to decide they were intentional than participants who had more time available.

We turn now to teleological reasoning. Kelemen (1999) argued that children are prone to a "promiscuous teleology" in which numerous animals, artifacts, and natural objects are believed to exist for a given purpose. For example, many children believe rocks are pointy so animals will not sit on them.

Kelemen and Rosset (2009) focused on teleological beliefs in university students. These students decided whether various statements were correct; of most relevance were sentences including unwarranted teleological explanations (e.g. "The sun radiates heat because warmth nurtures life"). When participants were required to respond rapidly (and so had reduced ability to use analytic processes), they incorrectly accepted significantly more unwarranted teleological explanations than when they had more time available (61 per cent vs. 52 per cent incorrect decisions, respectively).

Kelemen, Rottman, and Seston (2013) wondered whether the tendency for adults to endorse teleological beliefs of natural phenomena when their information-processing resources were limited would be found even among professional physicists. They found these physicists were more likely to endorse unwarranted teleological explanations (e.g. "Lamps shine brightly so they can produce light") when they had to respond rapidly than when they did not (29 per cent vs. 15 per cent, respectively). These findings are dramatic in that physicists explicitly reject teleological explanations in their professional lives. The implication is that almost everyone is susceptible to such explanations when having only limited processing resources available.

So far we have considered evidence indicating that individuals who are using only some of their processing resources have a heightened tendency to make use of various cognitive biases. What about the further prediction that individuals who process analytically should exhibit the opposite pattern? Gervais and Norenzayan (2012a) found that inducing analytic processing temporarily decreased religious belief suggesting this belief is anchored in intuitive biases.

One of the most important analytic processes is cognitive inhibition, which involves overriding prepotent attentional processes and/or responses generated by intuitive or heuristic processes (Nigg, 2000). The possible role of cognitive inhibition in supernatural beliefs was investigated by Lindeman, Svedholm, Riekki, Raij, and Hari (2013). Believers in the supernatural (e.g. traditional religious beliefs, witchcraft, spiritualism, precognition) and sceptics imagined themselves in various life situations (e.g. threatened end of an intimate relationship) each of which was followed by an emotionally charged picture of inanimate objects or scenery (e.g. a brick wall).

Supernatural believers were twice as likely as sceptics to see signs in the pictures concerning how the situations were going to turn out. Of most importance, the right inferior frontal gyrus (associated with cognitive inhibition) was activated more strongly in sceptics than in those believing in the supernatural. In addition, the amount of activation within the right inferior frontal gyrus correlated negatively with sign seeing in each group considered separately.

Intelligence, cognitive style and analytic processing

More intelligent individuals often (but by no means always) make more use of analytic processing than less intelligent ones. Accordingly, we can predict that intelligence will correlate negatively with religious belief. As predicted, Zuckerman et al. (2013) in a meta-analysis of 63 studies mentioned earlier found the strength of religious beliefs correlated on average −.24 with intelligence. Razmyar and Reeve (2013) replicated that finding on a sample of 150 undergraduate students.

Stanovich (2012) clarified the relationship between intelligence and use of analytic thinking by distinguishing between the algorithmic and reflective minds. The algorithmic mind contains mindware, which consists of "the rules, knowledge, procedures, and strategies that a person can retrieve from memory in order to aid decision making and problem solving" (p. 355). In approximate terms, the algorithmic mind relates to individual differences in fluid intelligence (the ability to think in novel and productive ways).

According to Stanovich (2012), successful intelligent or analytic thinking depends on the functioning of the reflective mind as well as the algorithmic mind. An individual's analytic processes are only used when he/she realises (based on processing within the reflective mind) that they are necessary and that he/she has the necessary motivation to initiate them. Thus, cognitive ability (algorithmic mind) and a cognitive style involving a willingness to use his/her cognitive ability (reflective mind) are required for an individual to use effective analytic processes to inhibit cognitive biases.

Individual differences in the tendency to use the reflective mind has frequently been assessed by means of the Cognitive Reflection Test (Frederick, 2005). As predicted, it has been found in several studies that there is a negative relationship between the willingness to engage in analytic reasoning (as assessed by the Cognitive Reflection Test) and adherence to religious beliefs (see Pennycook, 2014, for a review).

Conclusions

Mentalising ability is used to think about (and to interact with) God and thus plays an important role in religious beliefs. Individuals with severely deficient mentalising ability (e.g. those with autism) are much less likely than others to have religious beliefs. Cognitive biases such as mind-body dualism and teleological beliefs are stronger in religious believers than non-believers and are associated with mentalising ability. Most people make more use of cognitive biases of relevance to religious beliefs when their processing is heuristic or intuitive rather than analytic. Such findings suggest there is a "natural" tendency to use these biases. This tendency can be overridden only by engaging effortful, analytic processes (e.g. cognitive inhibition) and this requires sufficient cognitive ability and the willingness to use it. As Boyer (2008, p. 1039) argued, "Religious thoughts seem to be an emergent property of our standard cognitive abilities. . . . Some form of religious thinking seems to be the path of least resistance for our cognitive systems. By contrast, disbelief is generally a result of deliberate, effortful work against our natural cognitive dispositions".

It is clearly oversimplified to assign most (or all) cognitive processes to only two categories (Keren & Schul, 2009). As Fiedler and von Sydow (2015) pointed out, the two processes "are pretended to differ in too many attributes at the same time". For example, analytic processes are allegedly rule based, require high cognitive capacity and effort expenditure, and so on. There is very little evidence that all these attributes are anywhere near as highly correlated as has been assumed theoretically.

Religion and evolutionary psychology

So far we have focused mostly on proximate factors that help us to understand why billions of people have been motivated to adopt religious beliefs. However, several attempts have been made to account for the prevalence of religious beliefs worldwide in ultimate terms making use of explanations expressed in evolutionary terms (see Crespi & Summers, 2014, for a review).

The fundamental underlying notion is that this prevalence and the enormous impact that religion has had over the centuries (e.g. causing people to kill or die for their beliefs) strongly suggest that religion has evolutionary value.

The above notion was expressed succinctly by Marek Kohn (cited in Dawkins, 2006, p. 190): "To an evolutionary psychologist, the universal extravagance of religious rituals, with their costs in time, resources, pain and privation, should suggest as vividly as a mandrill's bottom that religion may be adaptive". In other words, evolutionary psychologists claim that religion has direct survival value and this explains why its impact has been so great throughout the entire world for thousands of years.

One of the most interesting of such evolutionary theories was proposed by Crespi and Summers (2014) but owes its origins to the theoretical ideas of Alexander (e.g. 2006, 2013). Whereas most theories of the origins of religious beliefs focus on individuals attempting to make sense of their lives and the world, Alexander emphasised the importance of the group:

> The concept of God may be hypothesised to derive from a particular set of feelings that we share with members of our group: warm, pleasant feelings of good will, agreement, cooperativeness, commitment and power as a result of power associated directly with the cooperativeness of the group. Because everyone in an integrated group tends to share these feelings, all members of such a group can accept God as denoting a unifying force so real that the collective agreement upon which the concept is based can easily be expanded to symbolise a superhuman entity.
>
> (Alexander, 2006)

Crespi and Summers (2014) developed the notion that an individual's immediate social group (especially his/her kin or family group) is of special importance. According to them, "The concept of God is represented by one's circle of kin and social salience, such that serving God and serving this circle become synonymous" (p. 313). In essence, religious beliefs have great evolutionary importance within this conceptualisation because they tend to maximise inclusive fitness (Hamilton, 1964). Inclusive fitness is "the notion that natural selection favours organisms that maximise replication of their genes. This can occur *directly* via reproduction or *indirectly* by helping genetically related individuals" (Eysenck, 2004, p. 36). It is assumed that religious beliefs enhancing altruism within families increase the indirect replication of an individual's genes.

It is indisputable that inclusive fitness is of great importance. However, much more research is required to establish the extent to which inclusive fitness is increased or maximised by religious beliefs.

Dawkins (2006) argued that religion probably does not have any direct survival value. Instead, he proposed that, "Religious behaviour may be a misfiring, an unfortunate by-product of an underlying psychological propensity which in other circumstances is, or once was, useful" (p. 202). This approach makes much sense (as we have seen already). However, it suffers from the problem that it is not easy to identify the "underlying psychological propensity". Indeed, for once the typically decisive Dawkins is reduced to various speculations. One such propensity which he emphasises is the claimed tendency for children to believe whatever their parents tell them. This propensity is of great value because much of children's knowledge and understanding of the world derive from what they have been told rather than from direct experience. However, the downside of this propensity is that it can lead children into what Dawkins calls "slavish gullibility" with respect to religious beliefs.

Children's propensity to believe most of what they hear from their parents clearly has adaptive value and certainly could play an important role in the perpetuation of religious beliefs. However, as the father of three children, I don't remember any of them believing all (or even most) of what I said to them when they were growing up!

Conclusions

In sum, evolutionary psychologists have provided several interesting potential explanations for the durability and strength of religious beliefs. However, it is important to note that this entire approach is intrinsically limited. It is by its very nature *post hoc*. In general terms, it is difficult to manipulate the factors identified as crucial to test their causal relevance to the development of religious beliefs.

Content of religious beliefs

We have discussed several of the main factors determining whether or not any given individual has religious beliefs. It is now time to consider the *content* of those beliefs – how can we explain religious believers' conceptualisations of the God or gods in whom they believe? According to Xenophanes, a Greek philosopher from the sixth century BC, these conceptualisations are strongly influenced by the ways we conceptualise human beings. The essence of his approach was expressed as follows (Lesher, 1992): "If cattle or lions had hands, so as to paint with their hands and produce works of art as men do, they would paint their gods and give them bodies like their own – horses like horses, cattle like cattle". In other words, religious believers create God in their own image.

Two main approaches have been taken to shed light on the issues raised in the previous paragraph. First, some research has focused on individuals' descriptions of gods, alien creatures and so on to see how closely they resemble descriptions of human beings. Second, other research has compared religious people's judgements concerning God's beliefs against their own beliefs.

Descriptions

Ward (1992) found that individuals instructed to imagine alien creatures typically drew ones resembling vertebrate creatures on earth with bilateral symmetry, sense organs such as ears and eyes, and animal-like body parts such as arms or legs. The findings were similar even when individuals were explicitly instructed to invent creatures widely different from those on earth (Ward & Sifonis, 1997).

De Cruz (2013) asked participants to imagine an alien very different from life forms on earth and also to imagine a religious supernatural being believed in by such aliens. Her findings with respect to descriptions of aliens were similar to those of Ward (1992) and Ward and Sifonis (1997) in that 54 per cent of these descriptions mentioned body parts (e.g. eyes, ears). In contrast, only 13 per cent of the descriptions of the religious supernatural beings mentioned body parts.

De Cruz (2013) found that the religious supernatural beings were more often categorised as spatial entities (e.g. clouds, flames, shadows) than aliens (50 per cent vs. 21 per cent). Of importance, the religious beings were described in less counterintuitive terms than the aliens. For example, if a religious being was described as a cloud than the rest of the description was typically consistent with the known features of clouds.

An important study was reported by Barrett and Keil (1996). Religious students read a story in which God was explicitly *not* described in anthropomorphic (human-like) terms. After that, they reconstructed the story. The key finding was that the story was changed in the reconstruction to give God human-like limitations not present in the original story. For example, some participants misremembered the story as stating that God needed perceptual information to know about events or that he could perform only one action at a time.

In sum, the findings suggest that religious believers can effortfully construct descriptions of Gods that differ in many ways from humans. However, there is in addition a "natural" tendency to describe Gods in human-like terms if relatively few processing resources are devoted to the task.

Beliefs

Many different factors influence our beliefs about another person's beliefs. For example, we may use episodic knowledge about that person (e.g. remembering views they expressed at a recent party) or semantic knowledge (e.g. they typically vote for right-wing candidates at elections and belong to a golf club). Egocentric processes are also involved: most people assume that other people's beliefs are more similar to their own than is actually the case (Epley, Keysar, Van Boven, & Gilovich, 2004).

Epley, Converse, Delbosc, Monteleone, and Cacioppo (2009) carried out several experiments to test whether religious people's reasoning about God's beliefs also exhibited egocentricity. In one experiment, they found patterns of brain activation did not differ when religious believers thought about their own beliefs and when they thought about God's beliefs. In another brain-imaging experiment, Epley et al. obtained evidence that egocentric biases among religious believers are stronger with God's beliefs than those of other people: reasoning about God's beliefs activated areas associated with self-referential thinking more than did reasoning about another person's beliefs.

Further experiments by Epley et al. (2009) indicated that religious believers are especially likely to use their own beliefs when reasoning about God's beliefs compared to reasoning about other people's beliefs. In essence, they manipulated religious believers' own beliefs on various issues including abortion, same-sex marriage, and affirmative action. These manipulations influenced their estimates of God's beliefs more than it influenced their estimates of other people's beliefs. This finding can be explained on the basis that religious believers typically have more direct evidence concerning the actual beliefs of other people than those of God.

In sum, it has often been argued that God provides religious believers with a moral compass to guide them. In contrast, Epley et al.'s (2009) findings suggest that, "Unlike an actual compass, inferences about God's beliefs may instead point people further in whatever direction they are already facing" (p. 21,537). This reminds me of Voltaire reporting a Pope as saying, "If God made us in His own image, we have certainly returned the favour".

Summary and conclusions

Until comparatively recently, most psychologists (with the honourable exception of William James, 1902) were sceptical as to the feasibility of providing a scientific account of faith-based religious beliefs. It has become increasingly clear that such scepticism was misplaced. The motivation for the development of religious beliefs has various sources. However, perceived lack of control (caused by poverty, old age, and life experiences) is of central importance in providing that motivation.

Several cognitive processes and cognitive biases (e.g. mentalising ability, mind-body dualism, teleological beliefs, egocentric bias) designed for other purposes are all of major importance in understanding how religious beliefs develop. These cognitive biases represent the "default" position in human thinking, and much effortful, deliberate cognitive processing is required to override them. In other words, religious beliefs "go with the grain" of our everyday heuristic thinking.

11
PSYCHIC FRAUD

Richard Wiseman

It's easier to fool people than to convince them that they have been fooled.

Mark Twain

Introduction

Many individuals claim to possess psychic ability. For example, faith healers and psychic surgeons state that they are able to cure illness. Psychic readers claim to be able to accurately divine the past and predict the future, and mediums often seem able to contact the dead. Also, law enforcement agencies are approached by individuals offering "psychic tips" that they feel might help solve a crime, and alleged psychics have also been used within industry and business. Investigations into these claims have often revealed evidence of trickery (Hansen, 1990), and recently academics have started to explore the psychology behind this rather unusual form of deception (Hansen, 1990; Wiseman & Morris, 1995a; Lamont & Wiseman, 1999).

Developing an understanding of "psychic fraud" is important for several reasons. First, both the lay public and professionals sometimes turn to alleged psychics in times of need, and failure to detect trickery could result in serious negative consequences. For example, in the 1970s the "Reverend" Jim Jones attracted several hundred followers to his US cult, often maintaining their faith by faking biblical miracles, such as healing and "walking on water" (Mills, 1979). Unfortunately, the personal power that Jones possessed is reflected in the fact that he was able to instigate the mass suicide of nearly all his followers.

Second, some scientists wish to investigate psychics and need to be able to identify whether alleged abilities are genuine or fake. The importance of detecting fakery during such work was illustrated when James Randi (an American magician and sceptic of the paranormal) sent two young magicians to be assessed at the McDonnell Parapsychology Laboratory in the USA. Whilst at the laboratory, both magicians used conjuring techniques to fake various "psychic" feats including metal bending and extrasensory perception. Although the researchers at the laboratory made no formal statements as to the validity of the claimants' psychic ability, neither did they manage to detect the trickery used by the two young men. Randi's revelation of the hoax contributed to the loss of funding and eventual closure of the McDonnell Laboratory (Randi, 1986).

Finally, an understanding of the techniques used to fake psychic ability may yield insight into the types of cognitive and social biases that disrupt perception, reasoning and memory. Cognitive psychologists attempt to understand how observers attend to, perceive, comprehend and store information from the environment. In addition, they are also concerned with how this information is recalled and utilised during thinking and problem solving. Research into psychic fraud may reveal novel types of bias and, like the study of optical illusions can provide important new insights into the weaknesses of human information processing. Also, the further analysis of psychic fraud may allow cognitive psychologists to undertake research into novel areas of enquiry which are recognised as important but, up to this point in time, have proved problematic to investigate.

One aspect of the research into the psychology of psychic fraud has involved identifying strategems used by fake psychics. This has involved collecting and collating information from several sources including magazines, books, and videos outlining methods for faking psychic ability (e.g. Fuller, 1975, 1980), investigations of fake psychics (e.g. Delanoy, 1987), and literature relating to the "folk" psychology of magic and psychic fraud (e.g. Lamont & Wiseman, 1999). Additional work has involved experiments designed to help evaluate the efficacy of some of these strategems. This chapter briefly outlines some of the key findings from both strands of research.

Misframing

Sociologists use the term "frame" to refer to abstract structures which observers use to define situations in a certain way (Goffman, 1974). Many situations can be framed in different ways. For example, before observing an alleged medium, sceptics might be expecting to see some kind of trickery, whereas believers may expect a display of genuine mediumistic ability. Such expectations can play a large role in determining the way in which the observer approaches the situation:

> the frame of mind in which a person goes to see magic and to a medium cannot be compared. In one case he goes either purely for amusement or possibly with the idea of discovering "how it was done", whilst in the other he usually goes with the thought that it is possible that he will come into direct contact with the other world. (Dingwall, 1921, p. 211)

Recent research has supported this notion, suggesting that expectation does indeed influence the observer's perception and memory of a "psychic" demonstration. Jones and Russell (1980) asked both believers in the paranormal (termed "Sheep") and disbelievers ("Goats") to observe a staged demonstration of extrasensory perception (ESP). In one condition the demonstration was successful (i.e. ESP appeared to take place) whilst in the other it was not. All observers were then asked to recall the demonstration. Sheep who saw the unsuccessful demonstration distorted their memories of it and often stated that ESP had occurred. Goats tended to correctly recall the demonstration, even if it appeared to support the existence of ESP.

Wiseman and Morris (1995b) also carried out two studies investigating the effect that belief in the paranormal has on the observation of conjuring tricks. In both experiments observers were first shown a film containing fake psychic demonstrations. They were then asked to rate the "paranormal" content of the film and complete a set of recall questions. Observers were then told that the film contained magic tricks and were asked to complete a second set of recall questions. The recall questions contained information both "important" and "unimportant" to the method of the tricks. Overall, the results suggested that Sheep rated the demonstrations as more "paranormal" than Goats and Goats recalled significantly more "important" information than Sheep. Perhaps most interesting of all, even when told that the film contained trickery, Goats still recalled more "important" information than Sheep.

In a similar study, M. D. Smith (1993) investigated the effect that instructions (given prior to watching a film which contained a demonstration of apparent psychic ability) had on the recall of the film. Observers were split into two groups. One group were told that the film contained trickery whilst the other group were told that it contained genuine paranormal phenomena. The former group recalled significantly more information about the film than the latter group. Given that this is the case, it is perhaps not surprising that fake psychics are eager to encourage observers to view their supposed abilities as genuine. Several strategems have been developed for this purpose. For example, a fake faith healer may assure an observer that he never accepts payment for his services, insinuating that he has no motive to deceive. However, Morris (1986) has noted how fake psychics can be motivated by many other factors, including personal fame, raised self-esteem, a desire to be socially helpful, and increased personal power. Various authors have also suggested that some observers deceive simply for enjoyment (e.g. Ekman, 1985). Randi (1982) has suggested that this, in part, may account for the success enjoyed by the two girls who fabricated the "Cottingley" fairies (see Box 11.1):

> The two girls had no stake in the deception that could have brought them money. . . . The assumption made is that only money and notoriety are plausible motives. Ego and just plain fun are not thought to be sufficient. (p. 37)

BOX 11.1 THE COTTINGLEY FAIRIES

The story of the Cottingley fairies dates from 1917 when two young girls Frances Griffiths and Elsie Wright living in Cottingley, a small village in Yorkshire, produced a number of photographs of fairies. The girls had been teased about their claims of seeing fairies near Cottingley Beck and so Elsie borrowed a camera from her father and went off with Frances into the area near the family home. They returned soon after. When the pictures were developed later that evening in Elsie's father's dark room they showed the girls with fairies. Finally in 1983 Elsie confessed that the pictures had been faked, stating that the girls had drawn the fairies, cut them out and fastened them to the ground with hatpins.

The fake psychic may also deliberately produce the type of psychic phenomena that the observer finds believable. For example, an observer may believe that psychokinesis (PK) can rarely be used to produce really large physical effects and the fake psychic may therefore cause an object to simply move a small distance along a table top, as opposed to making it levitate above the table. The fake psychic may exploit an observer's physical and emotional needs. If an observer has a serious illness a fake psychic may claim to possess psychic healing powers. If an observer has recently suffered a bereavement the fake psychic may promise some form of communication with deceased friends and relatives. Scientists may not be immune from such manipulation. One parapsychologist, after working with a fake psychic, noted:

> We are all familiar with the difficulties arising from the so-called "elusive nature of psi". In short, we cannot study a phenomenon unless we can first produce it. Thus, Tim's [the fake psychic] claims, that he could produce macro PK at will, suggested exciting possibilities. **I wanted his claims to be true and this desire may have influenced my evaluation of his performance**. [Emphasis mine] (Delanoy, 1987, p. 256)

Attention and distraction

During a demonstration it is often vital to the fake psychic that observers do not attend to the parts of their performance that might give some insight into the use of trickery. Fake psychics have developed several strategems to achieve this. For example, some fake psychics may say that they have little control over their ability and therefore cannot predict the phenomena that will occur. This strategy also helps the psychic should a performance not go according to plan – a point recognised as long ago as 1878 by magician Robert-Houdin:

> However skilful the performer may be, and however complete his preparations for a given trick, it is still possible that some unforseen accident may cause a

> failure. The only way to get out of such a difficulty is to finish the trick in another manner. But to be able to do this, the performer must have strictly complied with this important rule: **never announce beforehand the nature of the effect which you intend to produce**. [Emphasis mine] (p. 33)

Also, most observers only start to fully concentrate their attention when they believe that paranormal phenomena are about to take place. A fake psychic may take advantage of this by making secret preparations long before the beginning of the demonstration. This technique is especially effective when the performer is able to anticipate the phenomena which might be requested by observers. A well-known Scottish conjurer named John Ramsey often used this technique to fool fellow magicians:

> Another John Ramsey saying was "Hold and Hide". It simply meant, be prepared well in advance. Before John went into company, he always palmed a coin or a thimble so that if anyone asked him to do a trick, he was ready. . . . At one of the conventions he was having tea with some of his "disciples". . . . They asked him if he would perform his cups and balls routine. . . . John took out the cups and wand and went straight into the routine. This puzzled the onlookers because they knew that according to John's book, at the start of the effect the performer must have four balls palmed in the right hand and they had not seen him make any steal. The explanation was simple. John had them palmed long before his friends asked him to do the trick. In fact he had eaten a meal with the balls concealed in his hand. (Galloway, 1969, pp. 2–3)

Competent fake psychics can also manipulate the focal point of observers' attention. Fitzkee (1945) has outlined how the carefully planned introduction of movement, colour, sound and body language (including the positioning of the feet, hands and eye contact) can be used to attract observers' attention to a desired location. Also, Fuller (1975), in his manual of psychic fraud, has described how confusion can be generated to prevent attention being focused in any one location:

> When you're working for a group, keep talking and moving fast. Create maximum chaos. Flit from one task to another. Fail on one thing, put it aside, try something else, then go back and try again, and so on. (p. 15)

Switching methods

A fake psychic may develop several ways of fabricating a certain type of psychic ability, thus allowing him or her to switch methods during a performance. For example, many texts on magic and psychic trickery contain several different methods for achieving just one effect. Tamariz (1988) has described eighteen methods for performing one particular card effect, whilst Harris (1985) explains a whole range of methods that may be employed to fabricate PK metal bending. The fake psychic may then switch methods to create what Diaconis (1985) has referred to as the "bundle of sticks phenomena":

> An effect is produced several times under different circumstances with the use of a different technique each time . . . the weak points of one performance are ruled out because they were clearly not present during other performances. The bundle of sticks is stronger than any single stick. (p. 572)

Controlling performing conditions

Psychics often state that their ability only manifests itself under certain conditions. A fake psychic can exploit this concept by insisting upon working under conditions which are favourable to fraud. For example, Randi (1986) describes how in Project Alpha, the two fake psychics complained about electronic equipment putting out "bad vibes", such that the researchers were not able to videotape the demonstrations. In addition, Eugene Burger (1986) outlines how fake mediums insist that all of the sitters must link hands during a séance (see Box 11.2). The fake medium may state that this is necessary to bring forth spirit communication. In reality it is designed to prevent curious sitters from reaching out into the séance room, and possibly discovering various forms of trickery (such as reaching rods and accomplices).

BOX 11.2 THE PSYCHOLOGY OF THE SÉANCE

Many individuals have reported experiencing extraordinary phenomena during dark room séances. Eyewitnesses claim that objects have mysteriously moved, strange sounds have been produced or ghostly forms have appeared, and that these phenomena have occurred under conditions which render normal explanations practically impossible. Believers argue that conditions commonly associated with a séance (such as darkness, anticipation and fear) may act as a catalyst to produce these phenomena. Sceptics suggest that reports of séances are unreliable and that eyewitnesses are either fooling themselves or being fooled by fraudulent mediums.

The author carried out an experiment to assess the reliability of testimony relating to séance phenomena. Twenty-five people attended three séances. They were first asked to complete a short questionnaire, noting whether they believed that genuine paranormal phenomena might sometimes take place during séances.

A séance room had been prepared. All of the windows and doors in the room had been sealed and blacked out, and twenty-five chairs had been arranged in a large circle. Various objects – a book, a slate and a bell – had been treated with luminous paint and placed on a small table situated in the middle of the circle.

Everyone was led into the darkened séance room and shown to a chair. An actor played the part of the medium. He first pointed out the presence of a small luminous ball, approximately 5cm in diameter that was suspended on a piece of rope from the ceiling. Next, he extinguished the lights and asked everybody to join hands. The medium first asked the participants to concentrate on trying to move the luminous ball and then to try the same with the objects on the table.

After leaving the séance room, the participants completed a short questionnaire which asked them about their experience of the séance. In the séances, the slate, bell, book and table remained stationary. Despite this, 27 per cent of participants reported movement of at least one of these. An interesting pattern develops if the results are analysed by separating the participants by belief. The ball, suspended from the ceiling, did not move at any time. 76 per cent of disbelievers were certain that it hadn't moved. In contrast, the same certainty among believers was only 54 per cent. In addition, 40 per cent of believers thought that at least one other object had moved, compared to just 14 per cent of disbelievers. The answers to the question "Do you believe you have witnessed any genuine paranormal phenomena?" perhaps provide the most conclusive result for the believer/disbeliever divide. One in five believers stated that they thought they had seen genuine phenomena. None of the disbelievers thought so.

The results suggest that whilst we are all vulnerable to trickery, a belief or expectation of paranormal phenomena during séances may add to that vulnerability.

Further details about the experiment can be found in:

Wiseman, R., Smith, M., & Wiseman, J. (1995). Eyewitness testimony and the paranormal. Skeptical Inquirer, November/December, 29-32.

Have "outs" ready in case something goes wrong

Fake psychics have developed many types of "outs" to escape, or minimise, the damage caused by something not going according to plan during their performance. Should the planned method of trickery prove problematic, the skilled fake psychic may be forced to switch methods during a demonstration. For this reason, fake psychics often consider the ways in which a trick may go wrong, and develop various ways to switch the method of that trick, to salvage the demonstration. These are referred to as "outs". During a demonstration a fake psychic may find that the controls imposed prevent the type of trickery he intended to employ. If this is the case, the fake psychic may explain away such failure by stating that the conditions of the demonstration were not psi conducive. For example, Burger (1986) notes that, if a fake medium is unable to fabricate phenomena, he can state:

> "Well, my friends, conditions sometimes are just not right for this sort of thing". You see . . . there's always an "out" – a non-humiliating, non-embarrassing,

> perfectly reasonable (given the folk-accepted assumptions about séances and how they "work"), perfectly acceptable out for a failure. (p. 107)

Alternatively, the observer may have discovered evidence of possible fraud. The competent fake psychic may have anticipated such a problem, and created excuses to "explain away" such evidence. For example, Baggally, Johnson, Feilding, Taylor and Lobb (1906) report how, during a séance given by the fake medium Christopher Chambers, a false moustache (used to fabricate materialisations of spirits) was discovered in the séance room. Chambers attempted to explain away such evidence by telling sitters that it was difficult to materialise whiskers and moustaches, so the "guide" had made a false moustache, and left it as a souvenir!

The fake psychic may make such excuses part of the "lore" which govern his psychic ability. For example, Randi (1982) has reported that one researcher, Dr Lincoln (a specialist in blood group serology and forensic medicine at London Hospital Medical College), investigated the claims being made by Philippino psychic surgeons. Lincoln surreptitiously obtained some of the apparently "bad tissue" removed from a patient, by an alleged psychic surgeon, and analysed it. Lincoln discovered that the blood sample was from a cow, and that the "tumour" was a piece of chicken intestine. However, the surgeons attempted to explain away this evidence stating that it was a well-known fact that "supernatural forces" convert the tumours into innocuous substances once they have left the patient's body.

Conclusions

This chapter has presented a brief outline of some of the main psychological strategems used to fake psychic ability. It has discussed how fake psychics encourage observers to misframe a demonstration, focus their attention away from trickery and reject normal explanations. In addition, the chapter has outlined how good fake psychics will control performing conditions and be prepared to explain away potential evidence of fraud.

A full and thorough understanding of psychic fraud would have advantages for both the public and academics alike. As noted in the introduction, the public are often impressed with the performances staged by alleged psychics. Unfortunately, some fake psychics can use the status and power gained from such performances to exert a negative influence over others, and thus the public would benefit from ways of identifying trickery.

Also, parapsychologists are aware that many individuals claiming to be psychic use magic tricks to fabricate paranormal phenomena. Failure to detect such fraud can lead to serious consequences, including loss of funding and negative publicity. For this reason parapsychologists need to understand the psychology used by fake psychics to prevent being fooled during their investigations. Unfortunately, most of the previous literature on psychic fraud has tended to concentrate upon the specific tactics of such trickery, usually taking the form of case studies or "cookbooks" of methods for fabricating psychic ability. This emphasis is unfortunate because observers interested in countering psychic fraud may find it more helpful to know about the stratagems of psychic fraud, as opposed to the specific means to achieve it. This is, in part, because although there are only a limited number of stratagems involved in the fabrication of psychic abilities, there are an enormous number of methods used to implement these stratagems. Trying to detect these specific tactics may be problematic. For example, the literature of magic, and psychic fraud, is not well organised, such that it may be difficult for an observer to discover all the ways in which an ostensible psychic phenomena can be fabricated. Second, both magicians and fake psychics are continually inventing new methods by which to fabricate psi. It would be problematic to discover the nature of these innovations, especially as some of this information is not widely disseminated, even within certain sections of the magical, and fake psychic, communities. It is hoped that the current emphasis on broad strategies over distinct techniques will help those scientists wishing to investigate strong psychic claims (see Wiseman & Morris, 1995a).

Suggested further reading

Lamont, P., & Wiseman, R. (1999). *Magic in theory: An introduction to the theoretical and psychological elements in conjuring*. University of Hertfordshire Press: Hatfield, UK.

Randi, J. (1986). The Project Alpha experiment: Part 1. The first two years. In K. Frazier (Ed.), *Science confronts the paranormal*. Prometheus Books: Buffalo, New York.

Smith, M. D. (1993). The effect of belief in the paranormal and prior set upon the observation of a "psychic" demonstration. *European Journal of Parapsychology*, 9, 24–34.

12

CONSPIRACY THEORIES

Robert Brotherton and Christopher C. French

It is a general human weakness to allow things uncertain and unknown, to set us up in hope, or plunge us into fear.

Gaius Caesar

Conspiracy theories

According to assorted popular conspiracy theories, the terrorist attacks of September 11, 2001, were orchestrated not by members of al-Qaeda but by the United States government; Princess Diana's death was the result not of a tragic accident but of a secret plot concocted by the British Monarchy; government-run water treatment programs are designed not simply to provide potable drinking water but to spike it with chemicals intended to control or kill unsuspecting citizens.

From philandering spouses to drug cartels to high-level political corruption, there's no denying that conspiracy is a popular human pastime. The kinds of claims that attract the label *conspiracy theory*, however, tend to propose a different variety of scheme. A precise, succinct definition of the term is elusive. Yet, as the three preceding examples demonstrate, claims commonly labelled conspiracy theories typically purport to reveal sensational and hitherto undisclosed plots carried out by inordinately powerful and sinister conspirators. Moreover, they tend to be based on negative evidence, and are resistant to falsification (see Brotherton, 2013, 2015). Why, then, do large numbers of people claim to believe unsubstantiated and seemingly implausible allegations such as these to be true?

One possible reason for the prevalence of belief in conspiracy theories is simply that believers derive their opinions from rational and impartial evaluation of the available evidence. Information presented as evidence supporting many of the most popular conspiracy theories is readily available. Indeed, many theories generate cottage industries of books, websites, speaking tours, and documentaries (Byford, 2011). However, the evidence presented by proponents is generally criticised by credentialed experts as being of poor quality; relevant epistemic authorities generally regard conspiracy theories as unverified and lacking credibility at best, or conclusively disconfirmed by multiple lines of converging evidence at worst (e.g. Bugliosi, 2007; Dunbar & Reagan, 2006). Despite the ubiquity of conspiracy theories, critical analyses of various conspiracy theories are readily available in print, broadcast media and online. According to a recent survey of 3,000 Internet articles pertaining to conspiracy theories, considerably more than half portrayed the theories in a negative light (often accompanied by words like "fantasy", "bizarre", and "debunked"). Just one fifth of the articles sampled offered unqualified endorsements of conspiracy theories; the remainder presented the theories neutrally (Uscinski & Parent, 2014).

Regardless of the ultimate evidential basis for or against any particular conspiracist claim, there are other indications that beliefs in conspiracy theories might not be simply the product of objective scrutiny of the facts. Conspiracy theories are often quick to arise following an event, becoming widely endorsed even before many of the facts can be ascertained and analysed (Birdwell & Littler, 2011; Brotherton, 2014, 2015). In addition, endorsement of one conspiracy theory correlates positively with endorsement of other ostensibly unrelated theories. Certain individuals will even endorse mutually contradictory conspiracy theories (Wood, Douglas, & Sutton, 2012) and entirely novel, fictitious theories made up by researchers for the purpose of their research (Swami et al., 2011).

These observations do not in themselves indicate that any particular conspiracy theory is necessarily *false*. In the context of psychological enquiry the veracity of any particular conspiracy theory is not at issue. However, the observations do suggest that endorsing a conspiracy theory may be, at least in part, a product of factors other than impartial examination of the evidence. Whether or not any given conspiracy theory accurately describes reality, it appears likely that psychological factors influence the formation, adoption, maintenance, and transmission of conspiracist beliefs. Until recently, however, conspiracy theories attracted relatively little interest from psychologists. Between the late-1970s and 2005, only a sporadic trickle of studies on the psychology of conspiracy theories was published (Abalakina-Paap, Stephan, Craig, & Gregory, 1999; Bird & Bogart, 2003; Butler, Koopman, & Zimbardo, 1995; Goertzel, 1994; McCauley & Jacques, 1979; McHoskey, 1995; Parsons, Simmons, Shinhoster, & Kilburn, 1999; Simmons & Parsons, 2005). It is only within the last decade that conspiracist beliefs have begun to attract the sustained interest of a larger number of researchers. This body of research demonstrates that psychology can provide important insights into conspiracism.

Despite the increasing number of publications, however, research on the topic remains somewhat unfocused. The purpose of this chapter is to outline the relevant psychological literature to date, with the objective of systematising the available findings. For the purposes of this review, the existing research will be divided into four categories: *Associations between conspiracy beliefs*, *Sociodemographic correlates*,

Individual differences, and *Cognitive biases and heuristics*. It should be noted that these categories do not denote mutually exclusive categories or rigid psychological divisions, but are intended as convenient subheadings which serve to organise existing findings into a meaningful framework. This chapter also includes consideration of the relationship between belief in conspiracies and paranormal beliefs.

Associations between conspiracy beliefs

One of the most robust findings to emerge from the available literature concerns the relationships *between* different conspiracist beliefs. In short, the best predictor of belief in any particular conspiracy theory is usually belief in other conspiracy theories. Thus, engagement with conspiracy theories can be conceptualised as a singular personality trait. This trait – the extent to which an individual tends to accept or reject conspiracy theories in general – has been termed "conspiracy mentality" (Bruder, Haffke, Neave, Nouripanah, & Imhoff, 2013; Moscovici, 1987) or "conspiracist ideation" (Swami et al., 2011).

The homogeneity of attitudes towards various claims of conspiracy has most commonly been demonstrated by way of simple bivariate correlations or multiple regression analyses. Such studies have found that endorsement of 9/11 conspiracy theories (Swami, Chamorro-Premuzic, & Furnham, 2010), theories about the July 7, 2005, London bombings (Swami et al., 2011), moon landing hoax theories (Lewandowsky, Oberauer, & Gignac, 2013; Swami et al., 2013), conspiratorial explanations for the disappearance of Amelia Earhart (Swami & Furnham, 2012), the abduction of an Austrian child (Stieger, Gumhalter, Tran, Voracek, & Swami, 2013), and rejection of climate change as a scientific hoax (Lewandowsky, Gignac, & Oberauer, 2013) are all successfully predicted by endorsement of unrelated conspiracy theories. Moreover, Swami et al. (2011, Study 2) assessed belief in a number of entirely fictitious conspiracy theories made up by the researchers for the purposes of their study. Again, the strongest predictor of endorsement of these fictional theories perceived as real was general conspiracist ideation.

Several studies have used factor analysis and indicators of scale reliability to examine the structure of measures of general conspiracist ideation. Most existing measures have been composed of between 6 and 30 items, with each item referring to a different popular conspiracy theory. Despite the variety in item content, factor analyses have found most such measures to have a single-factor structure (Bruder et al., 2013; Goertzel, 1994; Imhoff & Bruder, 2013; Swami et al., 2011, 2010). In addition, most existing measures have demonstrated high internal reliability as assessed by Cronbach's alpha (Abalakina-Paap et al., 1999; Brotherton, French, & Pickering, 2013; Crocker, Luhtanen, Broadnax, & Blaine, 1999; Darwin, Neave, & Holmes, 2011; Douglas & Sutton, 2011; Goertzel, 1994; Leman & Cinnirella, 2007; Swami et al., 2011, 2010; Wood et al., 2012).

It should be noted that not all scales have demonstrated a single-factor structure. For instance, some measures with numerous items pertaining to a single conspiratorial theme have been found to consist of two factors, one encompassing relatively passive theories (e.g. the U.S. government deliberately allows racial discrimination to persist or allowed the 9/11 attacks to take place) and another encompassing more active plots (e.g. the government itself created and spread HIV/AIDS or planned the 9/11 attacks) (Parsons et al., 1999; Swami et al., 2010). Brotherton et al. (2013) found a measure of generic conspiracist ideation to comprise five factors, including government-centric claims, claims about extraterrestrial cover-ups, claims about small but influential secret societies, claims about the unethical control of information, and allegations which directly impinge upon citizens' health and liberty. Despite the emergence of distinct factors in some studies, however, in most cases the different factor scores correlate strongly and positively. Thus, while there may be different sub-varieties of conspiracy theory, it appears that belief in one type of conspiracy is associated with belief in other types, and different categories of beliefs are predicted by largely similar variables.

While the majority of such research has been correlational, Jolley and Douglas (2014b) provide experimental evidence that beliefs about one conspiracy theory can affect endorsement of unrelated theories. The authors had one group of participants read information critical of conspiracy theories about the death of Princess Diana, while another group read information supportive of the theories. Those who read evidence supportive of the theories later tended to endorse other unrelated conspiracy theories more strongly than did those who read disconfirming evidence. Other research suggests that this influence of conspiracy theories is surreptitious. When an individual's attitudes have been influenced by conspiracist information, the individual is likely to remain unaware that their opinions have been influenced at all (Douglas & Sutton, 2008).

Goertzel (1994) speculated that beliefs in conspiracy theories may be intercorrelated because entertaining one theory logically leads to entertaining others; while the alleged conspirators may differ, the assumed truth of one conspiracy theory could be taken as evidence for the probable existence of other similar plots. However, not all conspiracy theories are mutually supportive in this way. Wood et al. (2012) observed positive correlations in endorsement of conspiracy theories which *explicitly contradict* one another, such as the claim that Princess Diana faked her own death and the competing idea that she was assassinated by elements of the British government. The authors argued that such correlations may be observed not because of any direct logical relationship between individual conspiracy theories, but rather because each theory is in agreement with higher-order beliefs about the world which can promote and sustain a multitude of theories. The authors found that the positive correlation between two contradictory beliefs concerning Osama Bin Laden was fully mediated by endorsement of the more general allegation that the U.S. government is hiding important information about the raid. Thus, Wood et al. (2012) suggest that conspiracist beliefs may be the result of a more generic assumption that "official" narratives are not to be trusted. Consistent with this, Wood and Douglas (2013, 2015) found that conspiracy theory advocates who posted comments on Internet news forums were more likely to argue against the mainstream explanation of events rather than espousing alternative theories of their own.

The conspiracy mentality appears to colour attitudes not just towards unverified conspiracy theories, but towards real conspiracies. One recent study (Wood, 2015) presented speculative conspiracist statements alongside statements alluding to documented historical conspiracies, such as "How likely is the idea that federal government officials have taken bribes from industry leaders in exchange for favorable government contracts?" (in reference to incidents like the "Teapot Dome" scandal of the early 1920s). Endorsement of the unsubstantiated conspiracy theories correlated positively with endorsement of real documented conspiracies; conversely, participants who tended to discount the controversial conspiracy theories tended also to express scepticism of the documented conspiracies. Thus, disinclination to entertain conspiracy theories may lead in some cases to excessive scepticism of verifiably true claims.

Sociodemographic correlates

Few sociodemographic factors have emerged as consistent correlates of conspiracist ideation. Several studies report no significant relationships between belief in conspiracy theories and age, gender, income, occupational category, or level of education (Abalakina-Paap et al., 1999; Crocker et al., 1999; Darwin et al., 2011; Goertzel, 1994; Herek & Capitanio, 1994; Jolley & Douglas, 2014b; Parsons et al., 1999; Simmons & Parsons, 2005; Swami et al., 2011, 2013), or report weak, inconsistent, or indirect relationships (Goertzel, 1994; Stempel, Hargrove, & Stempel, 2007; Swami et al., 2010; Swami & Furnham, 2012; Uscinski & Parent, 2014). These largely negative findings suggest that, contrary to some popular stereotypes, conspiracy theories do not appeal disproportionately to males, the young, the poor, or the uneducated. Rather, conspiracist beliefs are largely equally prevalent amongst almost all sectors of society.

One demographic factor which has been found to correlate with conspiracist ideation is ethnicity. Members of ethnic minorities appear to be more open to conspiracy theories. Racial differences in endorsement of conspiracy theories are particularly pronounced for theories with specific racially-motivated content, such as the idea that HIV/AIDS was created in a government laboratory to infect black people (Goertzel, 1994; Ross, Essien, & Torres, 2006). However, even conspiracy theories with no specific racial connotations tend to be endorsed more strongly by Hispanics, African Americans and Asian Americans as compared to Caucasians (Abalakina-Paap et al., 1999; Goertzel, 1994; Stempel et al., 2007).

An explanation which has been offered for this finding is based on the social marginality hypothesis: members of socially marginalised and less powerful groups may turn to conspiracy theories in reaction to their disadvantaged position in society (Stempel et al., 2007). However, increased conspiracist ideation has not reliably been observed within other marginalised groups, such as females, youths, or those with low income. In addition, Crocker et al. (1999) found that ethnicity fully mediated the relationship between socioeconomic status and conspiracist ideation, while Simmons and Parsons (2005) observed no difference in endorsement of conspiracy theories between African Americans of differing social status. Rather than being an effect of general social marginalisation, therefore, the observed differences appear to be specific to racial or ethnic marginalisation.

One possibility is that the discrimination faced by ethnic minorities promotes alienation and distrust of authorities and institutions seen as perpetuating racial discrimination. Lending some support to this speculation, African Americans who believe they have been the victims of police harassment because of their race, who believe that African Americans have little political influence, and who blame the problems faced by the African American community on institutional racism, are more likely to endorse conspiracy theories than African Americans who do not report these experiences or attitudes (Abalakina-Paap et al., 1999; Crocker et al., 1999; Simmons & Parsons, 2005). Also of potential relevance, Goertzel (1994) found that scores on measures of interpersonal distrust and pessimism about the world were generally higher among African Americans and Hispanics than among Caucasians, partially mediating the relationship between conspiracist ideation and minority status. A problem with this explanation, as with much of the individual differences literature discussed later, is that the direction of causality is unclear. It is possible that greater susceptibility to conspiracy theorising among ethnic minorities for other reasons causes increased alienation, distrust and system blame independent of racial discrimination.

A related possibility is that documented historical injustices contribute to elevated conspiracist ideation. The United States has a history of social and institutional mistreatment of African Americans, particularly in matters of health and autonomy. In recent history, the "Tuskegee Study of Untreated Syphilis in the Negro Male" involved collusion and deception by medical authorities to study the progression of untreated syphilis in impoverished African Americans in the rural South. The study ran for more than four decades between the 1920s and 70s. Participants were not given the opportunity to provide informed consent, and when an effective treatment for syphilis was discovered during the study, it was withheld from participants (Thomas & Quinn, 1991). Contemporary research has found that African Americans who know about the Tuskegee experiment are more likely to believe conspiracy theories alleging that AIDS was manufactured by the United States government to harm the black community (Mays, Coles, & Cochran, 2012). More generally, surveys find that African Americans are generally less trusting of scientists and doctors than other demographics, and are more likely to believe that they could be used as guinea pigs in medical research without their consent and to doubt that physicians fully explain research participation information (Goertzel, 1994; Herek & Capitanio, 1994).

Highly emotive rumours are more likely to be passed on than less emotive claims (Heath, Bell, & Sternberg, 2001). Given the specific relevance and emotiveness to African Americans of claims of a conspiracy victimising the black population, it is possible that such a claim is more likely to be transmitted within African American communities than within other minorities or Caucasians. It has been demonstrated that mere exposure to conspiracist information can increase endorsement of the claims, though individuals may be unaware that their attitudes have been influenced (Butler et al., 1995; Douglas & Sutton, 2008; Jolley & Douglas, 2014b; Swami et al., 2013). This "conspiracy cascade" (Sunstein & Vermeule, 2009) effect may account, at least in part, for stronger endorsement (or weaker rejection) among African Americans of conspiracy theories relevant to their ingroup (Crocker et al., 1999; Goertzel, 1994; Herek & Capitanio, 1994; Ross et al., 2006). However, this explanation remains to be directly tested, and cannot account for stronger endorsement among minorities of conspiracy theories unrelated to their own ethnic group (Abalakina-Paap et al., 1999; Goertzel, 1994; Ross et al., 2006; Stempel et al., 2007).

It should be noted that all studies concerning ethnicity to date have been carried out on U.S. samples, and so the findings are of questionable generalisability. Conspiracy theorising amongst African Americans in particular may be a response to the deeply ingrained history of social and institutional discrimination against black people in the United States. It is possible that the relationship between ethnicity and conspiracist ideation is different in other countries with different ethnic populations and different histories of institutional discrimination.

Individual differences

Paranoia

Much of the literature on conspiracist ideation concerns the search for personality correlates. Several clusters of reliable correlates have emerged. One revolves around paranoid ideation and schizotypy. Goertzel (1994) reported that stronger conspiracist ideation was modestly associated with lower levels of interpersonal trust and higher levels of anomie (the pessimistic belief that the world is generally getting worse, measured by asking participants the degree to which they believed that it is unfair to bring a child into the world, for example). Subsequent studies have found small-to-modest correlations with interrelated variables, including high levels of hostility, cynicism, defiance of authority, impulsive nonconformity, proneness to boredom, and low agreeableness (Abalakina-Paap et al., 1999; Brotherton & Eser, 2015; Imhoff & Bruder, 2013; Parsons et al., 1999; Swami et al., 2010). A handful of studies report mixed findings – relationships with Big-5 agreeableness are not entirely consistent (e.g. Imhoff & Bruder, 2013; Swami et al., 2010, 2013), and Wood and Douglas (2013) found that conspiracist comments posted online exhibited less hostility than anti-conspiracist comments (perhaps because of the self-presentational concerns associated with attempts to persuade an anonymous audience). Yet, on the whole, the general pattern of results supports a relationship between conspiracist ideation and a cluster of traits revolving around interpersonal suspicion and hostility.

Darwin et al. (2011) suggested that these relationships may result from subclinical paranoid and schizotypal personality traits. The authors assessed paranoid ideation and schizotypy within a university undergraduate sample. These two measures reflect elements of many of the individual difference variables previously mentioned.

Higher scores on both scales were associated with stronger endorsement of conspiracy theories, and confirmatory factor analysis found a best fit model of conspiracist ideation to include both personality measures (see also Barron, Morgan, Towell, Altemeyer, & Swami, 2014). The authors argue that extreme forms of these traits lead to maladaptive behaviours and experiences, such as serious persecutory delusions, which can have a detrimental effect on individuals' mental health and social relationships. Milder versions of the same traits, however, may actually prove adaptive. Being slightly suspicious of the intentions of others could lead to the avoidance of personal harm if the suspicions turned out to be correct. Thus conspiracy theories may be a by-product of mild paranoid and schizotypal traits which promote some degree of distrust, hostility, pessimism, and magical thinking. People high in these traits are likely to reject "official" explanations which appear to be handed down by authorities whom the individual distrusts, and conspiracy theories may offer an appealing alternative explanation. Additionally, as conspiracy theories are predicated on the sinister intentions of hidden conspirators they may seem especially attractive and plausible due to congruence with the individual's existing worldview.

Self-efficacy

A second cluster of personality variables pertains to perceptions of self-efficacy and uncertainty. Abalakina-Paap et al. (1999) assessed participants' beliefs about their capacity to control and change aspects of their life. Regression analysis found higher scores on the measure to predict stronger endorsement of various specific conspiracy theories. The authors also measured locus of control, finding external locus of control to predict acceptance of the existence of conspiracies generally (but not endorsement of specific conspiracy theories). Likewise, Sullivan, Landau, and Rothschild (2010) found that people dispositionally low in perceived control tended to endorse conspiracist attributions more strongly than individuals higher in self-efficacy. Potentially related variables, including lack of self-esteem, dissatisfaction with life, and anxiety, have also been reliably found to correlate positively with conspiracist ideation (Abalakina-Paap et al., 1999; Grzesiak-Feldman, 2013; Newheiser, Farias, & Tausch, 2011; Swami et al., 2011). Additionally, as discussed in a previous section of this chapter, some studies focusing on African American samples report perceived lack of control over political processes to be the most important variable for explaining the belief that the U.S. government routinely conspires against the African American population (Parsons et al., 1999; Simmons & Parsons, 2005; however, see Crocker et al., 1999).

Consistent with this correlational data, several studies provide experimental evidence that temporarily lacking control increases susceptibility to conspiracy theories. Whitson and Galinsky (2008) manipulated participants' sense of control by having some recall a situation in which they lacked control and others recall a situation in which they possessed control. All participants then completed a task requiring them to reason about the possible existence of a conspiracy in an ambiguous situation. Participants made to feel powerless were more likely to perceive the existence of a conspiracy than participants whose sense of control was not diminished. Likewise, Sullivan et al. (2010) manipulated perceived control by reminding participants either of uncontrollable external threats (such as exposure to disease and natural disasters) or more controllable phenomena (such as television consumption and romantic partner choice). Those reminded of chaotic hazards were more likely to endorse conspiracy theories about a hypothetical election. Outside the laboratory, Grzesiak-Feldman (2013) found that students in an anxiety-inducing situation (awaiting an exam) were especially susceptible to conspiracy theorising. Notably, however, Imhoff (2015) failed to find an effect of a self-efficacy manipulation on generic conspiracist ideation, suggesting that situational factors may have more influence on spontaneous endorsement of specific conspiracy theories than on an individual's stable conspiracy mentality.

In total, it appears that individuals experiencing aversive psychological states relating to diminished self-efficacy, either as a temporary state or a stable disposition, are more receptive to conspiracy theories. In light of these findings, it has been suggested that conspiracy theories offer a form of "compensatory control" – an appealing explanatory tool for individuals seeking to alleviate the negative psychological consequences of low self-efficacy by restoring the perception of personal control and understanding, and perhaps also justifying and externalising blame for the situation (Kay, Whitson, Gaucher, & Galinsky, 2009; Sullivan et al., 2010; Whitson & Galinsky, 2008). Thus, a function of conspiracy theories may be the potential attribution of negative or uncontrollable events to a mysterious external agency or a specific identifiable outgroup.

Openness

A third cluster of variables concerns individual differences in information-seeking strategies. One relevant hypothesis which has not found support is that conspiracist ideation results from a preference for simple and concrete explanations over complexity and ambiguity. Abalakina-Paap et al. (1999) assessed individual differences in need for cognition, tolerance of ambiguity, and attributional complexity, predicting negative correlations between these variables and conspiracist ideation. Contrary to expectations, all three variables failed to predict conspiracist ideation. Likewise, Leman and Cinnirella (2013) found no difference between conspiracy believers and sceptics in terms of individual differences in need for cognitive closure. On reflection, while the conspiracist mindset may in some regards constitute a relatively simplified view of the world, individual conspiracy theories are themselves often nuanced and complex. Believers can exert significant cognitive effort in seeking out evidence in favour of certain theories, and the task of maintaining belief in a conspiracy theory despite the existence of compelling evidence to the contrary may be cognitively demanding.

A hypothesis which has found more support is that individuals who believe conspiracy theories, rather than being intellectually rigid and closed, are in fact more open to new and unusual ideas than sceptics. Conspiracist ideation has been found to correlate positively with other unorthodox beliefs, including the paranormal (Darwin et al., 2011; Lobato, Mendoza, Sims, & Chin, 2014), pseudoscience (Lobato et al., 2014), superstitions (Stieger et al., 2013), New Age beliefs (Newheiser et al., 2011), and urban legends (Drinkwater, Dagnall, & Parker, 2012), as well as with self-reported anomalous experiences (Swami et al., 2013). However, the generality of this apparent openness to unusual ideas is unclear. Some studies employing the Big-5 personality inventory report weak but statistically significant relationships with trait openness (Swami et al., 2010, 2011, 2013). However, other studies have produced mixed findings (Swami & Furnham, 2012), or failed to reproduce the relationship (Bruder et al., 2013; Furnham, 2013; Imhoff & Bruder, 2013). Thus, it is possible that the intercorrelations between conspiracist ideation and various anomalous beliefs reflect domain-general openness, but a seemingly more likely possibility is that the relative open-mindedness of conspiracists is limited to certain specific kinds of unconventional claims.

Summary of individual differences

In sum, certain clusters of personality traits appear to reliably correlate with conspiracist ideation. However, since much of the existing research is correlational and thus does not establish the direction of causality, speculation about "conspiracy-prone" personality types remains unproven. A relatively paranoid disposition may predispose an individual to endorsement of conspiracy theories, for example; however, an alternative explanation for the relationship is that acceptance of conspiracy theories increases feelings of distrust, hostility and alienation. Similarly, open-mindedness may promote acceptance of conspiracy theories, or perhaps believing in the ubiquity of hidden plots promotes open-mindedness. While there is some experimental evidence that lacking control increases conspiracy theorising, this does not rule out the possibility that conspiracy theories, in postulating a world controlled from behind the scenes by a powerful elite, erode individuals' sense of self-efficacy. A likely possibility is that the relationships are reciprocal, such that an existing paranoid, powerless or intellectually open disposition promotes the acquisition of conspiracist beliefs, creating a worldview which validates and strengthens the prior disposition, which in turn reinforces the conspiracist beliefs, and so on. It should also be noted that the list of personality variables which have been studied in relation to conspiracist ideation is far from exhaustive. It is likely that other individual difference variables yet to be examined are associated with conspiracist ideation.

Cognitive biases and heuristics

A growing number of studies provide evidence that conspiracist ideation, like other anomalous beliefs, may be a product in part of certain sociocognitive biases and heuristics. Note that the distinction between cognitive and personality variables is not always clear, and interactions between variables from either category are likely (Irwin, 1993, 2009); however, while the previous section focused on the role of largely stable and domain-general personality traits, this section focuses on context-specific biases and heuristics in information processing.

Proportionality

The proportionality bias refers to the tendency to attribute an outcome to a cause proportional to the magnitude of the event. Put simply, major events are judged to have major causes while minor events are assumed to have minor causes (Kahneman & Tversky, 1972). Since conspiracy theories tend to explain events of national or international significance as the outcome of a proportionally grand conspiracy, it seems likely that the proportionality bias might imbue the theories with an intuitive appeal which the "official" explanations lack. Several studies offer qualified support for this notion. McCauley and Jacques (1979) created two versions of a newspaper headline reporting the shooting of a president. One headline read "Man shoots at the President and misses" while the other read "Man shoots at the President and kills him". Consistent with the proportionality bias, participants judged the fatal assassination (and thus more momentous event) more likely to be the result of a conspiracy, while the nonfatal assassination attempt was judged more likely the result of a lone assassin. However, follow-up studies suggested that participants expected a conspiracy to be generally more likely to succeed in killing a president than a lone assassin. The authors suggested that rather than being influenced by an automatic proportionality heuristic, perhaps participants inferred conspiracy as the most likely cause of a successful assassination using a rational calculation based on the prior expected efficacy of a conspiracy as compared to a lone gunman.

Leman and Cinnirella (2007) attempted to rule out the effect of prior expected efficacy by creating two additional scenarios. In one, a president was reported to have been hit by an assassin's bullet, but survived by sheer luck. In another, it was reported that an assassin's bullet narrowly missed the president, but that he died a short time later due to an unrelated heart attack. Despite breaking the causal link between the apparent skill of the assassin and the president's ultimate fate, participants were more likely to attribute the gunman to a conspiracy when the president died. LeBoeuf and Norton (2012) created vignettes in which the consequences of an assassination were even more far removed from the efficacy of the shooter. The authors created two vignettes, both reporting the successful assassination of a foreign leader. The vignettes went on to inform participants that a British newspaper had subsequently criticised the assassinated leader, and that the criticism had incited attacks against Britain. In a large-magnitude condition, participants were told that the attacks had led to the British Prime Minister declaring war. In a small-consequence condition, participants were told that the British Prime Minister responded peacefully, subduing the attacks. Thus, the magnitude of the consequences of the assassination – whether Britain became embroiled in a war – was arbitrarily determined by the British Prime Minister's reaction. Despite the absence of a direct causal link between the assassination and the ultimate consequences, participants preferred the conspiratorial explanation for the assassination when the magnitude of the consequences was large.

Most recently, van Prooijen and van Dijk (2014) found that the effect of the proportionality bias on reasoning about conspiracies is mediated by the degree to which participants empathise with the people affected by the event in question. Following previous studies, the researchers created fictional news reports of a successful or unsuccessful assassination attempt on the leader of a foreign country. In one study the researchers first measured individual differences in the ability to empathise. Higher scores correlated positively with susceptibility to the proportionality bias. In a subsequent experimental study, some participants were instructed to imagine themselves in the shoes of a citizen of the nation whose president was the subject of an assassination attempt when making their judgment of the likelihood of the alleged conspiracy, while others were instructed to make an objective judgment. The proportionality bias appeared to influence the judgments of the former group, but not the latter.

The conjunction fallacy

The conjunction fallacy refers to the misperception that the co-occurrence of two events is more likely than the occurrence of either constituent event alone – a probabilistic impossibility. The fallacy was first explored at length by Tversky and Kahneman (1983). After reading a description designed to portray a fictional individual, Linda, as having several stereotypically feminist traits, participants rated the likelihood that Linda was either a bank teller, or a feminist and a bank teller. Since the more general category of "bank tellers" includes the more restrictive category of "feminist bank tellers", selecting the latter option is seen as committing a conjunction fallacy error. Between 50 per cent and 90 per cent of Tversky and Kahneman's participants committed the conjunction fallacy across several variations of the Linda scenario. These figures have generally been borne out by subsequent research using a wide variety of conjunction scenarios (Agnoli & Krantz, 1989; Fiedler, 1988; Fisk & Pidgeon, 1996, 1997, 1998; Rogers, Davis, & Fisk, 2009; Rogers, Fisk, & Wiltshire, 2011; Wolford, Taylor, & Beck, 1990). Notably, people who believe in the paranormal have been found to be more susceptible to the conjunction fallacy (Rogers et al., 2009, 2011). The fallacy appears to be most alluring when the conjunction response option suggests a motive or causal relationship (Nestler, 2008; Tversky & Kahneman, 1983).

Brotherton and French (2014) suggested that conspiracy theories often depend on the assertion that ostensibly unrelated observations are, in fact, more likely to be related by the proposed conspiracist narrative. Thus, conspiracy theories may represent a type of conjunction fallacy error. Following from research on the link between paranormal beliefs and the conjunction fallacy (Rogers et al., 2009, 2011), the authors created a measure of susceptibility to the conjunction fallacy consisting of both neutral and conspiracy-themed conjunction scenarios. Each item offered a brief description of an event or circumstance, after which participants rated the probability of three outcomes (two singular options and a conjunction of the two). In the case of the conspiracy items, the conjunction response option implied the existence of a conspiracy. For example, one item implied that a journalist's mysterious death was brought about by the secret society he was investigating. As expected, endorsement of conspiracy theories correlated positively with the number of conjunction errors that participants made. This was true of both the conspiracy and neutral conjunction items (and, in another study, paranormal-themed items), suggesting that the heightened susceptibility to the conjunction fallacy exhibited by conspiracy-believers is domain-general.

Intentionality

Three recent studies, using markedly different measurement approaches, offer evidence that endorsement of conspiracy theories is positively correlated with a relatively heightened tendency to perceive agency and to interpret ambiguous actions as having been intended rather than accidental.

First, van der Tempel and Alcock (2015) assessed hyperactive agency detection using the Belief in the Purpose of Random Events (BPRE) scale (Lindeman & Aarnio, 2007). The scale asks participants to imagine 18 positive, neutral or negative hypothetical events befalling them ("A stone falls from a scaffold and seriously injures you", for example), and to rate each item on a 5-point scale with endpoints labelled "The event had no purpose" and "The event clearly had a purpose". Scores on the measure correlated positively and moderately with a measure of conspiracist ideation.

Second, Brotherton and French (2015) adapted a measure of susceptibility to the intentionality bias from Rosset (2008). Participants were presented with twelve sentences describing an ambiguous action, such as "she kicked the dog". Each could be interpreted as an intentional act or an accident. Participants were asked to describe what came to mind as they read each sentence, and to clarify whether they had pictured something done on purpose or by accident. The number of items participants interpreted as intentional correlated weakly but significantly with scores on a measure of conspiracist ideation (and the relationship was successfully replicated in a second study).

Third, Douglas, Sutton, Callan, Dawtry, and Harvey (2016) adapted a measure created by Heider and Simmel (1944). In Heider and Simmel's classic study, participants viewed a short animated film clip in which three simple shapes (a big triangle, a small triangle and a circle) interact with one another and with a rectangular structure. When asked to describe the action, most participants offered detailed narratives which attributed complex mental states and intentions to the rudimentary shapes, suggesting that it takes little more than non-random movement to invoke intentional attributions. Rather than having participants freely describe their interpretation of the film, Douglas et al. (2016) simply asked participants to rate on numerical scales the extent to which they saw the shapes as conscious and acting purposefully. Again, scores on this measure correlated weakly but significantly with a measure of conspiracist ideation.

In sum, these studies suggest that the opportunity to attribute events to a purposeful conspiracy, as opposed to unintended consequences or pure chance, may account in part for the appeal of conspiracy theories. It is worth noting that each study measured hyperactive agency detection outside the context of conspiracies, suggesting that it is a domain-general bias.

Projection

Projection simplifies the complex task of reasoning about the social environment by attributing one's own tendencies to others, leading to a bias towards believing that others will generally think, feel, and behave in the same way as one does oneself (Ames, 2004). Douglas and Sutton (2011) provided evidence that projection plays a role in conspiracist ideation. The authors first conducted a correlational study which examined beliefs in a number of conspiracy theories and participants' perceptions that, if in the same position themselves, they would have personally participated in the alleged conspiracies. Machiavellianism, an indicator of willingness to manipulate others for one's own gain, was also assessed. Analysis found that greater personal willingness to conspire predicted stronger conspiracist ideation. In addition, the relationship between Machiavellianism and belief in conspiracies was fully mediated by personal willingness to conspire, suggesting that moral qualities are related to conspiracist ideation only in as much as those qualities influence personal willingness to conspire. A second study experimentally manipulated participants' perceptions of their own moral tendencies. An experimental group was primed with positive moral qualities by recalling an event in which they had helped another person. A control group was not exposed to any moral prime. All participants subsequently rated their belief in various conspiracies and their personal willingness to conspire. Those primed with positive moral qualities perceived themselves as less likely to conspire than the control group. As predicted, they also displayed weaker endorsement of conspiracy theories than the control group, and the relationship was fully mediated by personal willingness to conspire.

As the authors note, conspiracy theories arise when conflicting or incomplete information prevents an individual from arriving at a clear and satisfying explanation of an event. Uncertain situations such as these are likely to elicit projection; rather than relying on objective facts, an individual may attempt to infer the mental state and intentions of the alleged conspirators. In this case, an individual's personal willingness to have conspired may affect their judgement of whether the alleged conspirators did in fact conspire. If an individual supposes that they would have been willing to conspire to fake the moon landing, for instance, the process of projection may lead the individual to believe that most other people would be equally willing to have participated in such a conspiracy – and if most other people would, then by implication it is more likely that those accused did in fact go through with it.

Illusory pattern perception

The cognitive system is adept at detecting meaningful patterns in complex and chaotic stimuli. Without this ability essential tasks such as perceiving threats in the environment or identifying familiar faces would not be possible. However, because the costs of failing to perceive a genuine pattern often exceed the costs of identifying an illusory pattern, seemingly meaningful relationships are occasionally detected where objectively none exist (see Haselton & Nettle, 2006). Belief in the paranormal has been found to be associated with illusory pattern detection, suggesting that paranormal attributions may result from having a low threshold for pattern recognition (e.g. Blackmore & Moore, 1994).

Recent studies suggest that the same may be true of belief in conspiracy theories. Whitson and Galinsky (2008) demonstrated that the tendency to perceive illusory patterns across a number of modalities increases under conditions of low perceived self-efficacy (the relationship between individual differences in self-efficacy and conspiracist ideation was discussed earlier in this chapter). Following a manipulation designed to decrease participants' sense of control, participants were more likely to perceive visual images in purely random visual noise, to perceive illusory correlations in the financial market, and to make superstitious causal attributions for events. Crucially, the manipulation also increased the tendency to attribute ambiguous events to conspiracy. In addition to lack of control (see also Sullivan et al., 2010), similar tendencies have been demonstrated in response to ambivalence (van Harreveld, Rutjens, Schneider, Nohlen, & Keskinis, 2014), and uncertainty (van Prooijen & Jostmann, 2013; Whitson, Galinsky, & Kay, 2015).

Whitson and Galinsky (2008) argue that conspiracy theories may be just one possible product of a cognitive-perceptual bias towards finding meaning within ambiguous stimuli – a bias which is accentuated under aversive conditions including reduced control, conflicting cognitions, and uncertainty. Conspiracy theories are often predicated upon the perception of meaningful causal relationships between anomalies within a large, complex, and often ambiguous dataset. To take one illustrative example, it has been claimed that a man who conspicuously opened an umbrella moments before President John F. Kennedy was fatally shot must have been a co-conspirator signalling to the assassin (see Bugliosi, 2007). The alternative explanation – that the temporal relationship between umbrella and gunfire was merely a coincidence – does not satisfy the need to perceive order in the environment, and so may be less intuitively appealing. The findings also provide a possible explanation as to why conspiracy theories inevitably follow shocking events such as unexpected deaths, terrorist attacks, and natural disasters. Such unpredictable and uncontrollable events are likely to threaten people's sense of control and understanding over their immediate environment, thus increasing the tendency to seek patterns which may provide a satisfying causal explanation. By incorporating a large amount of anomalies and errant data into a coherent explanatory framework (Keeley, 1999) and thus maximising the perception of meaning, conspiracy theories may be more psychologically satisfying than their non-conspiratorial alternatives.

Confirmation bias

People often selectively seek and interpret information in ways that confirm their existing preconceptions (e.g. Lord, Ross, & Lepper, 1979). This bias has been observed in abstract deductive tasks as well as in reasoning about complex, real-world issues (e.g. Powell, Hughes-Scholes, & Sharman, 2012; Wason, 1960). The much-replicated finding that people who believe one conspiracy theory tend also to endorse others (and people who reject one theory tend to reject others) may reflect confirmatory reasoning, though to date only a few studies have specifically examined the role of confirmation biases in conspiracist ideation.

McHoskey (1995) surveyed participants to ascertain their opinions towards conspiracist and "lone gunman" theories of the assassination of President Kennedy. Participants were then presented with summaries of evidence relating to each version of events. Each summary contained an equal number of arguments and counterarguments. After exposure to this information, participants rated the persuasiveness of each of the arguments, and re-rated their endorsement of the conspiracy theory and the lone gunman theory. Analysis revealed biased assimilation of the evidence: people who began the study believing that a conspiracy took place found arguments supporting this position to be more persuasive than evidence in favour of the lone-gunman theory. On the other hand, participants who were initially sceptical of the conspiracy theory rated arguments consistent with the lone gunman account as more persuasive. Moreover, the extent of this biased assimilation was proportional to the extremity of the initial attitude; participants with a weak initial leaning demonstrated modest biased assimilation while those with an extreme initial belief displayed stronger biased assimilation. The end result of exposure to the mixed evidence was attitude polarisation – participants endorsed their pre-existing position even more strongly following exposure to the (deliberately ambivalent) evidence.

Information refuting conspiracy theories can diminish people's beliefs; as mentioned previously, Jolley and Douglas (2014b) found that presenting (randomly selected) participants with evidence disputing conspiracy theories about Princess Diana reduced their conspiracist beliefs as compared to participants who were presented with pro-conspiracist evidence. Yet other studies show that when an individual has strong prior beliefs, exposure to information refuting a conspiracy theory can inadvertently reinforce the belief. Nyhan et al. (2009) reported that presenting evidence against the idea that President Barack Obama is secretly Muslim *increased* some people's belief that Obama is Muslim – specifically, Republicans who did not graduate from high school. Likewise, attempts to correct misconceptions about the Affordable Care Act secretly authorising "death panels" increased belief in the reality of death panels among supporters of the politician who originated the death panel rumours (Nyhan, Reifler, & Ubel, 2013). Nyhan, Reifler, Richey, and Freed (2014) found that information correcting the idea that vaccines cause autism successfully reduced the belief that vaccines cause autism; yet, it also reduced some participants' intentions to vaccinate (perhaps because the correction brought to mind other fears about vaccine side effects).

Confirmation bias suggests a possible reason why conspiracy theories can endure over time, even in the face of substantial contradictory evidence. When a body of evidence can be construed as mixed, complex, and uncertain, as is often the case with the events which attract popular conspiracy theories, exposure to this ambiguous evidence can nevertheless result in the strengthening of an initial attitude. Thus people on opposite sides of an argument can feel that the same body of evidence supports their own pre-existing belief. It should be emphasised that this bias not only helps perpetuate belief in conspiracy theories, but also rejection of conspiracy theories.

Summary of cognitive biases and heuristics

The available findings suggest that certain cognitive biases and heuristics play a role in the formation and maintenance of conspiratorial beliefs, making the theories appear more plausible than their non-conspiratorial alternatives. Note that it is not necessarily the case that conspiracy theorists are uniquely susceptible to reasoning biases; rather, the content of conspiracist claims may preferentially invoke certain biases. It is likely that other biases yet to be examined play a role in the formation and maintenance of conspiracy beliefs.

Taking a broader perspective, Swami, Voracek, Stieger, Tran, and Furnham (2014) report a small but significant correlation between endorsement of conspiracy theories and intuitive thinking style, and a similarly sized negative correlation with analytic thinking style. Moreover, experimental manipulations designed to promote analytic thinking slightly reduced endorsement of conspiracy theories. This suggests that susceptibility to the biases and heuristics previously mentioned, and the accompanying tendency towards relatively greater endorsement of conspiracy theories, may be the product of a general proclivity towards intuitive thinking. Conversely, analytic thinking, either as a stable disposition or a situational response, may serve to attenuate susceptibility to reasoning biases, and thus to reduce belief in conspiracy theories. However, there are other possible explanations. For example, individuals primed to think analytically may simply be using a different heuristic, preferring responses that appear more stereotypically "rational". Given that analytic thinking has also been associated with disbelief in religious and paranormal claims (Gervais & Norenzayan, 2012a; Pennycook, Cheyne, Seli, Koehler, & Fugelsang, 2012), it could be the case that analytic thinking simply promotes a response set whereby the individual is more inclined to doubt any unconventional statement.

Belief in conspiracies and paranormal beliefs

Some readers may be wondering why a chapter on belief in conspiracies has been included in a book primarily focussed upon paranormal beliefs and experiences. We feel that the inclusion of this chapter is appropriate for a number of reasons.

First, some conspiratorial beliefs explicitly involve paranormal claims. To take but one example, it is widely believed that governments and intelligence services around the world are fully aware of the existence and activities of aliens but keep this information from the general public. It is claimed, for example, that the military have recovered crashed flying saucers and even make use of back-engineered alien technology in weapon systems. Depending upon one's preferred definition of the term *paranormal*, the very idea that UFOs are alien spaceships can legitimately be considered to be a paranormal belief. Even if one were to insist on a strict definition of the term to include only evidence relating to extrasensory perception and psychokinesis, alien abduction claims would still often involve a paranormal aspect as it is widely believed that aliens communicate with humans telepathically.

Secondly, as already noted, a number of empirical studies have found that belief in conspiracies reliably correlates with belief in the paranormal (e.g. Darwin et al., 2011; Lobato et al., 2014) as well as associated beliefs such as superstitions (Stieger et al., 2013) and New Age concepts (Newheiser et al., 2011). This strongly suggests that conspiracism and paranormal beliefs may well have common psychological roots.

Thirdly, a number of personality dimensions correlate with both conspiracist thinking and paranormal belief, including paranoia and schizotypy (Darwin et al., 2011) and, albeit somewhat inconsistently, openness (Bruder et al., 2013; Imhoff & Bruder, 2013; Swami et al., 2010, 2011, 2013; Swami & Furnham, 2012). With respect to clinical paranoia, delusions that one's mind is being read or that one can read others' minds are a common symptom. Those scoring highly on schizotypy may experience a range of anomalous experiences and infer that these are being caused by powerful and malicious outsiders. If the correlation between openness and conspiracism is real, this may well be reflected in a stronger tendency to consider and ultimately endorse a wide range of unconventional beliefs, including paranormal claims.

Finally, a number of cognitive biases associated with belief in conspiracies also appear to be associated with paranormal beliefs, including susceptibility to the conjunction fallacy, intentionality bias, and illusory pattern perception as already discussed. It can be reasonably argued that many of these biases have their roots in our evolutionary history (French & Stone, 2014) and that they are the price we pay for evolving cognitive systems that are better suited for keeping us alive as opposed to unerringly perceiving the way the world really is.

It is useful to consider both belief in conspiracies and paranormal beliefs as examples of magical thinking, along with traditional superstitions, belief in various pseudosciences, New Age beliefs and, arguably, religious beliefs. It is noteworthy that the tendency towards all forms of magical thinking increases in situations where individuals feel that events are beyond their control. The similarities and differences in terms of the psychological factors underlying each type of magical thinking remain to be fully explored in future research.

Conclusions

Conspiracy theories are sometimes regarded as a trivial curiosity, a harmless pastime, or even a potentially beneficial safeguard against genuine malfeasance (Clarke, 2002; Coady, 2012; Pigden, 2007). At least some conspiracy theories, however, have been shown to have potentially harmful consequences, from fostering political alienation (Bartlett & Miller, 2010; Butler et al., 1995; Jolley & Douglas, 2014b) to discouraging environmentalism (Jolley & Douglas, 2014b) and non-adherence to medical interventions (Bogart, Wagner, Galvan, & Banks, 2010; Jolley & Douglas, 2014a). A psychological understanding of people's reasons for endorsing conspiracy theories could lead to effective safeguards or interventions against these side effects. Moreover, understanding the psychological factors underlying belief in conspiracy theories can enhance our understanding of the psychology of attitude formation more generally, for example by illuminating the types of information most likely to invoke certain reasoning biases.

As this review has summarised, important advances are being made in understanding the psychology of conspiracy theories, particularly from the perspectives of individual differences and reasoning biases. Other fruitful avenues are just beginning to receive investigation, including attentional and perceptual biases (van Elk, 2015), the rhetorical effects of the label "conspiracy theory" (Wood, 2015), and the unique features of particular conspiracy theories (Douglas & Sutton, 2015). As the field progresses, it will be important to integrate existing insights. Van Elk (2015), for example, notes that schizotypal traits are associated with illusory pattern perception. There are likely many more interactions between and among various demographic, personality, and cognitive factors.

Clearly, there is much need for further research. However, it is possible to begin speculating about what a general model of conspiracist ideation might look like. It appears that certain personality traits and information-processing styles are associated with a generic conspiracy mentality, which describes the extent to which an individual assumes that conspiratorial activity is commonplace. To the extent that these assumptions are applicable to events and observations on hand from the real world, conspiracy theories of events may be adopted or rejected as viable explanations. People in aversive psychological states, either due to stable personality traits or temporary situational factors, may be more inclined to entertain conspiracy theories. Likewise, the content of conspiracy theories may invoke certain information-processing biases and heuristics, imbuing the theories with intuitive plausibility which "official stories" often lack. Belief in the paranormal has been conceptualised in similar terms (e.g. French & Stone, 2014; Irwin, 1993, 2009). Given the correlations between conspiracist ideation and other anomalous beliefs, and the apparently similar psychological underpinnings, it seems that conspiracist ideation can be usefully situated within the wider context of anomalous beliefs.

13

SCIENCE AND EXPERIENCE

Ron Roberts

> *The fantasies of the past determined by the needs of the present have a direct impact on the realities of the future.*
>
> Svetlana Boym

How we propose to understand reality is central to the pursuit of scientific activity, though by no means confined to it. Many lay people would be surprised to discover that the question of what specific characteristics distinguish scientific practice from other human activities has provoked fierce debate amongst scientists. Shortly we will consider some of the main points to emerge from these debates and their relevance for confronting the unusual and mysterious aspects of human experience which form the subject matter of this book.

First of all, however, let us be clear about what is fundamental to the nature of scientific enquiry about which few scientists would argue. Simply put, this is that the nature of scientific knowledge does not and ought not to rely on authority – that is, the truth of a proposition is not deemed to be true simply by virtue of the social status of the person uttering it. Sadly, in practice of course, this is rarely true – and for this both the media and the scientific community are culpable. In this idealised respect science is different from almost all other forms of knowledge. According to Karl Marx, what we think of as history are just the tales told by the victorious. Our modernist mental habit of assuming linear progress in all human affairs – including epistemology – leaves no space for the dignity of the defeated (Boym, 2010) – those whose ideas and practices lie off the beaten track of received wisdom. As a result we have assumed that what is most current in the world of science is most true.

The alternative renderings which the vanquished might have bequeathed are thereby lost or misplaced. In the contemporary world, what makes for good art is increasingly decided not by popular or critical judgement, but by the whims of collectors whose assessments are tainted by the influence of the potential economic value of works. The postmodern society we all inhabit would propose that of all the values, morals and judgements which muster expression, none may lay claim to any special status compared to others. In the totalitarian nightmare which was Orwell's 1984, this principle was elevated to encompass our very definitions of reality. What was real and true was whatever was decreed in the name of Big Brother to be real and true. The assault on the notion of objective truth however is far from fictitious. Orwell's own story was rooted in the chilling reality of Stalinist Russia, since when there have been other appalling variations on the same theme. In the present day, just a few years subsequent to the global banking crisis we see an upsurge in anti-Semitism, holocaust denial and bigotry which can leave no sensible person comfortable. The distortions of truth are not confined to distant historical periods or foreign countries.

Science, in theory at least, stands fundamentally opposed to such philosophies which decree truth on the basis of political convenience. The challenge which science throws down does not claim that scientists have access to any absolute knowledge or ultimate truth. Rather, what is asserted is that the relationships between events which it describes, in some way mirror or approximate to events assumed to occur in a world which is real and exists in some way outside of any human sensory contact with it. This is referred to as the correspondence theory of truth (Chalmers, 2013). The doctrine is known as scientific realism. For example, consider how knowledge of the mathematical relationships which describe motion enable spacecraft to be placed in orbit. These mathematical descriptions are not arbitrary in any postmodern sense – they do not depend upon a social or public consensus that they are correct. They must fit with reality in some deep sense otherwise the spacecraft could not remain in orbit – and the practical possibilities of satellite communications and human space travel could not be brought into being. Science in practice however is often subject to forces from the realms of culture and politics.

Science, belief and truth?

Science is not without its critics – some from within its own camp. Like Kuhn (1962), Feyerabend (1975) took the view that shifts in scientific paradigms owe more to the dominating influence of powerful interest groups and particular belief systems within the scientific community than to any logically and empirically derived truths. Indeed the physicist Max Planck famously remarked:

> a new scientific truth does not triumph by convincing its opponents and making them see the light, but rather because its opponents eventually die, and a new generation grows up that is familiar with it. (quoted in Kuhn, 1962, p. 151)

Because of this, many worthy and interesting hypotheses simply do not get to see the light of day or find their emergence into a wider public consciousness seriously delayed. Silvers (1997) provides an interesting collection of such ideas and the fates that befell them. What can we learn about the nature of science from these stories? Certainly they lead us to ask exactly what science is or is not. One of the recurring themes in the quest to pin its nature down has been whether to conceptualise it in terms of what scientists actually do – which is at times illogical, beset by personal and social bias, subject to cultural and ideological whims, and swayed by power politics, or instead to describe it in the ideal abstract terms of what scientists ought to do. In a nutshell – whether to depict it in a descriptive or a prescriptive language. Those who lean toward the latter position cite the views of Karl Popper (Popper, 1972), who argued that science progresses through cycles of hypothesis generation and refutation. However, he was acutely aware that the first half of this cycle – the business of generating hypotheses, could not be captured by any formal system of (hypothetico-deductive) rules. It is in essence a creative act. He was also cognisant that theories have frequently stood their ground and prevailed despite apparent falsifications and their inability to account for well-known observed phenomena. Newton's laws of motion for example were known during his own lifetime to be incapable of explaining the observed motion of the planet Mercury through the heavens.

Such difficulties, amongst others, lead Feyerabend to contend that no coherent account of a universal unchanging scientific method would suffice. In short that there is not, nor could ever be, such a thing as scientific method. It is furthermore true that science also embodies an article of faith – a fundamental principle if you like that the "laws of nature" are in principle comprehensible and consistent throughout the universe – in both time and place. Without such a guiding belief it is difficult to contemplate how science could be done at all. The historical embeddedness of all psychological phenomena in fact led Kenneth Gergen (1973) to argue that social psychology is not actually a science but a form of history – none of its findings capable of escaping the butterfly net of circumstance into the wide beyond of an assumed universal relevance for all times and places.

Beyond that one article of faith in universal laws of nature, however, no ideas are to be considered sacrosanct. A recent examination of the crises in Physics by Lee and Smolin (2015) has even begun to question whether the laws of nature are themselves invariant across the history of the universe and whether Physics itself could be reconsidered as an historical discipline. In this view laws are merely the best working descriptions for how nature currently works – that is they are descriptions and not prescriptions. For such laws to be useful it is not essential that they hold true for all time. But if science is so difficult to pin down, how is it possible that ideas come to fruition that in their structure and functioning seem to bear such a close correspondence with what is observable in the world? Consider our example of the laws of motion as set forth initially by Newton and later by Einstein. This we do need to understand if we are maintain that a scientific path offers the best prospect for coming to terms with human behaviour and the wealth of reported human experience which is on offer.

Though producing workable and testable hypotheses cannot be done by following a recipe, there are aspects of scientific activity which if viewed from a broad enough perspective do permit it to be distinguished from other activities which might also lay claim to truth. In opening this chapter we mentioned what is perhaps the most important of these – the disjunction between truth and authority. The proclamations of Nobel Prize–winning scientists and other eminent authorities are not true by virtue of who they are nor the position in the scientific community which they occupy. Certainly over short periods of time this can sometimes be obscured and the art of political persuasion triumph over reality. Boyle (2002) for example provides a convincing case for the abandonment of "schizophrenia" as a scientific concept because after almost 100 years there is no empirical evidence to support its validity. Perhaps we should be thankful that the work of Machiavelli does not form part of the scientific curriculum! However, because science is fundamentally pursued to solve intellectual and practical problems, the flaws in any proposed solutions which rely more on power and persuasion than reason tend, more often than not, to be eventually rooted out. That at least is the hope. Since the first edition of this book a number of critical issues pertinent to this interpretation have come increasingly to the fore.

Chief amongst the concerns provoking what some see as the beginnings of a crisis in science are the influence of global neoliberal politics on the funding, publishing and interpretation of scientific work (Itten & Roberts, 2014; Roberts, 2015). This has been most evident in medicine and the behavioural sciences where the influence of pharmaceutical companies (so-called Big Pharma) is having a detrimental effect on the integrity of scientific knowledge. Negative findings in respect to pharmacological products have been suppressed or simply not published, whilst many articles have been ghost-written by in-house writers for pharmaceutical companies (see https://en.wikipedia.org/wiki/Medical_ghostwriter). The introduction of market "logic" into higher education since the 1980s along with a host of dubious metrics (Burrows, 2012) has also contributed to reductions in academic freedom, producing a situation where the topics which are researched are more likely to be those which are deemed attractive to government and corporate sponsors. Not entirely unrelated to this is the problem of replication which other contributors to this volume have discussed. The desire of journal editors for continuously "novel" findings certainly has echoes with the capitalist ethos of continually bringing new products to the "market", and without doubt has nothing to do with any accepted notion of scientific practice. But the problem doesn't stop there. Even when replication is sought, the success rates are low. An attempt to replicate 100 research findings previously published in three top psychology journals were successful in only 39 cases (Baker, 2015). Added to these concerns are the inherent problems with peer review. The current anonymous system of review dates from the eighteenth century. It has been attacked by sociologists as a process susceptible to control by elites and beset by personal jealousy. On this Richard Horton (2000), the editor of the British Medical Journal, commented

> We portray it . . . to the public as a quasi-sacred process that helps to make science our most objective truth teller but we know that the system of

> peer review is biased, unjust, unaccountable, incomplete, easily fixed, often insulting, usually ignorant, occasionally foolish, and frequently wrong.

In addition to Horton's criticisms, evidence suggests it is a poor method for detecting errors in a paper (Baxt, Waeckerle, Berlin, & Callaham, 1998).

The self-correcting tendency which science (in any field worthy of the name) tends to exhibit over time is held as a hallmark which distinguishes science from other subjects – but as the issue of schizophrenia referred to above suggests – how long should we wait for this self-correction to occur? Here we witness the opposite problem to the obsession with novelty – a stasis in thinking encouraged by institutional and professional power – one which in Walter Benjamin's (2007, p. 255) terms one could easily describe as the "premeditated murder of reality". Often what is supposedly being corrected is the mismatch (or potential mismatch) between what is predicted from theory and what may be suggested by observation. In the case of "schizophrenia", neither its conceptual validity nor its reliability as a scientific construct has ever been satisfactorily demonstrated, yet its name lives on in journal after journal oblivious to these requirements. "Science" in this guise claims legitimacy not through adherence to practice or method but through its power as a form of rhetoric or discourse – one described by its critics as "scientism". "Schizophrenia" has much in common in its literary existence with both astrology and psychoanalysis. On the surface, work in all these areas exhibits features found in genuine scientific work: data collection, its representation in graphical form, occasionally the use of numbers and statistics and a grand theory to "explain" what is supposedly "in the data".

However, theories in truly scientific domains do not simply comprise ad hoc ideas, however interesting, nor nice pictures and fancy statistical tests. To qualify for the status of a theory, an idea must organise already existing data within a coherent explanatory framework, moreover one which allows new propositions to be logically derived – propositions which necessitate making new observations which in principle can either support or fail to support the theory. If more and more observations of sufficient quality are built up which challenge a particular theoretical stance, then pressure is generated to reject that stance and come up with an alternative. The alternative should be equally adept at explaining the old observations, be able to accommodate the new ones and permit further empirical testing of itself. As such, inconsistency or apparent inconsistency as expressed through people's ideas and theories is the fertile ground on which scientific theories are constructed. Neither astrology nor psychoanalysis nor psychiatry possesses an enviable track record for dealing with predictive failures. The same could be said for religion and politics.

This reiterative cycle of generating ideas and testing them has been likened to a form of artificial selection whereby "unfit" frameworks, theories and conjectures are progressively weeded out, leaving in the long run only those which tend to fit the facts well and thereby accord with reality. From this perspective when it operates in this manner unhindered by the corrupting influence of money, power and politics, science can be envisaged as a form of cultural evolution. Its environment is the world of competing theories and explanations. This allows us to understand those instances where theories persist even though they fail certain tests. What is crucial is the context within which they operate. Failure to account for known facts may not be fatal when the competition is no better and fares worse in other respects. A flawed order is deemed preferable to an unbridled intellectual chaos.

A science for experience: questions of method

All psychological science ultimately rests on real world experience – from introspection of our own mental processes to our experience of our own interactions with others – including in the experimental context. In this respect investigators in pursuit of a science of persons function as instruments of both data collection and data interpretation. In recent years a vehement argument has been unfolding about what methods are most appropriate for studying human beings. In close proximity to this debate has been another – whether the concept of truth in (psychological) science can be protected. Some advocates of qualitative research methods have questioned the very notion of objectivity. They contend that in psychological research it is inextricably bound up with the normative beliefs of groups (chiefly Western, economically powerful, white males), who have for so long occupied pivotal roles at the heart of political, economic, cultural and social life. Chiefly these notions pertain to maintaining emotional and physical distance between investigators and investigated and the perpetuation of this as a standard through the reproduction of existing power structures in each new generation. Under such conditions, our ideas of truth (which for example stress universality, emotional neutrality and freedom from moral values) mirror the means by which those in power have conducted themselves in the pursuit of both personal and public profit (see Figure 13.1 below).

Because of this it is argued that the use of impersonal methods – most notably those which describe aspects of human relationships in a quantitative fashion – contribute to our alienation and can tell us little useful about what it means to be human. The dismissal of quantitative methods of working have also frequently been accompanied by calls to reject repeatability as a necessary criterion for scientific truth – an ironic call in light of the replicability problem in psychological research. The call to reject replicability ultimately rests on the view that human meanings and actions conjoin at unique moments and may never be repeated.

There is undoubted force (both polemical and logical) behind this argument. Paradoxically, however, rejecting ideas of truth and objectivity would require that the very categories critics have used to locate the origins of the manufacture and distortion of "objectivity" and "truth" (e.g. social class, ethnicity, disability, and

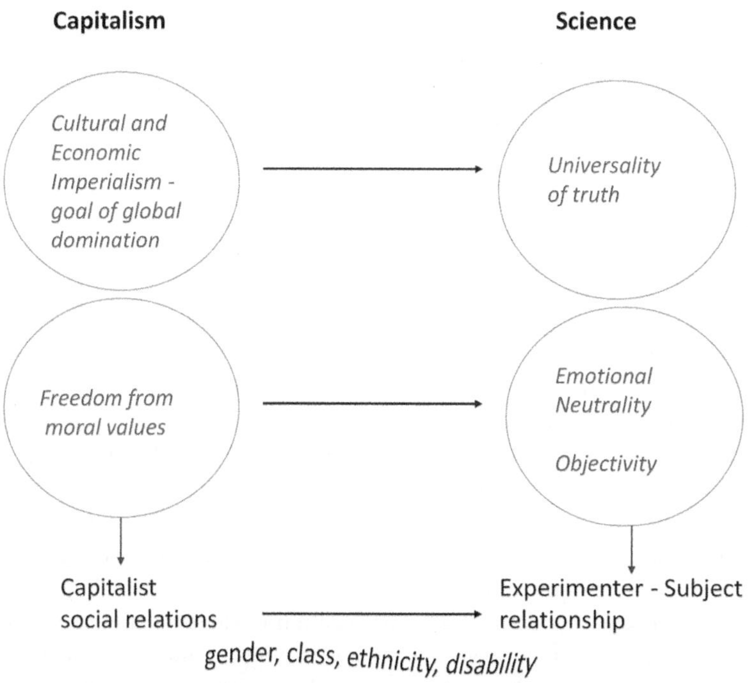

FIGURE 13.1 Capitalist social relations and science.

gender) must be reconsidered. Rather than universally objective categories these are regarded as socially constructed entities (see Berger & Luckman, 1967) active in particular historical periods and producing contingent effects within them. This perspective raises important questions about what the aims of knowledge are or could be. If they are merely linked to some competing ideological project, then the dangers of the political manufacture of scientific truth loom on the horizon. It can be argued that the questionable status of schizophrenia – as well as other mental health categories (e.g. ADHD) are already the consequences of the colonisation of science by ideology and power. History already bears witness to the costs of such colonisation. The rejection of Mendelian genetics in the Soviet Union during the Stalinist era for example led to mass famine – the promotion of racial science in the Nazi era to genocide and world war.

When we consider the problems of realism and replicability together we need to ask what goals should inform research. Despite inherent problems "truth" remains an important barometer. When it is rejected and replaced throughout a society by a state (or corporate) sanctioned substitute – i.e. where truth is what those with clout say it is – then tyranny appears a willing benefactor. And what begins with intellectual tyranny is usually the forerunner of physical tyranny to come.

A more considered criticism of scientific practise in both the quantitative and qualitative realms accepts the presence of bias emanating from certain interest groups and indeed regards the study of this as important in its own right. Furthermore the addition of qualitative research to extend the role of human meaning in scientific discourse is welcome. Proponents of "Critical Realism", as it has come to be called, accept the basic tenets of scientific realism (i.e. that the world exists independent of our attempts to describe it and that successful scientific theories describe relationships between theoretical constructs approximating to those which exist between real entities or processes in the world). Against this backdrop they seek simultaneously to reveal the distorting influences of specific social and historical processes as they bear upon the institutional organisation of science and the actual reasoning of practising scientists. Because historical analyses reveal that numerous changes in the fundamental tenets of scientific reasoning have occurred (see Chalmers, 2013) in line with Feyerabend's arguments, a universal conception of scientific method which is true for all time is rejected. However at any one time the process of asking questions and interpreting evidence is broadly similar in all scientific disciplines, although each favours the use of methods and techniques that are particularly well suited to handling the problems which arise in that domain. The more common elements of what comprises scientific method in the modern age do not require the use of mathematical or statistical computations per se. What is crucial is, as we have said, the gathering of data for the purpose of generating and testing ideas about what is or can be observed. The reiterative use of this process informing and in turn influenced by the cultural milieu is what leads over time to a more accurate and useful account of things (see Figure 13.2).

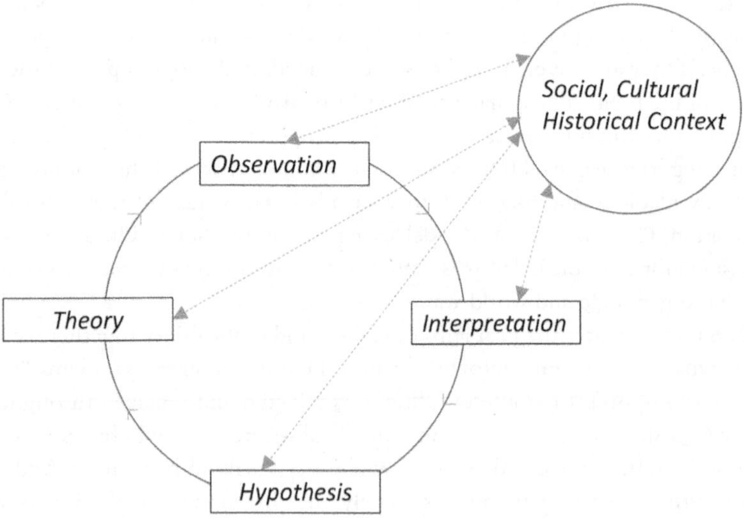

FIGURE 13.2 The contextual nature of science as an iterative cycle.

Experience and science: the moral landscape

The argument thus far is that although science does not follow perfectly prescribed rules, and is subject to a number of different sources of bias, its organisation and practice tend over time to favour the survival of well-ordered theoretical schemes able to coherently account for large bodies of data, whilst at the same time possessing sufficient flexibility to make novel testable predictions. The imperfect nature of this process requires continuous reflection on what is undertaken and due thought given to the external influences upon the work. This ideally requires a well-informed lay public to scrutinise it. The low value accorded to critical and independent thinking in contemporary society do not make this task easy.

To address the issue of whether science is a suitable vehicle for undertaking the study of experience we need to first look at the wider question of its moral fitness to do so. One of the fiercest objections to a scientific study of experience contends that science objectifies human beings, ignores our fundamental status as sentient, reasoning, feeling, self-conscious creatures and hence threatens our dignity. It must be admitted that in the name of science, many acts have been carried out which provide ammunition for this argument. The twentieth century witnessed the forging of ever-closer links between the global military industrial complex and the scientific community. The means to wage mass campaigns of technological and psychological war against civilian populations (Glover, 1999) has been made possible only because science increasingly serves the interests of big business – and the manufacture of the means to kill and terrorise people with ever greater "efficiency" is big business. To many this is a source of dismay and a grotesque parody of the beauty and elegance which are more fitting testaments to scientific enterprise.

One of the problems is that science was originally invented, constructed and elaborated for the study of natural objects. Unlike inanimate objects, however, the behaviour of people in objective three-dimensional space is a function of their experience of themselves, their experience of others and their experience of the world around them, as well as the behaviour of other persons and material objects. This poses unique challenges for the study of experience. The task of constructing an appropriate science of persons has for some been the holy grail of psychology. As an explicit goal it has been addressed by engineer turned psychologist George Kelly (Kelly, 1955) and psychiatrist R. D. Laing (Laing & Cooper, 1964; Laing, 1967). Through his theory of personal constructs, Kelly sought to develop an idea of the "person as scientist" actively constructing and reconstructing the building blocks of their mental life as they negotiated their way through the successive experiments which constituted their unfolding life. Highly influential though this has at times been, its radical premise of reconstructing psychology as an entire discipline has floundered. Meanwhile the emerging meta-disciplines of neuroscience, cognitive science, health science and social science threaten to pick off the various constituents of what appears increasingly to be a fragmented discipline.

Laing's efforts embodied a synthesis of Marxism, Psychoanalysis and Existentialism in which normality was depicted as an estranged and alienated state. He set out a radical agenda for a science of persons to support and discover pathways back to reality. As psychiatry became entrenched in biological reductionism and the optimism of the 1960s faded, Laing's critique was left on the sidelines (see Roberts & Hewer, 2015, for an update on its continuing relevance). The current dominance of global free market capitalism and its invasion of the private domain (through for example the multiple channels of pornography, the "talk show" and social media, whereby people bare their bodies, their souls and their personal photographs for mass market entertainment) only makes the need for us to reassess our position all the more urgent. The problem thus remains – how can we study experience in a way that does not do psychological violence to us?

Experience and method

A consistent difficulty for practitioners of the scientific method has been what status to accord the self-reported experiences of humans. Dreams, near-death experiences, apparent instances of telepathy, and alien abductions are just some of the reported experiences that scientists must contend with and yet the private unobservable nature of that experience seems to render it unsuitable for scientific scrutiny. Can systematic methods of enquiry be applied to both the empirical data of self-reports and within the experiential realm? If so, how are these to be approached?

Anchored in the philosophy of realism, one strategy is to seek correlations between such reports and other more easily observable phenomena and attempt to establish the conditions (e.g. biological, cognitive, social or cultural) under which such reports are made. Readers will note the ubiquity of this strategy in the scientific investigation of paranormal claims. This strategy might tell us something about the nature of the reports, but by itself is insufficient to establish the veracity of the putative experiences the reports allude to. Evidence for the existence of both sleep and dreaming for example (see Chapter 8) is reliant on the report of private experiences by human subjects (Malcolm, 1959). This remains the case no matter what the level of technological sophistication we have developed to investigate brain activity. In the case of sleep, these reports are validated by the appearance of particular behavioural and physiological indicators linked to levels of arousal which occur immediately prior to a report. Where dreams are concerned it is more the cognitive correlates of reporting, in combination with the temporal correlate of reporting them immediately subsequent to waking that points to the existence of a different mental state – which is unobservable to others, occurring under the conditions of sleep. This inference is further aided by the fact that an overwhelming majority of people report these experiences. We would stress that what is being validated here is the notion that dreaming as a different mental state occurs – not the contents of any one particular dream. Despite earlier misapprehensions, dreams are reported from all stages of sleep and not simply during the stage where rapid eye movements occur (REM sleep) (Foulkes, 1960). Applied to experiential reports, systematic investigations of their properties, correlates and implications are likely to yield valuable insights into what these mean – not just in framing causal explanations for these reports (i.e. what the reports can tell us about the internal and external realities in which people live) but what they also say to us about human life and the struggles which being human entail.

Similar rationales have been employed in the study of claimed alien abductions (Chapter 5) and near-death experiences (see Chapter 6). It is important to note however that once scientific practitioners are satisfied that a particular phenomenon is real, if they wish to explore further the nature of a particular type of conscious experience then they must orientate themselves with respect to the actual contents of the experience and systematically explore ways in which the experiences can be modified or transformed. Such means may be externally induced, e.g. through drugs, brain stimulation or sensory deprivation, but also through intended acts of will or cognition, which are themselves repeatable and which others may learn through instruction (as in meditation or mindfulness training). It may therefore be argued that a certain type of systematic questioning and evaluation of the nature of some kinds of experience and its attendant possibilities is possible only through someone having the experience. It is important to note here that this is only made possible through the replicable nature of a phenomenon. The initial stages of scientific exploration however must begin with establishing the veracity of experience – determining its boundary conditions – moving through exploring its content and structure and proceeding to ascertain the means to mould and transform the experience (see Figure 13.3 for a summary of this process).

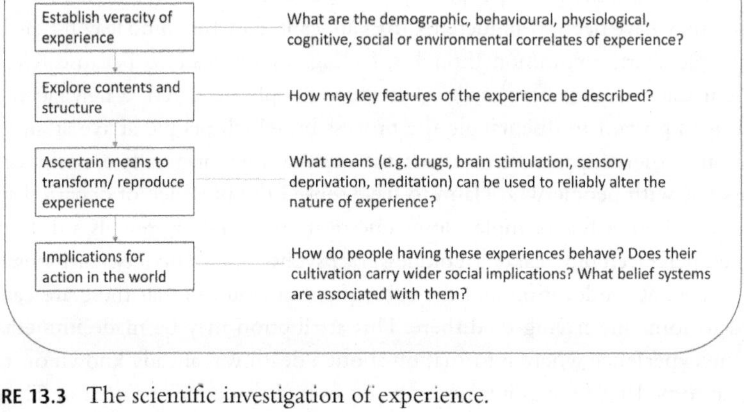

FIGURE 13.3 The scientific investigation of experience.

Although experiences such as dreaming, remembering and consciously experiencing the world are private, we assume their veracity in others, in part through our mutual identification with them as beings like us who have the same sort of conscious experiences we do, and live in the same world as us. When it comes to claims of more esoteric experiences such as alien abductions, this type of common ground simply does not exist.

In addition to exploring the veracity, content, form and malleability of experience, all psychologies of experience also invariably address some aspect of how experiential knowledge contributes to and transforms one's actions in the world. Such study can involve taking an anthropological stance toward the culture where certain experiences are cultivated or are held to occur. This may comprise asking how belief in particular experiences shapes the actions of those who adhere to it.

In the terms we have just described then, science is not opposed in any fundamental way to the study of experience – though it can certainly be argued that mainstream psychology has yet to give it its due importance (Itten & Roberts, 2014). Where science differs from common sense is in the interpretative stance adopted toward reported experience. "Seeing is believing" so the saying goes. And though Aristotle held reliance on the senses to be critical for establishing scientific truth, this criterion has long since been abandoned (Chalmers, 2013). By itself, experience cannot and is not regarded as sufficient evidence for the independent reality of what people observe. One's own conviction in the absolute reality of what one has experienced or in what one believes cannot stand as a criterion for truth – compelling though it may on occasion be. This does not mean that such conviction is ignored. However the difficulties of interpreting reports of certain experiences – particularly the kind addressed by the contributors to this book – are compounded by virtue of their being frequently presented in terms of an interpretation – an explanation of their origins, rather than an account only of the contents (the phenomenology) of the experience. This is a subtle but important point.

Reports of alien abductions, out-of-body experiences (OBEs) or apparent telepathy for example are usually described in terms which already presuppose the causes behind them, i.e. people report experiences of being abducted by aliens because they have been so abducted, OBEs are caused by the mind leaving the body and people sharing common thoughts, feelings or impressions because telepathy (thought transmission) between two or more people occurred. When faced with this, it is important to disentangle the process by which people arrive at an interpretation of their experience from what it was that they originally experienced. In discussions with people who claim to have sensed the presence of departed spirits in haunted houses for example, closer questioning frequently reveals a distinction between perceived physical (e.g. coldness) or psychological (anxiety, fear) sensations experienced at the location and the subsequent attribution that these are causally linked to someone having died there. This attribution may be made immediately after the experience where information about a death was already known or it may occur at some later time as information comes into someone's possession. The psychology of how and why people make attributions about the world they live in has much to offer here. It can help us throw light not just on the wild and wonderful reported experiences which people say they have, but also their beliefs about the very way the world is structured. One of the critical features which distinguish scientific from lay accounts of events concerns not just the methods adopted to arrive at an answer but also what is being accounted for. Pletcher (1987, p. 136) expressed this succinctly: "an important part of our understanding of the world lies in knowing what *not* to explain". Thus science begins with the report as the prime data, not the assumed reality of what is reported as experienced. Similarly it may be more instructive to investigate people's understanding of coincidence rather than to begin by assuming that some *acausal* connecting principle (e.g. synchronicity, telepathy) underlies the temporal juxtaposition of two events which to one person are highly meaningful. At the same time we must remain open to surprise and receptive to the myriad possibilities that the mystery of existence may throw us.

Let me repeat, this does not mean that science is antagonistic to experience – merely that something more is required before one moves from a person's expressed belief in a phenomenon to believing wholeheartedly in the reality of the phenomenon as described. The correct attitude of the scientist faced with reports of unusual experiences is to seek further evidence for or against their existence. It does not mean that such accounts must *necessarily* be dismissed. Absence of evidence is not of course the same as evidence of absence. However when very many people make persistent extraordinary claims – such as the presence of alien beings on Earth – in the absence of any compelling supporting evidence (which one would logically expect to exist were the claims actually true) and where ad hoc untestable explanations are continually proposed to account for the failure to produce evidence, one is entitled to remain sceptical until such evidence turns up (Sagan, 1997).

We need then to exercise considerable caution where beliefs are concerned, particularly those which are firmly held despite contradictory evidence and which appear to be unfalsifiable by any criterion – the same goes for dogmatic acceptance of scientific beliefs held in the face of contradictory evidence.

One stance investigators into unusual (or indeed controversial) beliefs can take is to contemplate the kind of contradictory evidence which might lead a rational person to give them up. Of course, to varying degrees we have all been guilty at one time or another of holding onto beliefs which have passed their sell-by date, and methods suited to investigating unusual beliefs and experiences, if they belong to the general corpus of scientific knowledge, will also very likely be fruitful in the study of more familiar aspects of human behaviour. It must be remembered however that beliefs cannot be validated in the same way that the existence of different states of consciousness can. No amount of neurophysiological reductionism will ever be able to point to the neurophysiological location of our everyday beliefs (Dennett, 1995). Beliefs are unavoidably grounded in our shared social realities. On their basis people may be deemed criminal, eccentric, worthy of psychiatric treatment or even murdered. But is there a paradox here? We are saying on the one hand that science is concerned with discovering what is real and true and on the other we are faced with a social reality which is grounded on consensus – a consensus which numerous studies of human history show us to be malleable. Under such conditions we are brought back to the question of how science can lay claim to any kind of objective truth about the world. We have seen that such claims can only be made providing the social consensus that exists is not one brought about by coercion or power alone, nor a collection of simple personal opinions (or shared common sense) – but which depends on adherence to broadly agreed conventions for collecting and reporting data, formulating conjectures or hypotheses to explain the data and logical and empirical argument to support them. The nature and limitations of science need to be well understood.

At the end of the day, no theories can lay claim to a final or ultimate truth (Chalmers, 2013). Scientific truths, unlike dogmatic assertion, must of necessity be approximate and temporal in their nature and open to revision. They are fallible but therein lies one of their major strengths. Science is of course not the only useful way to understand human experience – but if we are to use our experiences as a basis for understanding the world we live in – and not merely a source of recreation or wonder – then an alliance with a systematic critical outlook can yield useful rewards. Some of the claims made by people regarding their experiences present fundamental challenges to views of the world which are dominant in the scientific and political community. They must not be rejected simply on the basis of this discordance. Scientific dogma must never replace the fair and impartial assessment of unpopular ideas (Sheldrake, 2012). An in a fair and critical hearing, matters of evidence and logic must be given their due weight.

Suggested further reading

Chalmers, A. F. (2013). *What is this thing called Science?* (4th Edition). Maidenhead: Open University Press, McGraw Hill.

Popper, K. (1972). *Conjectures and refutations*. London: Routledge and Kegan Paul.

Sagan, C. (1997). *The demon-haunted world*. London: Headline Book Publishing.

14

COGNITION AND BELIEF

David Groome and Robin Law

Hamlet:	*Do you see yonder cloud that's almost in shape of a camel?*
Polonius:	*By the mass, and 'tis like a camel, indeed.*
Hamlet:	*Methinks it is like a weasel.*
Polonius:	*It is backed like a weasel.*
Hamlet:	*Or like a whale?*
Polonius:	*Very like a whale.*

William Shakespeare, *Hamlet*

Cognition

Cognition is the processing of information by the brain, in order to make sense of the world around us and to deal with it in an effective manner. This involves a number of different cognitive processes, including perception, memory and thinking. None of these processes are infallible, which means that we are all subject to misunderstandings, illusions and misjudgements. However, people differ from one another considerably in their cognitive abilities, and it is possible that those who are more prone to cognitive errors may also be more likely to acquire inaccurate beliefs. One possible example is our ability to make accurate judgements about chance events and coincidences.

Chance and coincidence

Unexpected events and coincidences happen from time to time, and when they do it is a matter of personal judgement whether we attribute them to chance or to some other factor such as paranormal influences. Consider the following examples, and try to decide whether they offer support for the occurrence of paranormal phenomena or whether they can be dismissed as merely chance events:

1. In an experiment on ESP, the experimenter turns over playing cards one at a time and tries to transmit to a partner whether he is looking at a red card or a black card. Although the partner cannot see the cards, he begins the experiment by guessing the correct colour three times in a row. Is this just luck or did he use ESP?
2. A student looking through a list of his classmates discovers that one of the other students has the same birthday as him. There are only 23 people in the class so this seems to him to be an extremely unlikely coincidence. Would you agree?
3. A woman dreams about a plane crash, then wakes up the next day to hear on the news that there actually has been an air crash. Was the dream a premonition, or was it just a coincidence?

In all of these examples we are faced with the same basic question – can the events be dismissed as mere chance, or were they just too improbable for such a mundane explanation? This question really is quite fundamental to every claim of a "psychic" or "paranormal" experience, and in order to answer it we need to be able to judge how probable it was that such an event could have occurred by chance alone.

Probability judgements

All of these examples require a judgement of how probable the events were to occur by chance. In some cases this level of probability can be precisely measured, and it is usually expressed either as a percentage or as a fraction. For example, the probability (P) of a coin falling down "heads" is one chance in two, which can be expressed as $P = 50$ per cent or alternatively $p = 0.5$.

In example (1) above (the ESP experiment), the probability of guessing the colour (i.e. red or black) of each card correctly is 50 per cent, so the chances of guessing a whole series of cards correctly will be halved with each card selected. This means that there is a 50 per cent chance of guessing the first card, a 25 per cent chance of guessing two in succession, and a 12.5 per cent chance of guessing three in a row. From this we can conclude that there is actually a fairly high probability of making three correct guesses in a row by sheer chance ($p = 0.125$), so there is no reason to look for any other explanation.

In example (2) above (the shared birthday) we can again calculate the probability of two people sharing the same birthday from a group of given size, though it is rather more complicated this time because we need to consider every possible comparison between each member of the group and every one of the other 23 members. This actually produces a surprisingly large number of pair comparisons, and consequently the chance of a shared birthday is higher than most people think. In fact the chance of finding a shared birthday in a group of 23 people is 50 per cent ($p = 0.5$), so such a coincidence is actually far from remarkable and can even be expected to occur as often as not. This surprisingly high probability illustrates how people tend to underestimate the chances of an event happening when there are a large number of possibilities or combinations to take into account.

In example (3) above (the plane crash premonition) we are dealing with events which cannot be readily quantified or measured. How likely are we to dream of a plane crash? And what are the chances of a real plane crash occurring on the same day? A precise probability figure cannot be calculated, so we will have to settle for a fairly rough estimate. What we do know is that air crashes are reported on the TV news fairly regularly, and dreams of disasters and accidents are also fairly common. If you multiply those odds by 60 million (the number of people in Britain) then the chances are that quite a large number of British people will dream of an air disaster the night before an air crash actually happens somewhere in the world. We must therefore conclude that the dream can be adequately explained by mere coincidence, so there is no need to assume any psychic or paranormal explanation.

These examples highlight the fundamental question we must ask when investigating claims of "paranormal" experiences. We need to estimate the probability of the particular event occurring by chance alone. If the event was reasonably likely, then we need look no further than chance or coincidence to provide an explanation. We should only start to consider the possibility of a non-chance explanation (e.g. the intervention of psychic forces) when the probability of a chance occurrence is extremely low. Even then, of course, we should not automatically accept the paranormal explanation, as there may be other possible causes which need to be ruled out. For example, in the ESP example above there could have been some subliminal cues passing between the two partners in the experiment, or one of them could have found some way of cheating. You should always look for any possible alternative explanations for claims of "paranormal" experiences, and ask yourself the question, "Could anything else have caused this?"

It is also important to bear in mind that accounts of psychic experiences tend to be reported selectively. Successful predictions and "premonitions" tend to attract publicity, whereas unsuccessful ones tend to go unreported.

One final point of caution about reports of paranormal experiences is that someone's personal experience is not scientific evidence. The example quoted above concerning the premonition about an air crash was based on a real event, told to me years ago by a friend. He claimed to have dreamed of a disaster the day before it happened, but this claim was based on a purely subjective experience which could easily have been subject to error or delusion. He could even have invented the whole episode, and indeed for all you know I might have done.

Probability judgements and belief in the paranormal

There is some evidence (Blackmore & Troscianko, 1985) that people who believe in paranormal phenomena may be less accurate in making judgements of probability than non-believers. More specifically, the believers are more likely to underestimate the probability of a chance event. This could help to explain why they are more likely to accept a paranormal account of their experiences, since they are likely to consider an unusual event as being so improbable as to be beyond coincidence, whereas those with a more accurate grasp of probability would judge the same event as falling within the bounds of chance.

A number of experiments have provided tentative support for the hypothesis that believers in the paranormal have a tendency to underestimate probabilities. These experiments have used a variety of tasks, including estimates of probability in computer-controlled coin-tossing (Blackmore & Troscianko, 1985), random number generation (Brugger et al., 1990), and estimations of the probability of shared birthdays (Matthews & Blackmore, 1995). Although these experiments provided some support for the "probability misjudgement" theory of paranormal belief, not all studies have found this (Blackmore, 1997).

Musch and Ehrenberg (2002) confirmed the finding that believers in the paranormal were more prone to making errors of probabilistic reasoning, but they also found that believers scored poorly on a range of different cognitive tests. They therefore suggested that the impaired probabilistic reasoning of the believers group could just be a reflection of a general lack of cognitive ability. Several other studies have reported similar findings. Wiseman and Watt (2006) carried out a review of previous studies and concluded that many did in fact report that believers in the paranormal scored lower on a variety of cognitive tests than did non-believers. Other studies failed to find such a difference, so this issue remains unresolved for the time being and requires further research. However, Wiseman and Watt conclude that there is considerable evidence for the "misattribution" hypothesis, which assumes that believers in the paranormal have a tendency to mistakenly attribute paranormal causes to experiences which have a normal explanation. The misattribution hypothesis receives further support from studies investigating the cognitive performance of those who believe in the paranormal, such as their tendency to find connections and images in their perceptual input. French (2012) sums up the influence of probability judgements on paranormal belief by concluding that "people are very poor intuitive statisticians".

Finding shapes and images in random patterns

You have probably had the occasional experience of seeing faces in the clouds, or noticing familiar shapes in a wallpaper pattern. Everyone probably has this kind of experience occasionally, but it seems that some individuals are particularly prone to seeing faces in the clouds, and these people also seem to be more likely to attribute coincidences to paranormal phenomena.

Several studies have shown that believers in the paranormal are more likely to find meaningful shapes in an array of random dots than are non-believers (Brugger et al., 1993; Blackmore & Moore, 1994). Believers are also more likely to find meaningful connections between randomly paired items (Brugger et al., 1994; Wiseman & Smith, 2002). Identifying shapes and patterns in our sensory input is of course crucial to our ability to make sense of the world, and Bartlett (1932) argued that the use of stored patterns in the brain ("schemas") to analyse our perceptual input was a fundamental part of the cognitive process. However, the brain would be unable to process an unlimited number of meaningful patterns and images impinging on it at a given moment, so there are probably neural mechanisms at work which limit or inhibit some of the weaker patterns. Brugger and Taylor (2003) suggest that some individuals have weaker inhibition of the activation of semantic networks than others, and will thus be more likely to find patterns and shapes in their perceptual input, even with the weakest of cues. Brugger and Taylor further speculate that such individuals are likely to be more prone to seeing shapes and patterns in their surroundings, and in extreme cases they may be more prone to experience delusions and hallucinations of the kind reported in schizophrenia. This view is entirely speculative, but it is at least consistent with the finding that schizophrenics are more likely to believe in the paranormal than are other groups (Thalbourne & French, 1995; Peltzer, 2003). However, this is not the same as saying that paranormal belief indicates a schizophrenic tendency, and it has been emphasised that there is no justification for regarding such beliefs as pathological (Williams & Irwin, 1991; Wiseman & Watt, 2006).

Suggestibility and fantasy proneness

There is some evidence that believers in the paranormal tend to be more vulnerable to suggestion than non-believers. For example, Wiseman et al. (2003) arranged a séance, during which the "medium" (actually an actor) suggested that the table was levitating (rising into the air). After the séance, believers were more likely than non-believers to agree that the table had levitated, though in reality it had not moved. In a similar experiment in which an alleged psychic suggested that a key was being bent by psychic powers, Wilson and French (2014) found that believers were more likely to be convinced that the key was actually bending. This effect was even stronger when other members of the audience commented to the group that they had seen the key bend, indicating the influence of social pressure.

As well as being more suggestible, it seems that believers in the paranormal are also more prone to fantasy, so that for example they may believe that they have actually experienced an event when in fact they have imagined it (Blackmore, 1984). In a study by Irwin (1990), participants were tested for their recall of childhood memories, and it was found that believers in the paranormal had more difficulty than others in distinguishing real from imagined events.

Wilson and French (2006) found that believers were more likely to hold false memories (i.e. memories for experiences which did not actually happen to them). They asked their participants to recall whether they had seen actual TV footage of several major news events which had been recorded on film, but they included one event (a nightclub bombing in Bali) for which no such footage actually existed. Those who described seeing such footage were therefore mistaken, and this occurred mainly among the paranormal believers.

Smith et al. (2009) used personality questionnaires to show that believers scored higher than non-believers on the "Openness to Experience" scale of the NEO Personality Inventory, and scored especially high on the "Fantasy" subscale. They found that believers also scored higher on the Zuckerman "Sensation Seeking" scale.

Irwin (1993) found that paranormal beliefs and fantasy proneness both tended to be more prevalent in individuals who had suffered physical abuse in childhood. Irwin suggested that fantasy and paranormal beliefs might help abused individuals to regain a sense of control over their lives, to counteract the sense of helplessness generated by physical abuse. Watt et al. (2007) also found a negative correlation between perceived control in childhood and adult paranormal belief. They argued that for some people paranormal belief is used as a psychological coping mechanism following early experiences of diminished control caused by abuse.

It is likely that individuals who hold on to paranormal beliefs, regardless of the lack of supporting evidence, must derive some benefit from these beliefs. Zusne and Jones (1982) suggested that a belief in the paranormal satisfies an individual's need to gain some kind of understanding of the events in their life. Perhaps they feel that such understanding will provide them with an advantage in dealing with events and with other people. Belief in the paranormal may also provide comfort and reassurance. For example, if you believe in astrology then you may think that you can predict future events and use this foreknowledge to make important decisions. If you believe in survival and mediumship then you may find it comforting to think that you can still communicate with friends and relatives who have died. And it is also comforting to believe that after your own death you will continue to function and survive in the afterlife, and perhaps even stay in touch with loved ones. Some of these forms of reassurance bear an obvious similarity to the comforting effects of religious belief. Indeed, Irwin (1993) showed that religious people are more likely to believe in the paranormal too, and Hergovich et al. (2005) suggest that in some cases people adopt paranormal beliefs as a replacement for previously held religious views.

Intuitive and analytic thinking

In recent years evidence has emerged that some individuals may be more prone to belief in the paranormal due to differences in the style of cognitive processing they tend to employ. It has been found that those who employ an "intuitive" rather than an "analytic" thinking style are more likely to believe in paranormal phenomena.

This research centres around what is known as the dual-process model of human processing, so named because it describes two divergent styles of problem solving and decision making (e.g. Kahneman, 2003, 2011; Evans & Stanovich, 2013). The first of these thinking styles is a fast, unconscious process, incorporating intuition and heuristics, and not requiring working memory (referred to as "type 1 processing" or "intuitive thinking"). In contrast, the second thinking style involves a slower and more effortful conscious process, which requires the use of working memory ("type 2 processing" or "analytic thinking"). While intuitive thinking is a faster process, it is also a somewhat error-prone method of problem solving. Analytic thinking involves complex assessment of the problem, including a critical evaluation of any initial intuition, and assessment of the logical steps involved in forming a solution. Although analytic thinking is slower and more effortful, it is a less error-prone process and better suited to forming logical conclusions (Evans & Curtis-Holmes, 2005; Kahneman, 2011).

These two thinking styles were first identified in a series of studies of human problem solving and decision making by Daniel Kahneman and Amos Tversky, and later reviewed in detail in the book *Thinking, fast and slow* (Kahneman, 2011). The dual-process model proposes that we employ an intuitive approach when first presented with a problem, which may continue unless we subsequently apply analytic processing which allows us to reflect upon, and potentially dismiss, our earlier intuitions (Kahneman, 2003; Evans & Curtis-Holmes, 2005). However, we may sometimes rely entirely on intuitive processing with little or no analytic thought, especially when we need to respond to something very quickly. Evans and Curtis-Holmes (2005) demonstrated this by having a group of participants try to solve syllogistic problems within a 10-second time limit. They found that under such a time restriction people tend to rely mainly on intuitive thought, and are thus more prone to belief bias and logically incorrect responses. It has also been suggested that whether or not we move beyond intuitive processing and engage in analytic thinking may also depend on whether we feel a sufficient sense of "rightness" from the initial intuition (Thompson & Morsanyi, 2012).

You can probably think of some examples of this in everyday life. When presented with a problem, we may sometimes rely on our immediate "gut feeling", or an unconscious "rule-of-thumb" to make sense of the problem and form a decision (intuitive thinking). We may persist with these intuitive ideas if they feel sufficiently "right" to us, or if we are under pressure to respond quickly. However, we are more likely to make logical errors if relying on these intuitions. In contrast, at other times we may make the effort to think in detail about our prior intuitions and prejudices, and apply a more abstract approach to the problem, weighing up the evidence for each potential solution before making a decision (analytic thinking), and in doing so we are less likely to make logical errors.

There is good evidence to show that people differ in the extent to which they rely on intuitive and analytical thought, and these differences in cognitive style have been shown to predict a wide range of beliefs and behavioural outcomes. It has been shown that those who tend to adopt an analytical cognitive style are less likely to believe in the paranormal (Pennycook et al., 2012; Bouvet & Bonnefon, 2015; Gray & Gallo, 2016), and this association is evident even when comparing individuals who are otherwise very similar in terms of their general cognitive abilities, prior religious belief, sex, age, political ideology, and education. Gray and Gallo (2016) tested over two thousand participants who were either firm believers or highly sceptical of the existence of psychic powers. The results of their study demonstrated that believers and non-believers performed similarly well on tests of both long-term and short-term memory, but that non-believers consistently out-performed believers across a range of tasks assessing analytical thinking and vocabulary, such as evaluating the strength of arguments and performing logical reasoning tasks. Notably, they found that both groups had reported a similar "need for cognition" and so the poorer analytical thinking of believers was not likely to be merely a result of low motivation.

The evidence therefore suggests that even if a person is very good at other cognitive tasks, they are still likely to hold paranormal beliefs if they tend to rely upon intuitive processing, and equally an individual who is very poor at other cognitive tasks may still be resistant to belief in the paranormal if they favour an analytic cognitive style. So the extent to which we are willing and able to engage in analytic thought may provide us with a very good explanation for why some people are prone to believing in the paranormal. A lack of analytical thinking may undermine a person's ability to critically examine the evidence presented in favour of paranormal belief.

In summary, it has been found that believers in the paranormal are more prone to fantasy, false beliefs, suggestion, probability misjudgements, finding patterns or connections in random arrays, and having a more intuitive and less analytic cognitive disposition. These findings would seem to offer a reasonable explanation for the fact that such individuals are more likely to acquire a belief in paranormal phenomena. Indeed, Wiseman and Watt (2006), in their review of studies linking paranormal belief and cognitive factors, conclude that most studies offer support for the misattribution hypothesis, which proposes that believers in the paranormal have a tendency to mistakenly attribute paranormal causes to what are basically normal experiences. However, this does not necessarily mean that believers in the paranormal are in some way inadequate or flawed individuals. Believers in the paranormal have a tendency to accept unproven beliefs more readily than the average person, which merely represents a particular point on a scale of belief proneness, just as people vary between extremes of introversion and extraversion. Nor is it clear that believers are disadvantaged by their acceptance of unproven phenomena. Whilst they are probably more likely to make incorrect judgements as a result of their beliefs, they may benefit from the reassurance gained from a perception of life as being more predictable, and an increased sense of control over events.

Many of the findings and observations about belief in the paranormal which have been discussed in this book also apply to other forms of belief, such as religious beliefs and political ideologies. It is to be hoped that the insights gained from studying paranormal beliefs offer a good starting point for the investigation of these other belief systems.

REFERENCES

Abalakina-Paap, M., Stephan, W. G., Craig, T., & Gregory, W. L. (1999). Beliefs in conspiracies. *Political Psychology*, 20(3), 637–647. http://doi.org/10.1111/0162-895X.00160.

Abu-Izzeddin, N. M. (1984). *The Druze: A new study of their history, faith and society*. Leiden: Brill.

Adler, S. R. (2011). *Sleep paralysis: Night-mares, nocebos, and the mind-body connection*. Piscataway, NJ: Rutgers University Press.

Agnoli, F., & Krantz, D. H. (1989). Suppressing natural heuristics by formal instruction: The case of the conjunction fallacy. *Cognitive Psychology*, 21(4), 515–550. http://doi.org/10.1016/0010-0285(89)90017-0.

Alexander, R. D. (2006). *The concept of God and the meaning of life*. Unpublished MS (cited in Crespi & Summers, 2014).

Alexander, R. D. (2013). Religion, evolution and the quest for global harmony. In K. Summers & B. Crespi (Eds.), *Human social evolution: The foundational works of Richard D. Alexander* (pp. 384–425). Oxford: Oxford University Press.

Ames, D. R. (2004). Inside the mind reader's tool kit: Projection and stereotyping in mental state inference. *Journal of Personality and Social Psychology*, 87(3), 340–353. http://doi.org/10.1037/0022-3514.87.3.340.

Appelle, S. (1996). The abduction experience: A critical evaluation of theory and evidence. *Journal of UFO Studies*, 6, 29–79.

Appelle, S., Lynn, S. J., Newman, L., & Malaktaris, A. (2014). Alien abduction experiences. In E. Cardeña, S. J. Lynn, & S. Krippner (Eds.), *Varieties of anomalous experience: Examining the scientific evidence*. 2nd ed. (pp. 213–240). Washington, DC: American Psychological Association.

Argyle, M. (1988). *Bodily communication* (2nd ed.). London: Methuen.

Aristotle (1996). *Poetics*. London: Penguin.

Augustine, K. (2007). Does paranormal perception occur in near-death experiences? *Journal of Near Death Studies*, 25(4), 203–236.

Augustine, K. (2008). *Hallucinatory near-death experiences*. Retrieved 2 August 2016 from http://infidels.org/library/modern/keith_augustine/HNDEs.html.

Baggally, W. W., Johnson, A., Feilding, E., Taylor, M., & Lobb, J. (1906). Sittings with Mr Chambers. *Journal of the Society for Psychical Research*, 12, 197–203.

Baker, M. (2015). First results from psychology's largest reproducibility test. *Nature News*, 30 April. Retrieved December 2015 from www.nature.com/news/first-results-from-psychology-s-largest-reproducibility-test-1.17433.

Baker, R. A. (1992). *Hidden memories: Voices and visions from within*. Buffalo, NY: Prometheus.

Baker, R. A. (1997a). The aliens among us: Hypnotic regression revisited. In K. Frazier, B. Karr, & J. Nickell (Eds.), *The UFO invasion: The Roswell incident, alien abductions, and government coverups* (pp. 210–227). Amherst, NY: Prometheus.

Baker, R. A. (1997b). No aliens, no abductions: Just regressive hypnosis, waking dreams, and anthropomorphism. In K. Frazier, B. Karr, & J. Nickell (Eds.), *The UFO invasion: The Roswell incident, alien abductions, and government coverups* (pp. 249–265). Amherst, NY: Prometheus.

Banerjee, K., & Bloom, P. (2014). Why did this happen to me? Religious believers' and non-believers' teleological reasoning about life events. *Cognition*, 133, 277–303.

Barber, N. (2011). A cross-national test of the uncertainty hypothesis of religious belief. *Cross-Cultural Research*, 45, 318–333.

Barber, N. (2012). Country religiosity declines as material security increases. *Cross-Cultural Research*, 47, 42–50.

Barker, D., & Pasricha, S. K. (1979). Reincarnation cases in Fatehabad: A systematic survey in North India. *Journal of Asian and African Studies*, 14, 231–240.

Barlow, D. H. (2002). *Anxiety and its disorders: The nature and treatment of anxiety and panic* (2nd ed.). New York: Guilford Press.

Barrett, J. L., & Keil, F. C. (1996). Conceptualising a non-natural entity: Anthropomorphism in God concepts. *Cognitive Psychology*, 31, 219–247.

Barron, D., Morgan, K., Towell, T., Altemeyer, B., & Swami, V. (2014). Associations between schizotypy and belief in conspiracist ideation. *Personality and Individual Differences*, 70, 156–159. http://doi.org/10.1016/j.paid.2014.06.040.

Bartholomew, R. E., & Howard, G. S. (1998). *UFOs and alien contact: Two centuries of mystery*. Amherst, NY: Prometheus.

Bartholomew, R. E., Basterfield, K., & Howard, G. S. (1991). UFO abductees and contactees: Psychopathology or fantasy proneness? *Professional Psychology: Research and Practice*, 22, 215–222.

Bartlett, F. C. (1932). *Remembering*. Cambridge: Cambridge University Press.

Bartlett, J., & Miller, C. (2010). *The power of unreason: Conspiracy theories, extremism and counter-terrorism*. London: DEMOS.

Basterfield, K. (2001). Paranormal aspects of the UFO phenomenon: 1975–1999. *Australian Journal of Parapsychology*, 1, 30–55.

Basterfield, K., & Thalbourne, M. A. (2002). Belief in, and alleged experience of, the paranormal in ostensible UFO abductees. *Australian Journal of Parapsychology*, 2, 2–18.

Bateson, M., Nettle, D., & Roberts, G. (2006). Cues of being watched enhance cooperation in a real-world setting. *Biology Letters*, 2, 412–414.

Baumeister, R. F., & Sommer, K. L. (1997). Patterns in the bizarre: Common themes in satanic ritual abuse, sexual masochism, UFO abductions, factitious illness, and extreme love. *Journal of Social and Clinical Psychology*, 16, 213–223.

Baxt, W. G., Waeckerle, J. F., Berlin, J. A., & Callaham, M. L. (1998). Who reviews the reviewers? Feasibility of using a fictitious manuscript to evaluate peer reviewer performance. *Annals of Emergency Medicine*, 32(3 Pt. 1), 310–317.

Beauregard, M., St-Pierre, E. L., Rayburn, G., & Demers, P. (2012). Conscious mental activity during a deep hypothermic cardiocirculatory arrest? *Resuscitation,* 83(1), e19. doi:10.1016/j.resuscitation.2011.09.027.

Bègue, L., Bushman, B. J., Giancola, P. R., Subra, B., & Rosset, E. (2010). "There is no such thing as an accident", especially when people are drunk. *Personality and Social Psychology Bulletin,* 36, 1301–1304.

Beischel, J., & Schwartz, G. (2007). Anomalous information reception by research mediums demonstrated using a novel triple-blind protocol. *Explore: The Journal of Science and Healing,* 3, 23–27.

Beischel, J., & Zingrone, N. (2015). Mental mediumship. In E. Cardeña, J. Palmer, & D. Marcusson-Clavertz (Eds.), *Parapsychology: A handbook for the 21st century* (pp. 301–313). Jefferson, NC: McFarland & Co.

Beloff, J. (1993). *Parapsychology: A concise history.* London: Athlone Press.

Bem, D. J. (2011). Feeling the future: Experimental evidence for anomalous retroactive influences on cognition and affect. *Journal of Personality and Social Psychology,* 100, 407–425.

Bem, D. J., & Honorton, C. (1994). Does psi exist? Replicable evidence for an anomalous process of information transfer. *Psychological Bulletin,* 115, 4–18.

Bem, D. J., Palmer, J., & Broughton, R. S. (2001). Updating the ganzfeld database: A victim of its own success? *Journal of Parapsychology,* 65, 207–218.

Benjamin, W. (2007). *Reflections.* New York: Schocken Books.

Bennett, A. (2006). Reincarnation, sect unity, and identity among the Druze. *Ethnology,* 45, 87–104.

Berger, P. L., & Luckmann, T. (1967). *The social construction of reality.* Harmondsworth: Penguin.

Bering, J. (2011). *The god instinct: The psychology of souls, destiny, and the meaning of life.* London: Nicholas Brealey Publishing.

Bering, J. M., McLeod, K. A., & Shackelford, T. K. (2005). Reasoning about dead agents reveals possible adaptive trends. *Human Nature,* 16, 60–81.

Bernstein, M. (1956). *The search for Bridey Murphy.* Garden City, NY: Doubleday.

Besterman, T. (1932). The psychology of testimony in relation to paraphysical phenomena: Report of an experiment. *Proceedings of the Society for Psychical Research,* 40, 363–387.

Betts, R. B. (1988). *The Druze.* New Haven: Yale University Press.

Beyerstein, B. L. (1988). Neuropathology and the legacy of spiritual possession. *Skeptical Inquirer,* 12, 248–262.

Beyerstein, B. L. (1996). Possession and exorcism. In G. Stein (ed.), *The encycopedia of the paranormal.* Amherst, NY: Prometheus.

Beyerstein, B. L. (2007). The neurology of the weird: Brain states and anomalous experience. In S. Della Sala (ed.), *Tall tales about the mind and brain: Separating fact from fiction* (pp. 314–335). Oxford: Oxford University Press.

Bird, S. T., & Bogart, L. M. (2003). Birth control conspiracy beliefs, perceived discrimination, and contraception among African Americans: An exploratory study. *Journal of Health Psychology,* 8(2), 263–276. http://doi.org/10.1177/1359105303008002669.

Birdwell, J., & Littler, M. (2011). *After Osama: What Londoners think.* London: Demos.

Blackmore, S. J. (1982). *Beyond the body: An investigation of out-of-body experiences.* London: Heinemann.

Blackmore, S. J. (1984). A postal survey of OBEs and other experiences. *Journal of the Society for Psychical Research,* 52, 225–244.

Blackmore, S. J. (1993). *Dying to live: Science and the near-death experience.* London: Grafton.

Blackmore, S. (1994). Alien abduction: The inside story. *New Scientist,* 144, 19 November 1994, pp. 29–31.

Blackmore, S. (1997). Probability misjudgment and belief in the paranormal: A newspaper survey. *British Journal of Psychology*, 88, 683–689.

Blackmore, S. (1999). *The meme machine*. Oxford: Oxford University Press.

Blackmore, S. (2004). *Consciousness: An introduction*. Oxford: Oxford University Press.

Blackmore, S. J., & Moore, R. (1994). Seeing things: Visual recognition and belief in the paranormal. *European Journal of Parapsychology*, 10, 91–103.

Blackmore, S., & Seebold, M. (2000). The effect of horoscopes on women's relationships. *Correlation*, 19, 14–23.

Blackmore, S., & Troscianko, T. (1985). Belief in the paranormal: Probability judgements, illusory control, and the "chance baseline shift". *British Journal of Psychology*, 81, 455–468.

Blackmore, S. J., & Troscianko, T. (1988). The physiology of the tunnel. *Journal of Near-Death Studies*, 8, 15–28.

Blanke, O. (2004). Out of body experiences and their neural basis. *British Medical Journal*, 329, 1414–1415.

Blanke, O., & Arzy, S. (2005). The out-of-body experience: Disturbed self-processing at the temporo-parietal junction. *The Neuroscientist*, 11(1), 16–24.

Blanke, O., & Dieguez, S. (2009). Leaving body and life behind: Out-of-body and near-death experience. In S. Laureys & G. Tononi (Eds.), *The neurology of consciousness: Cognitive neuroscience and neuropathology* (pp. 303–325). Amsterdam: Elsevier.

Blanke, O, Landis, T., Spinelli, L., & Seeck, M. (2004). Out-of-body experience and autoscopy of neurological origin. *Brain*, 127, 243–258.

Bloecher, T., Clamar, A., & Hopkins, B. (1985). *Summary report on the psychological testing of nine individuals reporting UFO abduction experiences*. Mount Rainier, MD. Fund for UFO Research.

Bloom, P. U. (2004). *Descartes' baby*. New York: Basic Books.

Bogart, L. M., Wagner, G. J., Galvan, F. H., & Banks, D. (2010). Conspiracy beliefs about HIV are related to antiretroviral treatment nonadherence among African American men with HIV. *Journal of Acquired Immune Deficiency Syndromes*, 53(5), 648–655. http://doi.org/10.1097/QAI.0b013e3181c57dbc.

Bottoms, B. L., & Davis, S. L. (1997). The creation of satanic ritual abuse. *Journal of Social and Clinical Psychology*, 16, 112–132.

Bouvet, R., & Bonnefon, J. F. (2015). Non-reflective thinkers are predisposed to attribute supernatural causation to uncanny experiences. *Personality and Social Psychology Bulletin*, 41, 955–961.

Boyer, P. (2008). Religion: Bound to believe? *Nature*, 455, 1038–1039.

Boyle, M. (2002). *Schizophrenia: A scientific delusion* (2nd ed.). London: Routledge.

Boym, S. (2005). Poetics and politics of estrangement: Victor Shklovsky and Hannah Arendt. *Poetics Today*, 26(4), 581–612.

Boym, S. (2010). *Another freedom*. London: University of Chicago Press.

Braithwaite, J. J. (2011). Magnetic fields, hallucinations and anomalous experiences: A sceptical critique of the current evidence. *The Skeptic*, 22(4)/23(1), 38–45.

Bransford, J. D., & Johnson, M. K. (1972). Contextual prerequisites for understanding: Some investigations of comprehension and recall. *Journal of Verbal Learning and Verbal Behavior*, 11, 717–726.

Braud, W. G. (1975). Psi-conducive states. *Journal of Communication*, 25, 142–152.

Brookesmith, P. (1996). *UFO: The government files*. London: Blandford.

Brookesmith, P. (1998). *Alien abductions*. New York: Barnes & Noble.

Brotherton, R. (2013). Towards a definition of "conspiracy theory". *PsyPAG Quarterly*, 88(3), 9–14.

Brotherton, R. (2014, March 20). Flight MH370: The allure of the conspiracy theory. Retrieved 12 August 2015 from www.newscientist.com/article/dn25260-flight-mh370-the-allure-of-the-conspiracy-theory/.

Brotherton, R. (2015). *Suspicious minds: Why we believe conspiracy theories*. London: Bloomsbury Sigma.

Brotherton, R., & Eser, S. (2015). Bored to fears: Boredom proneness, paranoia, and conspiracy theories. *Personality and Individual Differences*, 80, 1–5. http://doi.org/10.1016/j.paid.2015.02.011.

Brotherton, R., & French, C. C. (2014). Belief in conspiracy theories and susceptibility to the conjunction fallacy. *Applied Cognitive Psychology*, 28(2), 238–248. http://doi.org/10.1002/acp.2995.

Brotherton, R., & French, C. C. (2015). Intention seekers: Conspiracist ideation and biased attributions of intentionality. *PLOS ONE*, 10(5), e0124125. http://doi.org/10.1371/journal.pone.0124125.

Brotherton, R., French, C. C., & Pickering, A. D. (2013). Measuring belief in conspiracy theories: The generic conspiracist beliefs scale. *Frontiers in Personality Science and Individual Differences*, 4, 279. http://doi.org/10.3389/fpsyg.2013.00279.

Bruder, M., Haffke, P., Neave, N., Nouripanah, N., & Imhoff, R. (2013). Measuring individual differences in generic beliefs in conspiracy theories across cultures: Conspiracy Mentality Questionnaire. *Frontiers in Personality Science and Individual Differences*, 4, 225. http://doi.org/10.3389/fpsyg.2013.00225.

Brugger, P., & Taylor, K. I. (2003). ESP: Extrasensory perception or effect of subjective probability? *Journal of Consciousness Studies*, 10, 221–246.

Brugger, P., Landis, T., & Regard, M. (1990). A "sheep-goat effect" in repetition avoidance: Extrasensory perception as an effect of subjective probability? *British Journal of Psychology*, 76, 459–468.

Brugger, P., Regard, M., Landis, T., Cook, N., Krebs, D., & Niederberger, J. (1993). Meaningful patterns in visual noise: Effects of lateral stimulation and the observer's belief in ESP. *Psychopathology*, 26, 261–265.

Brugger, P., Regard, M., Landis, T., Krebs, D., & Niederberger, J. (1994). Coincidences: Who can say how meaningful they are? In E. W. Cook & D. L. Delanoy (Eds.), *Research in parapsychology* (pp. 94–98). Metuchen, NJ: Scarecrow Press.

Brunner, L. J. (1979). Smiles can be back channels. *Journal of Personality and Social Psychology*, 37, 728–734.

Bugliosi, V. (2007). *Reclaiming history: The assassination of president John F. Kennedy*. New York: W. W. Norton & Co.

Bull, P. (1987). *Posture and gesture*. Oxford: Pergamon.

Bullard, T. E. (1987). *UFO abductions: The measure of a mystery*. Mount Rainier, MD: Fund for UFO Research.

Bullard, T. E. (1989). Hypnosis and UFO abductions: A troubled relationship. *Journal of UFO Studies*, 1, 3–40.

Bullard, T. E. (1994). The influence of investigators on UFO abduction reports: Results of a survey. In A. Pritchard, D. E. Pritchard, J. E. Mack, P. Kasey, & C. Yapp (Eds.), *Alien discussions. Proceedings of the Abduction Study Conference held at MIT* (pp. 571–619). Cambridge, MA: North Cambridge Press.

Burger, E. (1986). *Spirit theatre*. New York: Kaufman and Greenberg.

Burrows, J. (2012). Living with the h-index? Metric assemblages in the contemporary academy. *The Sociological Review*, 60(2), 355–372.

Butler, L. D., Koopman, C., & Zimbardo, P. G. (1995). The psychological impact of viewing the film J.F.K.: Emotions, beliefs, and political behavioral intentions. *Political Psychology*, 16(2), 237–257. http://doi.org/10.2307/3791831.

Byford, J. (2011). *Conspiracy theories: A critical introduction*. London: Palgrave Macmillan.

Calin-Jageman, R. J., & Caldwell, T. L. (2014). Replication of the superstition and performance study by Damisch, Stoberock, and Mussweiler (2010). *Social Psychology*, 45, 239–245.

Carlson, S. (1985). A double-blind test of astrology. *Nature*, 318, 419–425.

Carpenter, J. C. (1965). An exploratory test of ESP in relation to anxiety proneness. In J. B. Rhine and Associates (Eds.), *Parapsychology from Duke to FRNM* (pp. 85–120). Durham, NC: Parapsychology Press.

Cartwright, R. (1977). *Night life: Explorations in dreaming*. Englewood Cliffs, NJ: Prentice Hall.

Chalmers, A. (2013). *What is this thing called science*? Open University Press. Maidenhead: McGraw Hill.

Chalmers, D. J. (1995). The puzzle of conscious experience. *Scientific American*, December 1995, 62–68.

Chari, C. T. K. (1978). Reincarnation research: Method and interpretation. In M. Ebon (ed.), *Signet Handbook of Parapsychology* (pp. 313–324). New York: New American Library.

Cheyne, J. A., Rueffer, S. D., & Newby-Clark, I. R. (1999). Hypnagogic and hypnopompic hallucinations during sleep paralysis: Neurological and cultural construction of the night-mare. *Consciousness and Cognition*, 8(3), 319–337.

Child, I. L. (1985) Psychology and anomalous observations: The question of ESP in dreams. *American Psychologist*, 40(2), 1219–1230.

Clancy, S. A. (2005). *Abducted: Why people come to believe they were kidnapped by aliens*. Cambridge, MA: Harvard University Press.

Clancy, S. A., McNally, R. J., Schacter, D. L., Lenzenweger, M. F., & Pitman, R. K. (2002). Memory distortion in people reporting abduction by aliens. *Journal of Abnormal Psychology*, 111, 455–461.

Clarke, D. (2012). *The UFO files: The inside story of real-life sightings*. London: Bloomsbury.

Clarke, D., & Roberts, A. (1990). *Phantoms of the sky: UFOs, a modern myth?* London: Robert Hale.

Clarke, S. (2002). Conspiracy theories and conspiracy theorizing. *Philosophy of the Social Sciences*, 32, 131–150. http://doi.org/10.1177/004931032002001.

Coady, D. (2012). *What to believe now: Applying epistemology to contemporary issues*. Chichester, West Sussex; Malden, MA: Wiley-Blackwell.

Committee on Ritual Abuse. (2012). *Ritual abuse and race*. Retrieved 24 February 2016 from www.theguardian.com/society/2012/jan/23/ritual-abuse-and-race.

Conway-Morris, S. (2005). *Life's solution: Inevitable humans in a lonely universe*. Cambridge: Cambridge University Press.

Cook, E., Greyson, B., & Stevenson, I. (1998). Do any near-death experiences provide evidence for the survival of human personality after death? *JSE*, 12, 377–406.

Crespi, B., & Summers, K. (2014). Inclusive fitness theory for the evolution of religion. *Animal Behaviour*, 92, 313–323.

Crick, F., & Mitchison, G. (1983). The function of dream sleep. *Nature*, 30, 111–114.

Crick, F., & Mitchison, G. (1986). REM sleep and neural nets. *The Journal of Mind and Behaviour*, 5, 81–98.

Crocker, J., Luhtanen, R., Broadnax, S., & Blaine, B. E. (1999). Belief in US government conspiracies against blacks among black and white college students: Powerlessness or system blame? *Personality and Social Psychology Bulletin*, 25(8), 941–953. http://doi.org/10.1177/01461672992511003.

Culver, R. B., & Ianna, P. A. (1979). *The Gemini Syndrome: Star wars of the oldest kind.* Tucson: Pachart.

Cuneo, M. W. (2001). *American exorcism: Expelling demons in the land of plenty.* New York: Doubleday.

Dahlitz, M., & Parkes, J. D. (1993). Sleep paralysis. Lancet, 341, 406–407.

Dahlstrom, W. G., Hopkins, D., Dahlstrom, L., Jackson, E., & Cumella, E. (1996). MMPI findings on astrological and other folklore concepts of personality. *Psychological Reports*, 78, 1059–1070.

Dalton, K. (1997). Exploring the links: Creativity and psi in the ganzfeld. In *The Parapsychological Association 40th Annual Convention: Proceedings of presented papers* (pp. 119–134). Durham, NC: Parapsychological Association.

Damisch, L., Stoberock, B., & Mussweiler, T. (2010). Keep your fingers crossed! How superstition improves performance. *Psychological Science*, 21, 1014–1020.

Darwin, C. (1859). *The origin of species.* London: Macmillan.

Darwin, H., Neave, N., & Holmes, J. (2011). Belief in conspiracy theories. The role of paranormal belief, paranoid ideation and schizotypy. *Personality and Individual Differences*, 50(8), 1289–1293. http://doi.org/10.1016/j.paid.2011.02.027.

Dawkins, R. (2006). *The God delusion.* London: Bantam Press.

de Bruin, A., & Della Sala, S. (2016). How biases inflate scientific evidence. *The Psychologist*, 29(1), 36–39.

De Cruz, H. (2013). Religious concepts as structured imagination. *The International Journal for the Psychology of Religion*, 23, 63–74.

De Ridder, D., Van Laere, K., Dupont, P., Menovsky, T., & Van de Heyning, P. (2007). Visualizing out-of-body experience in the brain. *New England Journal of Medicine*, 357, 1829–1833.

Dean, G. (2002). Is the Mars effect a social effect? *Skeptical Inquirer*, 26(3), 33–38.

Dean, G., & Kelly, I. W. (2003). Is astrology relevant to consciousness and psi? *Journal of Consciousness Studies*, 10(6–7), 175–198.

Deese, J. (1959). On the prediction of occurrence of particular verbal intrusions in immediate recall. *Journal of Experimental Psychology*, 58, 17–22.

Delanoy, D. L. (1987). Work with a fraudulent PK metal-bending subject. *Journal of the Society for Psychical Research*, 54, 247–256.

Dement, W. C., & Kleitman, N. (1957) The relation of eye movements during sleep to dream activity: An objective method for the study of dreaming. *Journal of Experimental Psychology*, 53(5), 339–346.

Denis, D., French, C. C., Rowe, R., Zavos, H. M. S., Nolen, P. M., Parsons, M. J., & Gregory, A. M. (2015). A twin and molecular genetics study of sleep paralysis and associated factors. *Journal of Sleep Research*, 24, 438–446.

Dennett, D. C. (1987). *The intentional stance.* Cambridge, MA: MIT Press.

Dennett, D. C. (1995). *Consciousness explained.* Harmondsworth: Penguin.

Devereux, P. (1989). *Earth lights revelation.* London: Blandford.

Devereux, P., & Brookesmith, P. (1997). *UFOs and ufology: The first 50 years.* London: Blandford.

Devinsky, O., Feldmann, E., Burrowes, K., & Bromfield, E. (1989). Autoscopic phenomena with seizures. *Archives of Neurology*, 46(10), 1080–1088.

Diaconis, P. (1985). Statistical problems in ESP research. In P. Kurtz (Ed.), *A skeptics handbook of parapsychology* (pp. 569–584). Buffalo, NY: Prometheus Books.

Diener, E., Tay, L., & Myers, D. G. (2011). The religion paradox: If religion makes people happy, why are so many dropping out? *Journal of Personality and Social Psychology*, 101, 1278–1290.

Dingwall, E. (1921). Magic and mediumship. *Psychic Science Quarterly*, 1(3), 206–219.

Douglas, K. M., & Sutton, R. M. (2008). The hidden impact of conspiracy theories: Perceived and actual influence of theories surrounding the death of Princess Diana. *Journal of Social Psychology*, 148(2), 210–221. http://doi.org/10.3200/SOCP.148.2.210-222.

Douglas, K. M., & Sutton, R. M. (2011). Does it take one to know one? Endorsement of conspiracy theories is influenced by personal willingness to conspire. *British Journal of Social Psychology*, 50(3), 544–552. http://doi.org/10.1111/j.2044-8309.2010.02018.x.

Douglas, K. M., & Sutton, R. M. (2015). Climate change: Why the conspiracy theories are dangerous. *Bulletin of the Atomic Scientists*, 71(2), 98–106. http://doi.org/10.1177/0096340215571908.

Douglas, K. M., Sutton, R. M., Callan, M. J., Dawtry, R. J., & Harvey, A. J. (2016). Someone is pulling the strings: Hypersensitive agency detection and belief in conspiracies. *Thinking and Reasoning*, 22(1), 57–77. doi: 10.1080/13546783.2015.1051586.

Drinkwater, K., Dagnall, N., & Parker, A. (2012). Reality testing, conspiracy theories and paranormal beliefs. *Journal of Parapsychology*, 76(1), 57–77.

Druffel, A, & Rogo, D. S. (1980). *The Tujunga Canyon contacts*. Englewood Cliffs, NJ: Prentice Hall.

DuBreuil, S. C., Garry, M., & Loftus, E. F. (1998). Tales fom the crib: Age regression and the creation of unlikely memories. In S. J. Lynn & K. M. McConkey (Eds.), *Truth in memory* (pp. 137–160). New York: Guilford Press.

Dunbar, D., & Reagan, B. (2006). *Debunking 9/11 myths: Why conspiracy theories can't stand up to the facts*. New York: Hearst Books.

Duncan, S., & Fiske, D. W. (1977). *Face-to-face interaction: Research methods and theory*. Hillsdale, NJ: Erlbaum.

Dwairy, M. (2006). The psychosocial function of reincarnation among Druze in Israel. *Culture, Medicine and Psychiatry*, 30, 29–53.

Earle, L. (1990). *The classic cold reading*. USA: Binary Star Publications.

Edwards, P. (1996a). *Reincarnation: A critical examination*. Amherst, NY: Prometheus.

Edwards, P. (1996b). Reincarnation. In G. Stein (ed.), *Encyclopedia of the paranormal* (pp. 621–652). Amherst, NY: Prometheus.

Ekman, P. (1985). *Telling lies: Clues to deceit in the marketplace, politics and marriage*. New York: W. W. Norton and Co.

Empson, J. (1989). *Sleep and dreaming*. London: Faber and Faber Ltd.

Epley, N., Akalis, S., Waytz, A., & Cacioppo, J. T. (2008). Creating social connection through inferential reproduction. *Psychological Science*, 19, 114–120.

Epley, N., Converse, B. A., Delbosc, A., Monteleone, G. A., & Cacioppo, J. T. (2009). Believers' estimates of God's beliefs are more egocentric thanestimates of other people's beliefs. *Proceedings of the National Association of Sciences*, 106(51), 21,533–21,538.

Epley, N., Keysar, B., Van Boven, L., & Gilovich, T. (2004). Perspective taking as egocentric anchoring and adjustment. *Journal of Personality and Social Psychology*, 87, 327–339.

Evans, H. (1983). *The evidence for UFOs*. Wellingborough: Aquarian.

Evans, H. (1998). *From other worlds: The truth behind aliens, abductions, UFOs and the paranormal*. London: Carlton.

Evans, J. S. B., & Curtis-Holmes, J. (2005). Rapid responding increases belief bias: Evidence for the dual-process theory of reasoning. *Thinking & Reasoning*, 11(4), 382–389.

Evans, J. S. B., & Stanovich, K. E. (2013). Dual-process theories of higher cognition advancing the debate. *Perspectives on Psychological Science*, 8(3), 223–241.

Everett, H. C. (1963). Sleep paralysis in medical students. *Journal of Nervous and Mental Disease*, 135, 283–287.

Eysenck, H. J., & Nias, D. K. (1982). *Astrology: Science or superstition?* London: Maurice Temple Smith.

Eysenck, M. W. (2004). *Psychology: An international perspective*. Hove: Psychology Press.

Eysenck, M. W., & Keane, M. T. (2015). *Cognitive psychology: A student's handbook* (7th ed.). Hove, UK: Psychology Press.

Feilding, E., Baggally, W. W., & Carrington, H. (1909). Report on a series of sittings with Eusapia Palladino. *Proceedings of the Society for Psychical Research*, 23, 309–569.

Fenwick, P. (1997). Is the near-death experience only N-methyl-D-aspartate blocking? *Journal of Near-Death Studies*, 16, 43–53.

Fenwick, P., & Fenwick, E. (1996). *The truth in the light: an investigation of over 300 near-death experiences*. New York: Berkley Books.

Feyerabend, P. (1975). *Against method: Outline of an anarchist theory of knowledge*. London: New Left Books.

Fiedler, K. (1988). The dependence of the conjunction fallacy on subtle linguistic factors. *Psychological Research*, 50(2), 123–129. http://doi.org/10.1007/BF00309212.

Fiedler, K., & von Sydow, M. (2015). Heuristics and biases: Beyond Tversky and Kahneman's (1974) judgment under uncertainty. In M. W. Eysenck & D. Groome (Eds.), *Classic studies in cognitive psychology*. London: Sage.

Firro, K. M. (1992). *A history of the Druze*. London: Brill.

Fisk, J. E., & Pidgeon, N. (1996). Component probabilities and the conjunction fallacy: Resolving signed summation and the low component model in a contingent approach. *Acta Psychologica*, 94(1), 1–20. http://doi.org/10.1016/0001-6918(95)00048-8.

Fisk, J. E., & Pidgeon, N. (1997). The conjunction fallacy: The case for the existence of competing heuristic strategies. *British Journal of Psychology*, 88, 1–27. http://doi.org/10.1111/j.2044-8295.1997.tb02617.x.

Fisk, J. E., & Pidgeon, N. (1998). Conditional probabilities, potential surprise, and the conjunction fallacy. *Quarterly Journal of Experimental Psychology: Section A*, 51(3), 655–681. http://doi.org/10.1080/027249898391576.

Fisk, R. (1992). *Pity the nation: Lebanon at war*. Oxford: Oxford University Press.

Fitzkee, D. (1945). *Magic by misdirection*. Oakland, CA: Magic Limited.

Forer, B. R. (1949). The fallacy of personal validation: A classroom demonstration of gullibility. *Journal of Abnormal and Social Psychology*, 44, 118–123.

Foulkes, D. (1960). Dream reports from different stages of sleep. *Journal of Abnormal and Social Psychology*, 65(1), 14–25.

Foulkes, D. (1978). *A grammar of dreams*. New York: Basic Books.

Foulkes, D. (1979) Home and laboratory dreams: Four empirical studies and a conceptual re-evaluation. *Sleep*, 2, 233–251.

Foulkes, D. (1982a). A cognitive-psychological model of REM dream production. *Sleep*, 5(2), 169–187.

Foulkes, D. (1982b). *Children's dreams: Longitudinal studies*. New York: John Wiley.

Foulkes, D. (1985). *Dreaming: A cognitive-psychological analysis*. Hillsdale, NJ: Lawrence Erlbaum Associates.

Foulkes, D. (1993). Data constraints on theorising about dream function. In A. Moffitt, M. Kramer, & R. Hoffmann (Eds.), *The functions of dreaming* (pp. 11–20). New York: State University of New York Press.

Foulkes, D. (1999). *Children's dreaming and the development of consciousness*. Cambridge, MA: Harvard University Press.

Frazier, K., Karr, B., & Nickell, J. (Eds.). (1997). *The UFO invasion: The Roswell incident, alien abductions, and government coverups*. Amherst, NY: Prometheus.

Frederick, S. (2005). Cognitive reflection and decision making. *The Journal of Economic Perspectives*, 19, 25–42.

French, C. (2001). Dying to know the truth: Visions of a dying brain or false memories? *The Lancet*, 358, 2010–2011.

French, C. C. (2003). Fantastic memories: The relevance of research into eyewitness testimony and false memories for reports of anomalous experiences. *Journal of Consciousness Studies*, 10, 153–174.

French, C. C. (2005). Near-death experiences in cardiac arrest survivors. In S. Laureys (Ed.), *Progress in brain research, vol. 150: The boundaries of consciousness, neurobiology and neuropathology* (pp. 351–367). Amsterdam: Elsevier.

French, C. (2012). Astrologers and other inhabitants of parallel universes. Retrieved 24 February 2016 from www.theguardian.com/science/2012/feb/07/astrologers-parallel-universes.

French, C. (2014a). Pope Francis and the psychology of exorcism and possession. Retrieved 24 February 2016 from www.theguardian.com/science/2014/jul/09/pope-francis-psychology-exorcism-possession.

French, C. (2014b). Satanic abuse claims are almost certainly based upon false memories. Retrieved 24 February 2016 from www.theguardian.com/science/2014/nov/18/satanic-child-abuse-false-memories-scotland.

French, C. C. (in press). Close encounters of the psychological kind. *The Psychologist*.

French, C. C., & Ost, J. (in press). Beliefs about memory, childhood abuse, and hypnosis amongst clinicians, legal professionals and the general public. In R. Burnett (ed.), *Wrongful allegations of person abuse*. Oxford: Oxford University Press.

French, C. C., & Santomauro, J. (2007). Something wicked this way comes: Causes and interpretations of sleep paralysis. In S. Della Sala (ed.), *Tall tales about the mind and brain: Separating fact from fiction* (pp. 3–22). Oxford: Oxford University Press.

French, C. C., & Stone, A. (2014). *Anomalistic psychology: Exploring paranormal belief and experience*. Basingstoke, UK: Palgrave Macmillan.

French, C. C., & Wilson, K. (2006). Incredible memories: How accurate are reports of anomalous events? *European Journal of Parapsychology*, 21, 166–181.

French, C. C., Fowler, M., McCarthy, K., & Peers, D. (1991). A test of the Barnum Effect. *The Skeptical Enquirer*, 15, 66–72.

French, C. C., Haque, U., Bunton-Stasyshyn, R., & Davis, R. (2009). The "haunt" project: An attempt to build a "haunted" room by manipulating complex electromagnetic fields and infrasound. *Cortex*, 45, 619–629.

French, C. C., Santomauro, J., Hamilton, V., Fox, R., & Thalbourne, M. A. (2008). Psychological aspects of the alien contact experience. *Cortex*, 44, 1387–1395.

Freud, S. (1900/1976). *The interpretation of dreams*. Harmondsworth: Penguin.

Fuller, U. (1975). *Confessions of a psychic*. Teaneck, NJ: Karl Fulves.

Fuller, U. (1980). *Further confessions of a psychic*. Teaneck, NJ: Karl Fulves.

Furnham, A. (2013). Commercial conspiracy theories: a pilot study. *Frontiers in Personality Science and Individual Differences*, 4, 379. http://doi.org/10.3389/fpsyg.2013.00379.

Furnham, A., & Schofield, S. (1987). Accepting personality test feedback: A review of the Barnum Effect. *Current Psychological Research & Reviews*, 6, 162–178.

Gallagher, M. W., Bentley, K. H., & Barlow, D. H. (2014). Perceived control and vulnerability to anxiety disorders: A meta-analytic review. *Cognitive Therapy and Research*, 38, 571–584.

Galloway, A. (1969). *The Ramsay legend*. Birmingham, UK: Goodliffe Publications.

Gardner, M. (1957). *Fads and fallacies in the name of science*. New York: Dover.

Gauld, A. (1968). *The founders of psychical research*. London: Routledge and Kegan Paul.

Gauld, A. (1982). *Mediumship and survival: A century of investigations*. London: Heinemann.

Gauquelin, M. (1972). Planetary effect at the time of birth of successful professionals, an experimental control made by scientists. *Journal of Interdisciplinary Cycle Research*, 3(2), 381–389.

Gebauer, J. E., & Maio, G. R. (2012). The need to belong can motivate belief in God. *Journal of Personality*, 80, 465–501.

Gergen, K. J. (1973). Social psychology as history. *Journal of Personality and Social Psychology*, 26(2), 309–320.

Gervais, W. M. (2013). Perceiving minds and gods: How mind perception enables, constrains, and is triggered by belief in gods. *Perspectives on Psychological Science*, 8, 380–394.

Gervais, W. M., & Norenzayan, A. (2012a). Analytic thinking promotes religious disbelief. *Science*, 336, 493–496.

Gervais, W. M., & Norenzayan, A. (2012b). Like a camera in the sky? Thinking about God increases public self-awareness and socially desirable responding. *Journal of Experimental Social Psychology*, 48, 298–302.

Glanville, J. (1689). *Saducimus trimuphatus*. London: J. Collins and Lownds.

Gleick, J. (1992). *Genius: The life and science of Richard Feynman*. New York: Pantheon.

Glover, J. (1999). *Humanity: A moral history of the twentieth century*. London: Jonathan Cape.

Goertzel, T. (1994). Belief in conspiracy theories. *Political Psychology*, 15(4), 731–742. http://doi.org/10.2307/3791630.

Goffman, E. (1974). *Frame analysis*. Boston: Northeastern University Press.

Granqvist, P., Fredrikson, M., Unge, P., Hagenfeldt, A., Valind, S., Larhammar, D., & Larsson, M. (2005). Sensed presence and mystical experiences are predicted by suggestibility, not by the application of transcranial weak complex magnetic fields. *Neuroscience Letters*, 379, 1–6.

Gray, S., & Gallo, D. (2016). Paranormal psychic believers and skeptics: A large-scale test of the cognitive differences hypothesis. *Memory & Cognition*, 44(2), 242–261

Greasley, P. (2000). Management of positive and negative responses in a Spiritualist medium consultation. *Skeptical Inquirer*, 24(5), 45–49.

Green, C. (1968). *Lucid dreams*. Oxford: Institute of Psychophysical Research.

Greenaway, K. H., Louis, W. R., & Harvey, M. J. (2013). Loss of control increases belief in precognition and belief in precognition increases control. *PLoS ONE*, 8(8), e71327.

Gregory, R. L. (1977). *Eye and brain* (3rd ed). London: Weidenfeld and Nicholson.

Greyson, B. (1983). The near-death experience scale: Construction, reliability and validity. *Journal of Nervous and Mental Disease*, 171, 369–375.

Greyson, B. (1985). A typology of near-death experiences. *American Journal of Psychiatry*, 142, 967–969.

Greyson, B. (1998). The incidence of near-death experiences. *Medicine and Psychiatry*, 1, 92–99.

Greyson, B. (2014). Near-death experiences. In E. Cardeña, S. J. Lynn, & S. Krippner (Eds.), *Varieties of anomalous experience: Examining the scientific evidence*, 2nd ed. (pp. 333–367). Washington, DC: American Psychological Association.

Greyson, B., & Stevenson, I. (1980). The phenomenology of near-death experiences. *American Journal of Psychiatry*, 137, 1193–1196.

Griffin, J. (1997). *The origin of dreams*. Trowbridge, UK: Redwood Books.

Grosso, M. (1981). Toward an explanation of near-death phenomena. *Anabiosis: The Journal of Near-Death Studies*, 1, 3–26.

Grzesiak-Feldman, M. (2013). The effect of high-anxiety situations on conspiracy thinking. *Current Psychology*, 32(1), 100–118. http://doi.org/10.1007/s12144-013-9165-6.

Guazzo, F. M. (1608/1970). *Compendium maleficarum*. New York: Barnes and Noble.

Guiley, R. E. (1991). *Harper's encyclopedia of mystical and paranormal experience*. San Francisco: Harper Collins.

Hamilton, W. D. (1964). The genetical evolution of social behaviour, I and II. *Journal of Theoretical Biology*, 7, 1–52.

Hansen, G. P. (1990). Deception by subjects in psi research. *The Journal of the American Society for Psychical Research*, 84, 25–80.

Haraldsson, E. (1985). Representative national surveys of psychic phenomena: Iceland, Great Britain, Sweden, USA and Gallup's Multinational Survey. *Journal of the Society for Psychical Research*, 53, 145–158.

Haraldsson, E. (2002). *Children who speak of past-life experiences: Is there a psychological explanation?* Paper presented to the Parapsychological Association Congress, Paris, August 2002.

Haraldsson, E., & Abu-Izzeddin, M. (2002). Development of certainty about the correct deceased person in a case of the reincarnation type in Lebanon: The case of Nazih Al-Danaf. *Journal of Scientific Exploration*, 16, 363–380.

Haraldsson, E., & Houtkooper, J. (1992). Effects of perceptual defensiveness, personality and belief on extrasensory perception tasks. *Personality and Individual Differences*, 13, 1085–1096.

Haraldsson, E., Fowler, P. C., & Periyannanpillai, V. (2000). Psychological characteristics of children who speak of a previous life: A further field study in Sri Lanka, *Transcultural Psychiatry*, 37, 525–544.

Harris Poll (2013). Americans' belief in God, miracles and heaven declines: Belief in Darwin's theory of evolution rises. Retrieved 1 November 2015 from www.harrisinteractive.com/Insights/HarrisVault.aspx.

Harris, B. (1985). *Gellerism revealed*. Calgary: Micky Hades International.

Harris, M. (1986). *Investigating the unexplained*. Buffalo, NY: Prometheus.

Harris, W.V. (2009). *Dreams and experience in classical antiquity*. Cambridge: Harvard University Press.

Harvey, C. (1984). The stars look down: Meanwhile astrology is looking up. *Guardian*, 23 March 1984.

Harvey, C., & Harvey, S. (1999). *Principles of astrology*. London: Thorson.

Haselton, M. G., & Nettle, D. (2006). The paranoid optimist: An integrative evolutionary model of cognitive biases. *Personality & Social Psychology Review*, 10(1), 47–66. http://doi.org/10.1207/s15327957pspr1001_3.

Hastings, A. (1990). Psi and the phenomena of channeling. In L. A. Henkel & J. Palmer (eds.), *Research in parapsychology 1989* (pp. 99–123). Metuchen, NJ: Scarecrow Press.

Hearne, K. (1978). *Lucid dreams: An electrophysiological and psychological study*. Unpublished Ph.D. thesis, University of Hull.

Heath, C., Bell, C., & Sternberg, E. (2001). Emotional selection in memes: The case of urban legends. *Journal of Personality and Social Psychology*, 81(6), 1028–1041. http://doi.org/10.1037//0022-3514.81.6.1028.

Heider, F., & Simmel, M. (1944). An experimental study of apparent behavior. *American Journal of Psychology*, 57, 243–259. http://doi.org/10.2307/1416950.

Herek, G. M., & Capitanio, J. P. (1994). Conspiracies, contagion, and compassion: Trust and public reactions to AIDS. *AIDS Education and Prevention*, 6(4), 365–375.

Hergovich, A., Schott, R., & Arendasy, M. (2005). Paranormal belief and religiosity. *Journal of Parapsychology*, 69, 293–303.

Heywood, B. T. (2010). "Meant to be": How religious beliefs, cultural religiosity, and impaired theory of mind affect the implicit bias to think teleologically (Unpublished doctoral thesis). Queen's University of Belfast, Belfast, UK.

Heywood, B. T., & Bering, J. M. (2013). "Meant to be": How religious beliefs and cultural religiosity affect the implicit bias to think teleologically. *Religion, Brain, and Behavior*. http://dx.doi.org/10.1080/2153599X.2013.782888.

Hobrin (no initial) (1990). *Money-making cold reading*. Sheffield, England: Magick Enterprises.

Hobson, A. (1988). *The dreaming brain*. New York: Basic Books.

Hobson, J. A. (2005). *Dreaming: A very short introduction*. Oxford: Oxford University Press.

Hobson, A., & McCarley, R. (1977). The brain as a dream state generator: An activation-synthesis hypothesis of the dream process. *American Journal of Psy*chiatry, 134, 97–112.

Hodgson, R., & Davey, S. J. (1887). The possibilities of malobservation and lapse of memory from a practical point of view. *Proceedings of the Society for Psychical Research*, 4, 381–495.

Holden, K. J., & French, C. C. (2002). Alien abduction experiences: Clues from neuropsychology and neuropsychiatry. *Cognitive Neuropsychiatry*, 7, 163–178.

Holden, J. M., Greyson, B., & James, D. J. (2009). *The handbook of near-death experiences: Thirty years of investigation*. Denver, CO: ABC Clio.

Holden, J., Long, J., & MacLurg, B. J. (2009). Characteristics of Western near-death experiencers. In J. Holden, B. Greyson, & D. James (Eds.), *The handbook of near-death experiences: Thirty years of investigation* (pp. 109–133). Santa Barbara, CA: ABC-CLIO.

Holk, F. H. (1978). Life revisited. *Omega*, 9, 1–11.

Holt, N. J., Simonds-Moore, C., Luke, D., & French, C. (2012). *Anomalistic psychology*. Houndmills: Palgrave.

Honorton, C., & Harper, S. (1974). Psi-mediated imagery and ideation in an experimental procedure for regulating perceptual input. *Journal of the American Society for Psychical Research*, 68, 156–168.

Honorton, C., & Krippner, S. (1969). Hypnosis and ESP: A review of the experimental literature. *Journal of the American Society for Psychical Research*, 63, 214–252.

Hopkins, B. (1987). *Intruders: The incredible visitations at Copley Woods*. New York: Random House.

Hopkins, B., Jacobs, D. M., & Westrum, R. (1992). *Unusual personal experiences: An analysis of the data from three national surveys conducted by the roper organisation*. Las Vegas: Bigelow Holding Corporation.

Horton, R. (2000). Genetically modified food: consternation, confusion, and crack-up. *The Medical Journal of Australia*, 172(4), 148–149.

Hough, P., & Rogers, P. (2007–2008). Individuals who report being abducted by aliens: Core experiences and individual differences. *Imagination, Cognition & Personality*, 27, 139–161.

Houran, J., & Lange, R. (1998). Modelling precognitive dreams as meaningful coincidences. *Psychological Reports*, 83(3 Pt. 2), 1411–1414.

Hufford, D. J. (1982). *The terror that comes in the night*. Philadelphia: University of Pennsylvania Press.

Hunt, H. T. (1989). *The multiplicity of dreams: Memory, imagination, and consciousness*. New Haven, CT: Yale University Press.

Hunt, L. (2012). Why is child abuse tied to witchcraft on the rise? Retrieved 24 February 2016 from www.theguardian.com/society/2012/jan/18/child-abuse-witchcraft-exorcism-rise.

Hunter, J., & Luke, D. (2014). *Talking with the spirits: Ethographies from between the worlds*. Brisbane: Daily Grail Publishing.

Huntley, J. (2000). *Astrology: An introductory guide to the influence of the stars on your life*. Shaftsbury: Element Books.

Hyman, R. (1977). Cold reading: How to convince strangers that you know all about them. *Skeptical Enquirer*, 1, 18–37.

Hyman, R. (1981). The psychic reading. In T. A. Sebeok & R. Rosenthal (Eds.), *The clever Hans phenomenon* (pp. 169–181). New York: New York Academy of Sciences

Hyman, R. (2010). A meta-analysis that conceals more than it reveals: Comment on Storm et al. (2010). *Psychological Bulletin*, 136, 486–490.

Hyman, R., & Honorton, C. (1986). A joint communiqué: The psi ganzfeld controversy. *Journal of Parapsychology*, 50, 351–364.

Imhoff, R. (2015). Beyond (right-wing) authoritarianism: Conspiracy mentality as an incremental predictor of prejudice. In M. Bilewicz, A. Cichocka, W. Soral, & M. Kofta (Eds.), *The psychology of conspiracy* (pp. 122–142). New York: Routledge.

Imhoff, R., & Bruder, M. (2013). Speaking (un-)truth to power: Conspiracy mentality as a generalised political attitude. *European Journal of Personality*, advance online publication. http://doi.org/10.1002/per.1930.

Irwin, H. J. (1990). Fantasy proneness and paranormal beliefs. *Psychological Reports*, 66, 655–658.

Irwin, H. J. (1991). A study of paranormal belief, psychological adjustment, and fantasy-proneness. *Journal of the American Society for Psychical Research*, 85, 317–331.

Irwin, H. J. (1993). Belief in the paranormal: A review of the empirical literature. *Journal of the American Society for Psychical Research*, 87, 1–39.

Irwin, H. J. (2009). *The psychology of paranormal belief: A researcher's handbook*. Hatfield, UK: University of Hertfordshire Press.

Irwin, H. J., & Watt, C. A. (2007). *An introduction to parapsychology* (5th ed.). Jefferson, NC: McFarland & Co.

Itten, T., & Roberts, R. (2014). *The new politics of experience & the bitter herbs*. Monmouth: PCCS Books.

Iverson, J. (1977). *More lives than one?* London: Pan Books.

Jackson, M., & Fiebert, M. S. (1980). Introversion-extraversion and astrology. *Journal of Psychology*, 105, 155–156.

Jacobs, D. M. (1990). The rock and roll theory of UFOs. *Journal of UFO Studies*, 2, 141–143.

Jacobs, D. M. (1992). *Secret life: First-hand accounts of UFO abductions*. New York: Simon and Schuster.

Jacobs, D. M. (1998). *The threat: The secret agenda: What the aliens really want and how they plan to get it*. New York: Simon and Schuster.

James, W. (1902). *The varieties of religious experience: A study in human nature, being the Gifford lectures on natural religion delivered at Edinburgh in 1901–1902*. London: Longmans, Green & Co.

Jansen, K. L. R. (1997). The ketamine model of the near-death experience: A central role for the N-methyl-D-aspartate receptor. *Journal of Near-Death Studies*, 16, 5–26.

Jolley, D., & Douglas, K. M. (2014a). The effects of anti-vaccine conspiracy theories on vaccination intentions. *PLoS ONE*, 9(2), e89177. http://doi.org/10.1371/journal.pone.0089177.

Jolley, D., & Douglas, K. M. (2014b). The social consequences of conspiracism: Exposure to conspiracy theories decreases intentions to engage in politics and to reduce one's carbon footprint. *British Journal of Psychology*, 105(1), 35–56. http://doi.org/10.1111/bjop.12018.

Jones, W. H., & Russell, D. (1980). The selective processing of belief disconfirming information. *European Journal of Social Psychology*, 10, 309–312.

Judson, I. R., & Wiltshaw, E. (1983). A near-death experience. *The Lancet*, 3 September, 561–562.

Jung, C. G. (1959). *Flying saucers: A modern myth of things seen in the skies*. New York: Harcourt Brace.

Kahneman, D. (2003). A perspective on judgment and choice: Mapping bounded rationality. *American Psychologist*, 58, 697–720.

Kahneman, D. (2011). *Thinking, fast and slow.* New York: Farrar, Strauss, Giroux.

Kahneman, D., & Tversky, A. (1972). Subjective probability: A judgement of representativeness. *Cognitive Psychology*, 3, 430–439.

Kapogiannis, D., Barbey, A. K., Su, M., Zamboni, G., Krueger, F., & Grafman, J. (2009). Cognitive and neural foundations of religious belief. *Proceedings of the National Association of Sciences*, 106(12), 4876–4881. Published online 9 March 2009. doi: 10.1073/pnas.0811717106.

Kay, A. C., Gaucher, D., McGregor, I., & Nash, K. (2010). Religious belief as compensatory control. *Personality and Social Psychology Review*, 14, 37–48.

Kay, A. C., Whitson, J. A., Gaucher, D., & Galinsky, A. D. (2009). Compensatory control: Achieving order through the mind, our institutions, and the heavens. *Current Directions in Psychological Science*, 18(5), 264–268. http://doi.org/10.1111/j.1467-8721.2009.01649.x

Keeley, B. L. (1999). Of conspiracy theories. *Journal of Philosophy*, 96(3), 109–126.

Kelemen, D. (1999). Function, goals and intention: Children's teleological reasoning about objects. *Trends in Cognitive Sciences*, 3, 461–468.

Kelemen, D., & Rosset, E. (2009). The human function compunction: Teleological explanation in adults. *Cognition*, 111, 138–143.

Kelemen, D., Rottman, J., & Seston, R. (2013). Professional physical scientists display tenacious teleological tendencies: Purpose-based reasoning as a cognitive default. *Journal of Experimental Psychology: General*, 142, 1074–1083.

Kellehear, A., Heaven, P., & Gao, J. (1990). Community attitudes toward near-death experiences: A Chinese study. *Journal of Near-Death Studies*, 8, 163–173.

Kelly, G. W. (1955). *The psychology of personal constructs*. New York: W. W. Norton.

Kelly, I. W. (1998). Why astrology doesn't work. *Psychological Reports*, 82, 527–546.

Kennedy, J. E. (2013). Can parapsychology move beyond the controversies of retrospective meta-analysis? *Journal of Parapsychology*, 77, 21–35.

Keren, G., & Schul, Y. (2009). Two is not always better than one: A critical evaluation of two-system theories. *Perspectives on Psychological Science*, 4, 533–550.

Klass, P. J. (1983). *UFOs: The public deceived*. Buffalo, NY: Prometheus.

Klass, P. J. (1989). *UFO abductions: A dangerous game*. Buffalo, NY: Prometheus.

Klass, P. J. (1997a). Additional comments about the "Unusual Personal Experiences Survey". In K. Frazier, B. Karr, & J. Nickell (Eds.), *The UFO invasion: The Roswell incident, alien abductions, and government coverups* (pp. 207–209). Amherst, NY: Prometheus.

Klass, P. J. (1997b). *The real Roswell crashed-saucer cover-up*. Amherst, NY: Prometheus.

Klemenc-Ketis, Z., Grmec, S., & Kersnick, J. (2011). Near-death experiences and electrocardiogram patterns in out-of-hospital cardiac arrest survivors: A prospective observational study. *Signa Vitae*, 6, 31–35.

Kletti, R., & Noyes, R. (1981). Mental states in mortal danger. *Essence*, 5, 5–20.

Korff, K. K. (1997). *The Roswell UFO crash: What they don't want you to know.* Amherst, NY: Prometheus.

KPU study registry. Retrieved 1 November 2015 from https://koestlerunit.wordpress.com/study-registry/.

Kuhn, T. (1962). *The structure of scientific revolutions*. Chicago: University of Chicago Press.

La Fontaine, J. S. (1998). *Speak of the devil: Tales of Satanic abuse in contemporary England.* Cambridge: Cambridge University Press.

LaBerge, S., & Gackenbach, J. (2000). Lucid dreaming. In E. Cardeña, S. J. Lynn, & S. Krippner (Eds.), *Varieties of anomalous experience* (pp. 151–182). Washington, DC: American Psychological Association.

Laing, R. D. (1967). *The politics of experience and the bird of paradise*. Harmondsworth: Penguin.

Laing, R. D., & Cooper, D. G. (1964). *Reason and violence*. London: Tavistock.
Lamont, P., & Wiseman, R. (1999). *Magic in theory: An introduction to the theoretical and psychological elements in conjuring*. Hatfield, UK: University of Hertfordshire Press.
Lawrence, T., Edwards, C., Barraclough, N., Church, S., & Hetherington, F. (1995). Modelling childhood causes of paranormal belief and experience: Childhood trauma and childhood fantasy. *Personality and Individual Differences*, 19, 209–215.
Lawson, A. H. (1984). Perinatal imagery in UFO abduction reports. *Journal of Psychohistory*, 12, 211–239.
LeBoeuf, R. A., & Norton, M. I. (2012). Consequence-cause matching: Looking to the consequences of events to infer their causes. *Journal of Consumer Research*, 39(1), 128–141. http://doi.org/10.1086/662372.
LeDoux, J. (2012). Rethinking the emotional brain. *Neuron*, 73, 653–676.
Lee, C., Linkenauger, S. A., Bakdach, J. Z., Joy-Graba, J. M., & Parfitt, D. R. (2011). Putting like a pro: The role of positive contagion in golf performance and perception. *PLoS ONE*, 6, e26016.
Lee, L., & Smolin, R. (2015). *The singular universe and the reality of time*. Cambridge: Cambridge University Press.
Leman, P. J., & Cinnirella, M. (2007). A major event has a major cause: Evidence for the role of heuristics in reasoning about conspiracy theories. *Social Psychological Review*, 9, 18–28.
Leman, P. J., & Cinnirella, M. (2013). Beliefs in conspiracy theories and the need for cognitive closure. *Frontiers in Personality Science and Individual Differences*, 4, 378. http://doi.org/10.3389/fpsyg.2013.00378.
Lerner, M. J. (1980). *The belief in a just world: A fundamental delusion*. New York: Plenum.
Lesher, J. H. (1992). *Xenophanes of Colophon: Fragments*. Toronto: University of Toronto Press.
Levack, B. P. (2013). *The devil within: Possession and exorcism in the Christian West*. New Haven and London: Yale University Press.
Levitan, L., & LaBerge, S. (1993). Day life, night life: How waking and dreaming experiences relate. *NightLight*, 5(1), 4–6.
Lewandowsky, S., Gignac, G. E., & Oberauer, K. (2013). The role of conspiracist ideation and worldviews in predicting rejection of science. *PLoS ONE*, 8(10), e75637. http://doi.org/10.1371/journal.pone.0075637.
Lewandowsky, S., Oberauer, K., & Gignac, G. E. (2013). NASA faked the moon landing—therefore, (climate) science is a hoax: An anatomy of the motivated rejection of science. *Psychological Science*, 24(5), 622–633. http://doi.org/10.1177/0956797612457686.
Lewis, E. E. (1848). *A report of the mysterious noises heard in the house of Mr. John D. Fox, in Hydesville, Arcadia, Wayne County, NY: Authenticated by the certificates, and confirmed by the statements of the citizens of that place and vicinity*. Canandaigua, NY: E.E. Lewis.
Lewis, I. M. (1987). *Ecstatic religion*. New York: Routledge.
Lindeman, M., & Aarnio, K. (2007). Superstitious, magical, and paranormal beliefs: An integrative model. *Journal of Research in Personality*, 41(4), 731–744. http://doi.org/10.1016/j.jrp.2006.06.009.
Lindeman, M., & Svedholm, A. M. (2012). What's in a term? Paranormal, superstitious, magical, and supernatural beliefs by any other name would mean the same. *Review of General Psychology*, 16, 241–255.
Lindeman, M., Svedholm, A. M., Riekki, T., Raij, T., & Hari, R. (2013). Is it just a brick wall or a sign from the universe? An fMRI study of supernatural believers and sceptics. *Social, Cognitive & Affective Neuroscience*, 8, 943–949.
Lindeman, M., Svedholm-Häkkinen, A. M., & Lipsanen, J. (2015). Ontological confusions but not mentalising abilities predict religious belief, paranormal belief, and belief in supernatural purpose. *Cognition*, 134, 63–76.

Lindsay, D. S., & Read, J. D. (1995). "Memory work" and recovered memories of childhood sexual abuse: Scientific evidence and public, professional, and personal issues. *Psychology, Public Policy, and the Law*, 1, 846–908.

Littlewood, R. (2001). Social institutions and psychological explanations: Druze reincarnation as a therapeutic resource. *British Journal of Medical Psychology*, 74, 213–222.

Lobato, E., Mendoza, J., Sims, V., & Chin, M. (2014). Examining the relationship between conspiracy theories, paranormal beliefs, and pseudoscience acceptance among a university population. *Applied Cognitive Psychology*, 28(5), 617–625. http://doi.org/10.1002/acp.3042.

Loftus, E. F. (1993). The reality of repressed memories. *American Psychologist*, 48, 518–537.

Loftus, E. F., & Ketcham, K. (1994). *The myth of repressed memory: False memories and allegations of sexual abuse*. New York: St. Martin's Press.

Long, G. (1990). *Examining the earthlight theory*. Chicago: Center for UFO Studies.

Lord, C. G., Ross, L., & Lepper, M. R. (1979). Biased assimilation and attitude polarization: The effects of prior theories on subsequently considered evidence. *Journal of Personality and Social Psychology*, 37, 2098–2109.

Lynn, S. J., & McConkey, K. M. (Eds.). (1998). *Truth in memory*. New York: Guilford Press.

Lynn, S. J., & Rhue, J. W. (1988). Fantasy proneness: Hypnosis, developmental antecedents, and psychopathology. *American Psychologist*, 43, 35–44.

Lynn, S. J., Pintar, J., & Rhue, J. W. (1997). Fantasy proneness, dissociation, and narrative construction. In S. M. Powers & S. Krippner (Eds.), *Broken images, broken selves: Dissociative narratives in clinical practice* (pp. 274–302). New York: Brunner.

Mack, J. E. (1994). *Abduction: Human encounters with aliens*. New York: Scribners.

Makarem, S. (1974). *The Druze faith*. Delmar, NY: Caravan Books.

Malcolm, N. (1959). *Dreaming: Studies in philosophical psychology*. London: Routledge and Kegan Paul.

Mamelak, A., & Hobson, A. (1989). Dream bizarreness as the cognitive correlate of altered neuronal behaviour in REM sleep. *Journal of Cognitive Neuroscience*, 1, 201–222.

Maner, J. K., DeWall, C. N., Baumeister, R. F., & Schaller, M. (2007). Does social exclusion motivate interpersonal reconnection? Resolving the "porcupine problem". *Journal of Personality and Social Psychology*, 92, 42–55.

Maranise, A. M. J. (2013). Superstition and religious ritual: An examination of their effects and utilisation in sport. *Sport Psychologist*, 27, 83–91.

Martin, R. (1990). *The tarot reader's notebook*. Albuquerque: Flora & Company.

Masson, J. (1992). *The assault on truth*. London: Fontana.

Matheson, T. (1998). *Alien abductions: Creating a modern phenomenon*. Amherst, NY: Prometheus.

Matthews, R., & Blackmore, S. (1995). Why are coincidences so impressive? *Perceptual and Motor Skills*, 80, 1121–1122.

Mayo, J. White, O., & Eysenck, H. J. (1978). An empirical study of the relation between astrological factors and personality. *Journal of Social Psych*ology, 105, 229–236.

Mays, V. M., Coles, C. N., & Cochran, S. D. (2012). Is there a legacy of the U.S. public health syphilis study at Tuskegee in HIV/AIDS-related beliefs among heterosexual African Americans and Latinos? *Ethics & Behavior*, 22(6), 461–471. http://doi.org/10.1080/10508422.2012.730805.

McCauley, C., & Jacques, S. (1979). Popularity of conspiracy theories of presidential assassination: A Bayesian analysis. *Journal of Personality and Social Psychology*, 37(5), 637–644. http://doi.org/10.1037/0022-3514.37.5.637.

McGrath, M. J., & Cohen, D. B. (1978). REM sleep facilitation of adaptive waking behaviour: A review of the literature. *Psychological Bulletin*, 85, 24–57.

McHoskey, J. W. (1995). Case closed? On the John F. Kennedy assassination: Biased assimilation of evidence and attitude polarization. *Basic and Applied Social Psychology*, 17(3), 395–409. http://doi.org/10.1207/s15324834basp1703_7.

McNally, R. J., Lasko, N. B., Clancy, S. A., Macklin, M. L., Pitman, R. A., & Orr, S. P. (2004). Psychophysiological responding during script-driven imagery in people reporting abduction by space aliens. *Psychological Science*, 15, 493–497.

Meehl, P. E. (1956). Wanted – a good cookbook. *American Psychologist*, 11, 262–272.

Merckelbach, H., Horselenberg, R., & Muris, P. (2001). The Creative Experiences Questionnaire (CEQ): A brief self-report measure of fantasy proneness. *Personality and Individual Differences*, 31, 987–995.

Meyersburg, C. A., & McNally, R. J. (2011). Reduced death distress and greater meaning of life among individuals reporting past life memory. *Personality and Individual Differences*, 50, 1218–1221.

Meyersburg, C. A., Bogdan, R., Gallo, D. A., & McNally, R. A. (2009). False memory propensity in people reporting recovered memories of past lives. *Journal of Abnormal Psychology*, 118, 399–404.

Miller, S. M. (1979). Controllability and human stress: Method, evidence and theory. *Behaviour and Research Therapy*, 17, 287–304.

Mills, A., & Tucker, J. (2014). Past-life experiences. In E. Cardeña, S. J. Lynn, & S. Krippner (Eds.), *Varieties of anomalous experience: Examining the scientific evidence*. 2nd ed. (pp. 303–332). Washington, DC: American Psychological Association.

Mills, J. (1979). *Six years with God*. New York: A and W Publishers.

Milton, J. (1999). Should ganzfeld research continue to be crucial in the search for a replicable psi effect? Discussion paper and introduction to an electronic-mail discussion. *Journal of Parapsychology, 63*, 309–333.

Milton, J., & Wiseman, R. (1997). *Guidelines for extrasensory perception research*. Hatfield: University of Hertfordshire Press.

Milton, J., & Wiseman, R. (1999). Does psi exist? Lack of replication of an anomalous process of information transfer. *Psychological Bulletin*, 125, 387–391.

Mobbs, D., & Watt, C. (2011). There is nothing paranormal about near-death experiences: How neuroscience can explain seeing bright lights, meeting the dead, or being convinced you are one of them. *Trends in Cognitive Sciences*, 15(10), 447–449.

Montangero, J. (1993). Dream, problem-solving, and creativity, cited in C. Cavallero & D. Foulkes (Eds.), *Dreaming as cognition* (pp. 93–113). London: Harvester Wheatsheaf.

Moody, R. A. (1975). *Life after life*. New York: Bantam Books.

Moorcroft, W. H., Hoversten, E., & Foxworthy, C. (1993). Theories of dreaming. In W. H. Moorcroft (Ed.), *Sleep, dreaming, and sleep disorders*. Lanham, MD: University Press of America, Inc.

Morley, C. (2013) *Dreams of awakening: Lucid dreaming and mindfulness of dream and sleep*. London: Hay House.

Morris, R. L. (1986). Minimizing subject fraud in parapsychology laboratories. *European Journal of Parapsychology*, 6, 137–149.

Morris, R. L., Cunningham, S., McAlpine, S., & Taylor, R. (1993). Toward replication and extension of ganzfeld results. In *The Parapsychological Association 36th Annual Convention: Proceedings of Presented Papers* (pp. 177–191). Durham, NC: Parapsychological Association.

Morris, R. L., Dalton, K., Delanoy, D. L., & Watt, C. (1995). Comparison of the sender/no sender condition in the ganzfeld. In *The Parapsychological Association 38th Annual Convention: Proceedings of Presented Papers* (pp. 244–259). Durham, NC: Parapsychological Association.

Morse, M., & Moody, R. A. (1991). *Closer to the light: Learning from children's near-death experiences*. London: Souvenir.

Moscovici, S. (1987). The conspiracy mentality. In C. F. Graumann & S. Moscovici (Eds.), *Changing conceptions of conspiracy* (pp. 151–169). New York: Springer.

Musch, J., & Ehrenberg, K. (2002). Probability misjudgment, cognitive ability, and belief in the paranormal. *British Journal of Psychology*, 93, 169–177.

Myers, S. A. (1983). The Wilson-Barber Inventory of Childhood Memories and Imaginings: Children's form and norms for 1337 children and adolescents. *Journal of Mental Imagery*, 7, 83–94.

Narlikar, J.V. (2013). An Indian test of Indian astrology. *Skeptical Inquirer*, 37(2).

Nash, C. B. (1986). Comparison of subliminal and extrasensory perception. *Journal of the Society for Psychical Research*, 53, 435–455.

Nathan, D. (2011). *Sybil exposed: The extraordinary story behind the famous multiple personality case*. New York: Free Press.

Nathan, D., & Snedeker, M. (1995). *Satan's silence: Ritual abuse and the making of a modern American witchhunt*. San Jose: Author's Choice Press.

Nestler, S. C. (2008). Hindsight bias, conjunctive explanations and causal attribution. *Social Cognition*, 26(4), 482–493. http://doi.org/10.1521/soco.2008.26.4.482.

Neubauer, R. L. (2013). Prayer as an interpersonal relationship: A neuroimaging study. *Religion, Brain & Behavior*, 4(2), 92–103. doi:10.1080/2153599X.2013.768288.

Newberg, A. B., Wintering, N. A., Morgan, D., & Waldman, M. R. (2006). The measurement of regional cerebral blood flow during glossolalia: A preliminary SPECT study. *Psychiatry Research: Neuroimaging*, 148, 67–71.

Newheiser, A. K., Farias, M., & Tausch, N. (2011). The functional nature of conspiracy beliefs: Examining the underpinnings of belief in the Da Vinci Code conspiracy. *Personality and Individual Differences*, 58(8), 1007–1011. http://doi.org/10.1016/j.paid.2011.08.011.

Newman, L. S. (1997). Intergalactic hostages: People who report abduction by UFOs. *Journal of Social and Clinical Psychology*, 16, 151–177.

Newman, L. S., & Baumeister, R. F. (1996a). Toward an explanation of the UFO abduction phenomenon: Hypnotic elaboration, extraterrestrial sadomasochism, and spurious memories. *Psychological Inquiry*, 7, 99–126.

Newman, L. S., & Baumeister, R. F. (1996b). Not just another false memory: Further thoughts on the UFO abduction phenomenon. *Psychological Inquiry*, 7, 185–187.

Newman, L. S., & Baumeister, R. F. (1998). Abducted by aliens: Spurious memories of interplanetary masochism. In S. J. Lynn & K. M. McConkey (Eds.), *Truth in memory* (pp. 284–303). New York: Guilford Press.

Nickell, J. (1993). *Looking for a miracle: Weeping icons, relics, stigmata, visions and healing cures*. Amherst, NY: Prometheus.

Nickell, J. (1995). *Entities: Angels, spirits, demons, and other alien beings*. Amherst, NY: Prometheus.

Nickell, J. (1997). A study of fantasy proneness in the thirteen cases of alleged encounters in John Mack's Abduction. In K. Frazier, B. Karr, & J. Nickell (Eds.), *The UFO invasion: The Roswell incident, alien abductions, and government coverups* (pp. 207–209). Amherst, NY: Prometheus.

Nickell, J. (2001). Exorcism! Driving out the nonsense. *Skeptical Inquirer*, 20, Jan/Feb 2001, 20–24.

Nielsen, T. A., & Powell, R. A. (1992). The day-residue and dream-lag effects: A literature review and limited replication of two temporal effects in dream formation. *Dreaming*, 2(2), 67–77.

Nigg, J. (2000). On inhibition/disinhibition in developmental psychopathology: Views from cognitive and personality psychology and a working inhibition taxonomy. *Psychological Bulletin*, 126, 220–246.

Norenzayan, A., & Gervais, W. M. (2013). The origins of religious disbelief. *Trends in Cognitive Sciences*, 17, 20–25.

Norenzayan, A., Gervais, W. M., & Trzesniewski, K. H. (2012). Mentalising deficits constrain belief in a personal God. *PLoS ONE*, 7(5), e36880.

Noyes, R. (1972). The experience of dying. *Psychiatry*, 35, 174–184.

Noyes, R., & Kletti, R. (1976). Depersonalisation in the face of life-threatening danger: An interpretation. *Omega*, 7, 103–114.

Noyes, R., & Kletti, R. (1977). Depersonalisation in the face of life-threatening danger. *Comprehensive Psychiatry*, 18, 375–384.

Nyborg, H. (2009). The intelligence-religiosity nexus: A representative study of white adolescent Americans. *Intelligence*, 37, 81–93.

Nyhan, B., Reifler, J., & Ubel, P. A. (2013). The hazards of correcting myths about health care reform. *Medical Care*, 51(2), 127–132. http://doi.org/10.1097/MLR.0b013e318279486b.

Nyhan, B., Reifler, J., Edelman, C., Passo, W., Banks, A., Boston, E., et al. (2009). The effects of semantics and social desirability in correcting the Obama Muslim myth. Unpublished manuscript.

Nyhan, B., Reifler, J., Richey, S., & Freed, G. L. (2014). Effective messages in vaccine promotion: A randomized trial. *Pediatrics*, 2,013–2,365. http://doi.org/10.1542/peds.2013-2365.

O'Keeffe C., & Wiseman, R. (2005). Testing alleged mediumship: Methods and results. *British Journal of Psychology*, 96, 165–179.

Office for National Statistics (ONS) (2015). *Labour market statistics*. December 2015. Retrieved December 2015 from www.ons.gov.uk/ons/rel/lms/labour-market-statistics/december-2015/index.html.

Ofshe, R., & Watters, E. (1995). *Making monsters: False memories, psychotherapy, and sexual hysteria*. London: Andre Deutsch.

Okasha, S. (2002). *Philosophy of science: A very short introduction*. Oxford: Oxford University Press.

Opsasnick, M. (2000). The haunted boy. *Strange Magazine*, 20. Retrieved 24 February 2016. Serialised at www.strangemag.com/exorcistpage1.html.

Osis, K., & Haraldsson, E. (1977). *At the hour of death*. New York: Avon.

Otgaar, H., Candel, I., Merckelbach, H., & Wade, K. A. (2009). Abducted by aliens: Prevalence information affects young children's false memories for an implausible event. *Applied Cognitive Psychology*, 23, 115–125.

Owens, J. E., Cook, E. W., & Stevenson, I. (1990). Features of "near death experience" in relation to whether or not patients were near death. *Lancet*, 336, 1175–1177.

Paley, J. (1997). Satanist abuse and alien abduction: A comparative analysis theorizing temporal lobe activity as a possible connection between anomalous memories. *British Journal of Social Work*, 27, 43–70.

Parnell, J. O., & Sprinkle, R. L. (1990). Personality characteristics of persons who claim UFO experiences. *Journal of UFO Studies*, 2, 45–58.

Parsons, S., Simmons, W., Shinhoster, F., & Kilburn, J. (1999). A test of the grapevine: An empirical examination of conspiracy theories among African Americans. *Sociological Spectrum*, 19(2), 201–222. http://doi.org/10.1080/027321799280235.

Pasricha, S., & Stevenson, I. (1986). Near-death experiences in India: A preliminary report. *Journal of Nervous and Mental Disease*, 174, 165–170.

Pechey, R., & Halligan, P. (2012). Prevalence and correlates of anomalous experiences in a large non-clinical sample. *Psychology and Psychotherapy: Theory, Research and Practice*, 85, 150–162.

Peltzer, K. (2003). Magical thinking and paranormal beliefs among secondary and university students in South Africa. *Personality and Individual Differences*, 35, 1419–1426.

Pendergrast, M. (1996). *Victims of memory: Incest accusations and shattered lives*. London: HarperCollins.

Pennycook, G. (2014). Evidence that analytic cognitive style influences religious belief: Comment on Razmar and Reeve (2013). *Intelligence*, 43, 21–26.

Pennycook, G., Cheyne, J. A., Seli, P., Koehler, D. J., & Fugelsang, J. A. (2012). Analytic cognitive style predicts religious and paranormal belief. *Cognition*, 123(3), 335–346. http://doi.org/10.1016/j.cognition.2012.03.003.

Pennycook, G., Fugelsang, J. A., & Koehler, D. J. (2015). Everyday consequences of analytic thinking. *Current Directions in Psychological Science*, 24(6), 425–432.

Persinger, M. A. (1990). The tectonic strain theory as an explanation for UFO phenomena: A non-technical review of the research, 1970–1990. *Journal of UFO Stu*dies, 2, 105–137.

Persinger, M. A., & Valliant, P. M. (1985). Temporal lobe signs and reports of subjective paranormal experiences in a normal population. *Perceptual and Motor Skills*, 60, 903–909.

Persinger, M. A., Tiller, S. G., & Koren, S. A. (2000). Experimental simulation of a haunt experience and elicitation of paroxysmal electroencephalographic activity by transcerebral complex magnetic fields: Induction of a synthetic "ghost"? *Perceptual and Motor Skills*, 90, 659–674.

Pigden, C. (2007). Conspiracy theories and the conventional wisdom. *Episteme*, 4(2), 219–232. http://doi.org/10.3366/epi.2007.4.2.219.

Pletcher, G. K. (1987). Coincidence and explanation. In A. Flew (Ed.), *Readings in the philosophical problems of parapsychology* (pp. 128–137). New York: Prometheus Books.

Podmore, F. (1902) *Modern spiritualism: A history and a criticism (2 vol.)*. London: Methuen.

Popper, K. (1972). *Conjectures and refutations*. London: Routledge and Kegan Paul.

Powell, M. B., Hughes-Scholes, C. H., & Sharman, S. J. (2012). Skill in interviewing reduces confirmation bias. *Journal of Investigative Psychology & Offender Profiling*, 9(2), 126–134. http://doi.org/10.1002/jip.1357.

Powers, S. M. (1994). Dissociation in alleged extraterrestrial abductees. *Dissociation*, 7, 44–50.

Radner, D., & Radner, M. (1982). *Science and unreason*. Belmont, CA: Wadsworth.

Randi, J. (1981). Cold reading revisited. In K. Frazier (Ed.), *Paranormal borderlands of science*. Buffalo, NY: Prometheus.

Randi, J. (1982). *Flim-flam*. Buffalo, NY: Prometheus Books.

Randi, J. (1986). The Project Alpha experiment: Part 1. The first two years. In K. Frazier (Ed.), *Science confronts the paranormal*. Buffalo, NY: Prometheus Books.

Randle, K. D., Estes, R., & Cone, W. P. (1999). *The abduction enigma: The truth behind the mass alien abductions of the late twentieth century*. New York: Forge.

Randles, J., Roberts, A., & Clarke, J. (2000). *The UFOs that never were*. London: London House.

Randolph-Seng, B., & Nielsen, M. E. (2007). Honesty: One effect of primed religious representations. *International Journal for the Psychology of Religion*, 17, 303–315.

Razmyar, S., & Reeve, C. L. (2013). Individual differences in religiosity as a function of cognitive ability and style. *Intelligence*, 41, 667–673.

Rechtschaffen, A., & Kales, A. (1971). *A manual of standardised terminology, techniques and scoring system for sleep stages of human subjects*. Bethesda, MD: US Department of Health Education and Welfare.

Rhine, L.E. (1969). Case study review. *Journal of Parapsychology*, 33, 228–266.

Riekki, T., Lindeman, M., & Raij, T. T. (2014). Supernatural believers attribute more intentions to random movement than sceptics: An fMRI study. *Social Neuroscience*, 9, 400–411.

Ring, K. (1980). *Life after death: A scientific investigation of the near-death experience.* New York: Coward, McCann & Geoghegan.

Ring, K. (1984). *Heading toward Omega: In search of the meaning of the near-death experience.* New York: Quill.

Ring, K. (1992). *The Omega Project.* New York: William Morrow.

Ring, K., & Rosing, C. J. (1990). The Omega Project: A psychological survey of persons reporting abductions and other UFO encounters. *Journal of UFO Studies*, 2, 59–98.

Ritchie, S.J., Wiseman, R., & French, C.C. (2012). Replication, replication, replication. *The Psychologist*, 25(5), 346–348.

Robert-Houdin, J. E. (1878). *The secrets of conjuring and magic.* [Translated and edited with notes by Professor Hoffmann]. Cambridge: Cambridge Library Collection.

Roberts, G., & Owen, J. (1988). The near-death experience. *British Journal of Psychiatry*, 153, 607–617.

Roberts, P., & Greengrass, H. (1994), *The astrology of time twins.* Bishop Auckland: Pentland Press.

Roberts, R. (1981). Personal constructs & dreaming. *New Forum: Journal of the Psychology and Psychotherapy Association*, 7(3), 60–62.

Roberts, R. (1988). Recurring themes and images in a series of consecutive REM dreams. *Perceptual and Motor Skills*, 67, 767–777.

Roberts, R. (2015). *Psychology & capitalism.* Winchester: Zero Books.

Roberts, R., & Hewer, H. (2015). Memory, "madness" and conflict: A Laingian perspective. *Memory Studies*, 8(2), 169–182.

Robertson, T. J., & Roy, A. E. (2001) A preliminary study of the acceptance by non-recipients of mediums' statements to recipients. *Journal of the Society for Psychical Research*, 65, 91–106.

Rodeghier, M., Goodpaster, J., & Blatterbauer, S. (1991). Psychosocial characteristics of abductees: Results from the CUFOS abduction project. *Journal of UFO Studies*, 3, 59–90.

Rodin, E. A. (1980). The reality of near-death experiences: A personal perspective. *Journal of Nervous and Mental Disease*, 168, 259–263.

Roe, C. A. (1994). Subjects' evaluations of a Tarot reading. In *Proceedings of Presented Papers: The Parapsychological Association 37th Annual Convention,* 323–334.

Roe, C. A. (1995). Pseudopsychics & the Barnum Effect. *European Journal of Parapsychology*, 11, 76–91.

Roe, C. A. (1998). Belief in the paranormal and attendance at psychic readings. *Journal of the American Society for Psychical Research*, 90, 25–51.

Roe, C. A., & Roxburgh, E. C. (2013a). Non-parapsychological explanations of ostensibly mediumistic information: A review of the evidence. In A. J. Rock (Ed.), *The survival hypothesis: Essays on mediumship* (pp. 65–78). Jefferson, NC: McFarland.

Roe, C. A., & Roxburgh, E. (2013b). An overview of cold reading strategies. In C. Moreman (Ed.), *The spiritualist movement: Speaking with the dead in America and around the world. Volume 2: Belief, practice, and evidence for life after death* (pp. 177–203). Santa Barbara, CA: Praeger.

Roediger, H. L., III, & McDermott, K. B. (1995). Creating false memories: Remembering words not presented on lists. *Journal of Experimental Psychology: Learning, Memory, and Cognition*, 21, 803–814.

Roediger, H.L. III (2012). Psychology's woes and a partial cure: The value of replication. *APS Observer*, 25(2), 9.

Rogers, P., Davis, T., & Fisk, J. (2009). Paranormal belief and susceptibility to the conjunction fallacy. *Applied Cognitive Psychology*, 23(4), 524–542. http://doi.org/10.1002/acp.1472.

Rogers, P., Fisk, J. E., & Wiltshire, D. (2011). Paranormal belief and the conjunction fallacy: Controlling for temporal relatedness and potential surprise differentials in component events. *Applied Cognitive Psychology*, 25(5), 692–702. http://doi.org/10.1002/acp.1732.

Roney-Dougal, S. (1986). Subliminal and psi perception: A review of the literature. *Journal of the Society for Psychical Research*, 53, 405–434.

Ross, M. W., Essien, E. J., & Torres, I. (2006). Conspiracy beliefs about the origin of HIV/AIDS in four racial/ethnic groups. *Journal of Acquired Immune Deficiency Syndromes*, 41(3), 342–344. http://doi.org/10.1097/01.qai.0000209897.59384.52.

Rosset, E. (2008). It's no accident: Our bias for intentional explanations. *Cognition*, 108(3), 771–780. http://doi.org/10.1016/j.cognition.2008.07.001.

Rotter, J. B. (1966). Generalised expectancies for internal versus external control of reinforcement. *Psychological Monographs*, 80(1).

Rowland, I. (2002). *The full facts book of cold reading* (3rd ed.). London: Ian Rowland Ltd.

Roy, A. E., & Robertson, T. J. (2001). A double-blind procedure for assessing the relevance of a medium's statements to a recipient. *Journal of the Society for Psychical Research*, 65(3), 161–174.

Roy, A. E., & Robertson, T. J. (2004). Results of the application of the Robertson-Roy protocol to a series of experiments with mediums and participants. *Journal of the Society for Psychical Research*, 68(1), 18–34.

Rudski, J. (2004). The illusion of control, superstitious belief, and optimism. *Current Psychology*, 22, 306–315.

Rush, J. H. (1986). Parapsychology: A historical perspective. In H. L. Edge, R. L. Morris, J. Palmer, & J. H. Rush (Eds.), *Foundations of parapsychology: Exploring the boundaries of human capability* (pp. 9–44). London: Routledge & Kegan Paul.

Rutjens, B. T., van der Pligt, J., & van Harreveld, F. (2010). Deus or Darwin: Randomness and belief in theories about the origin of life. *Journal of Experimental Social Psychology*, 46, 1078–1080.

Rutkowski, C. A. (1984). Geophysical variables and human behavior. XVI. Some criticisms. *Perceptual and Motor Skills*, 58, 840–842.

Rutkowski, C. A. (1990). Critical comments about earth lights and the TST. *Journal of UFO Studies*, 2, 144–146.

Rutkowski, C. A. (1994). On Persinger. *Bulletin of Anomalous Experiences*, 5, 7.

Rutkowski, C. (2000). *Abductions and aliens: The psychology behind extraterrestrial experience.* London: Fusion Press.

Rycroft, C. (1981). *The innocence of dreams*. London: Oxford University Press.

Sabom, M. (1982). *Recollections of death: A medical investigation*. New York: Harper & Row.

Sabom, M. (1998). *Light and death*. Grand Rapids, MI: Zondervan Publishing House.

Sabom, M., & Kreutziger, S. (1982). Physiacians evaluate the near-death experience. In C. R. Lundahl (Ed.), *A collection of near-death research readings* (pp. 148–159). Chicago: Nelson Hall.

Sagan, C. (1997). *The demon-haunted world: Science as a candle in the dark*. London: Headline.

Saklofske, D. H., Kelly, I. W., & McKerracher, D. W. (1981). *Astrology and personality: Yet another failure to replicate*. Unpublished manuscript, University of Saskatchewan, Saskatoon.

Samarin, W. J. (1972). *Tongues of men and angels: The religious language of Pentecostalism*. New York: Macmillan.

Sanderson, W. C., Rapee, R. M., & Barlow, D. H. (1989). The influence of an illusion of control on panic attacks induced via inhalation of 5.5 percent carbon-dioxide enriched air. *Archives of General Psychiatry*, 46, 157–162.

Santomauro, J., & French, C. C. (2009). Terror in the night: The experience of sleep paralysis. *The Psychologist*, 22, 672–675.

Sartori, P. (2008). *The near-death experiences of hospitalized intensive care patients: A five-year clinical study*. New York: Edwin Mellen Press.

Schatzman, M., Worsley, A., & Fenwick, P. (1988). Correspondence during lucid dreams between dreamed and actual events. In J. Gackenbach & S. Laberge (Eds.), *Conscious mind, sleeping brain: Perspectives on lucid dreaming* (pp. 155–179). London: Plenum Press.

Schippers, M. C., & van Lange, P. A. M. (2005). The psychological benefits of superstitious rituals in top sport. *ERIM Report Series Research in Management*, ERS-2005-071-ORG.

Schjoedt, U., Stødkilde-Jørgensen, H., Geertz, A. W., & Roepstorff, A. (2009). Religious participants recruit areas of social cognition in personal prayer. *Social Cognitive and Affective Neuroscience*, 4, 199–207.

Schlitz, M. J., & Honorton, C. (1992). Ganzfeld psi performance within an artistically gifted population. *Journal of the American Society for Psychical Research*, 86, 83–98.

Schmeidler, G. R. (1988). *Psychology and parapsychology: Matches and mismatches*. Jefferson, NC: McFarland.

Schmeidler, G. R., & Edge, H. (1999). Should ganzfeld research continue to be crucial in the search for a replicable psi effect? Part II. Edited ganzfeld debate. *Journal of Parapsychology*, 63, 335–388.

Schnabel, J. (1994). *Dark white: Aliens, abductions, and the UFO obsession*. London: Hamish Hamilton.

Schorer, C.E. (1985/6). Two native American near-death experiences, *Omega*, 16, 111–113.

Schwartz, R. A. (1978). Sleight of tongue. *The Skeptical Inquirer*, 3(1), 47–55.

Schwartz, G. E. R., Russek, L. G. S., & Barentsen, C. (2002). Accuracy and replicability of anomalous information retrieval: replication and extension. *Journal of the Society for Psychical Research*, 66(3), 144–156.

Schwartz, G. E. R., Russek, L. G. S., Nelson, L. A., & Barentsen, C. (2001). Accuracy and replicability of anomalous after-death communication across highly skilled mediums. *Journal of the Society for Psychical Research*, 65(1), 1–25.

Shariff, A. F., & Norenzayan, A. (2007). God is watching you: Priming God concepts increases prosocial behavior in an anonymous economic game. *Psychological Science*, 18, 803–809.

Sharpless, B. A., & Barber, J. P. (2011). Lifetime prevalence rates of sleep paralysis: A systematic review. *Sleep Medicine Review*, 15, 311–315.

Sharpless, B., & Doghramji, K. (2015). *Sleep paralysis: Historical, psychological, and medical perspectives*. Oxford: Oxford University Press.

Shaughnessy, M. F., Neely, R., Manz, A., & Nystul, M. (1990). Effects of birth order, sex, and astrological sign on personality. *Psychological Reports*, 66, 272–274.

Sheaffer, R. (1998). *UFO sightings: The evidence*. Amherst, NY: Prometheus.

Sheldrake, R. (2012). *The science delusion*. London: Coronet.

Sherwood, S. J., & Roe, C. A. (2003). A review of dream ESP studies conducted since the Maimonides dream ESP programme. *Journal of Consciousness Studies*, 10(6–7), 85–109.

Showalter, E. (1997). *Hystories: Hysterical epidemics and modern culture*. New York: Columbia University Press.

Sibley, C. G., & Bulbulia, J. (2012). Faith after an earthquake: A longitudinal study of religion and perceived health before and after the 2011 Christchurch New Zealand earthquake. *PLoS ONE*, 7, 349648.

Silvers, R. B. (1997). *Hidden histories of science.* London: Granta.

Simmons, W. P., & Parsons, S. (2005). Beliefs in conspiracy theories among African Americans: A comparison of elites and masses. *Social Science Quarterly*, 86(3), 582–598. http://doi.org/10.1111/j.0038-4941.2005.00319.x.

Smith, C. (1993). REM sleep and learning: some recent findings, cited in A. Moffitt, M. Kramer, & R. Hoffmann (Eds.), *The functions of dreaming* (pp. 341–362). New York: State University of New York Press.

Smith, C., & Kelly, G. (1988). Paradoxical sleep deprivation applied two days after the end of training retards learning. *Physiology and Behaviour*, 43, 213–216.

Smith, C., & Lapp, L (1986). Prolonged increases in both PS and number of REMs following a shuttle avoidance task. *Physiology and Behaviour*, 36, 1053–1057.

Smith, C. L., Johnson, J. L., & Hathaway, W. (2009). Personality contributions to belief in paranormal phenomena. *Individual Differences Research*, 7, 85–96.

Smith, M. D. (1993). The effect of belief in the paranormal and prior set upon the observation of a "psychic" demonstration. *European Journal of Parapsychology*, 9, 24–34.

Smithers, A. G. (1984). The zodiac test. *Guardian*. 19–23 March 1984.

Smithers, A. G., & Cooper, H. J. (1984). Social class and season of birth. *Journal of Social Psychology*, 124, 79–84.

Snyder, C. R., & Schenkel, R. J. (1975). P. T. Barnum Effect. *Psychology Today*, 8, 52–54.

Snyder, T. J., & Gackenbach, J. (1988). Individual differences associated with lucid dreaming. In J. Gackenbach & S. LaBerge (Eds.), *Conscious mind, sleeping brain: Perspectives on lucid dreaming* (pp. 221–259). London: Plenum Press.

Solms, M. (2000) Dreaming and REM sleep are controlled by different brain mechanisms. *Behavioral and Brain Sciences*, 23(6), 843–850.

Somer, E., Klein-Sela, C., & Or-Chen, K. (2011). Beliefs in reincarnation and the power of fate and their association with emotional outcomes among bereaved parents of fallen soldiers. *Journal of Loss and Trauma*, 16, 459–475.

Spanos, N. P. (1989). Hypnosis, demonic possession, and multiple personality: Strategic enactments and disavowals of responsibility for actions. In C. A. Ward (ed.), *Altered states of consciousness and mental health: A cross-cultural perspective* (pp. 96–124). Newbury Park, CA: Sage Publications.

Spanos, N. P. (1994). Multiple identity enactments and multiple personality disorder: A sociocognitive perspective. *Psychological Bulletin*, 116, 143–165.

Spanos, N. P. (1996). *Multiple identities and false memories: A sociocognitive perspective.* Washington, DC: American Psychological Association.

Spanos, N. P., & Gottlieb, J. (1979). Demonic possession, mesmerism, and hysteria: A social psychological perspective on their historical interrelations. *Journal of Abnormal Psychology*, 88, 527–546.

Spanos, N. P., & Hewitt, E. C. (1979). Glossolalia: A test of the "trance" and psychopathology hypotheses. *Journal of Abnormal Psychology*, 88, 427–434.

Spanos, N. P., Burgess, C. A., & Burgess, M. F. (1994). Past-life identities, UFO abductions, and satanic ritual abuse: The social construction of memories. International *Journal of Clinical and Experimental Hypnosis*, 42, 433–446.

Spanos, N. P., Cross, P. A., Dickson, K., & DuBreuil, S. C. (1993). Close encounters: An examination of UFO experiences. *Journal of Abnormal Psychology*, 102, 624–632.

Spanos, N. P., Cross, W. P., Lepage, M., & Coristine, M. (1986). Glossolalia as learned behavior: An experimental demonstration. *Journal of Abnormal Psychology*, 95, 21–23.

Spanos, N. P., Menary, E., Gabora, N. J., DuBreuil, S. C., & Dewhirst, B. (1991). Secondary identity enactments during hypnotic past-life regression: A sociocognitive perspective. *Journal of Personality and Social Psychology*, 61, 308–320.

Sproull, L., Subramani, R., Kiesler, S., Walker, J., & Waters, K. (1996). When the interface is a face. *Human-Computer Interaction*, 11, 97–124.

Srivastava, M., Simakov, O., Chapman, J., Fahey, B., Gauthier, M. E. A., Mitros, T., et al. (2010). The Amphimedon queenslandica genome and the evolution of animal complexity. *Nature*, 466, 720–726.

Stanovich, K. E. (2012). On the distinction between rationality and intelligence: Implications for understanding individual differences in reasoning. In K. J. Holyoak & R. G. Morrison (Eds.), *The Oxford handbook of thinking and reasoning*. Oxford: Oxford University Press.

Stemman, R. (1998). Lebanese research among the Druze. *Reincarnation International*, 15, June 1998, 11–21.

Stempel, C., Hargrove, T., & Stempel, G. H. (2007). Media use, social structure, and belief in 9/11 conspiracy theories. *Journalism & Mass Communication Quarterly*, 84(2), 353–372. http://doi.org/10.1177/107769900708400210.

Stevenson, I. (1980). *Cases of the reincarnation type. Volume III. Twelve cases in Lebanon and Turkey*. Charlottesville: University Press ofVirginia.

Stevenson, I. (1994). A case of the psychotherapist's fallacy: Hypnotic regression to "previous lives". *American Journal of Clinical Hypnosis*, 36, 188–193.

Stevenson, I. (2001). *Children who remember past lives: A question of reincarnation*. Jefferson, NC: McFarland.

Stevenson, I. (2003). *European cases of the reincarnation type*. Jefferson, NC: McFarland.

Stieger, S., Gumhalter, N., Tran, U. S., Voracek, M., & Swami, V. (2013). Girl in the cellar: A repeated cross-sectional investigation of belief in conspiracy theories about the kidnapping of Natascha Kampusch. *Frontiers in Personality Science and Individual Differences*, 4(297). http://doi.org/10.3389/fpsyg.2013.00297.

Stires, L. (1997). 3.7 million Americans kidnapped by aliens? In K. Frazier, B. Karr, & J. Nickell (Eds.), *The UFO invasion: The Roswell incident, alien abductions, and government coverups* (pp. 203–206). Amherst, NY: Prometheus.

Stollznow, K. (2011). Running hot and cold: "psychic medium" Rebecca Rosen. *Skeptical Inquirer*. Retrieved September 2015 from www.csicop.org/specialarticles/show/running_hot_and_cold_psychic_ medium_rebecca_rosen.

Stone-Carmen, J. (1994). A descriptive study of people reporting abduction by unidentified flying objects (UFOs). In A. Pritchard, D. E. Pritchard, J. E. Mack, P. Kasey, & C. Yapp (Eds.), *Alien discussions: Proceedings of the Abduction Study Conference held at MIT* (pp. 309–315). Cambridge, MA: North Cambridge Press.

Storm, L., Tressoldi, P. E., & Di Risio, L. (2010a). Meta-analysis of free-response studies, 1992–2008: Assessing the noise reduction model and parapsychology. *Psychological Bulletin*, 136, 471–485.

Storm, L., Tressoldi, P. E., & Di Risio, L. (2010b). A meta-analysis with nothing to hide: Reply to Hyman (2010). *Psychological Bulletin*, 136, 491–494.

Strassman, R. (1997). Endogenous ketamine-like compounds and the NDE: If so, so what? *Journal of Near-Death Studies*, 16, 27–41.

Strieber, W. (1987). *Communion: A true story*. New York: Morrow.

Strieber, W. (1998). *Confirmation: The hard evidence*. London: Simon & Schuster.

Stuart, N. R. (2005). The Fox sisters: Spiritualism's unlikely founders. *American History Magazine*. Retrieved September 2015 from www.historynet.com/the-fox-sisters-spiritualisms-unlikely-founders.htm.

Sullivan, D., Landau, M. J., & Rothschild, Z. K. (2010). An existential function of enemyship: Evidence that people attribute influence to personal and political enemies to compensate for threats to control. *Journal of Personality and Social Psychology*, 98(3), 434–449. http://doi.org/10.1037/a0017457.

Sunstein, C. R., & Vermeule, A. (2009). Symposium on conspiracy theories. Conspiracy theories: Causes and cures. *Journal of Political Philosophy*, 17(2), 202–227. http://doi.org/10.1111/j.1467-9760.2008.00325.x.

Sutherland, C. (2009). "Trailing clouds of glory": The near-death experience of Western children and teens. In J. Holden, B. Greyson, & D. James (Eds.), *The handbook of near-death experiences: Thirty years of investigation* (pp. 87–107). Santa Barbara, CA: ABC-CLIO.

Swami, V., & Furnham, A. (2012). Examining conspiracist beliefs about the disappearance of Amelia Earhart. *The Journal of General Psychology*, 139(4), 244–259. http://doi.org/10.1080/00221309.2012.697932.

Swami, V., Chamorro-Premuzic, T., & Furnham, A. (2010). Unanswered questions: A preliminary investigation of personality and individual difference predictors of 9/11 conspiracist beliefs. *Applied Cognitive Psychology*, 24, 749–761. http://doi.org/10.1002/acp.1583.

Swami, V., Coles, R., Stieger, S., Pietschnig, J., Furnham, A., Rehim, S., & Voracek, M. (2011). Conspiracist ideation in Britain and Austria: Evidence of a monological belief system and associations between individual psychological differences and real-world and fictitious conspiracy theories. *British Journal of Psychology*, 102, 443–463. http://doi.org/10.1111/j.2044-8295.2010.02004.x.

Swami, V., Pietschnig, J., Tran, U. S., Nader, I. W., Stieger, S., & Voracek, M. (2013). Lunar lies: The impact of informational framing and individual differences in shaping conspiracist beliefs about the moon landings. *Applied Cognitive Psychology*, 27(1), 71–80. http://doi.org/10.1002/acp.2873.

Swami, V., Voracek, M., Stieger, S., Tran, U. S., & Furnham, A. (2014). Analytic thinking reduces belief in conspiracy theories. *Cognition*, 133(3), 572–585. http://doi.org/10.1016/j.cognition.2014.08.006.

Tamariz, J. (1988). *The magic way*. Madrid: Magic Books.

Tellegen, A., & Atkinson, R. P. (1974). Openness to absorbing and self-altering susceptibility. *Journal of Abnormal Psychology*, 83, 268–277.

Thalbourne, M. A. (2003). *A glossary of terms used in parapsychology*. 2nd ed. Charlottesville, VA: Puente Publications.

Thalbourne, M. A., & French, C. (1995). Paranormal belief, manic-depressiveness, and magical ideation: A replication. *Personality and Individual Differences*, 18, 291–292.

Theos Poll (2009). Poll of belief in ghosts and the supernatural, commissioned by Theos and published on 13 April 2009. Retrieved 1 November 2015 from www.comres.co.uk/polls/theos-ghosts-poll.

Thomas, S. B., & Quinn, S. C. (1991). The Tuskegee syphilis study, 1932 to 1972: Implications for HIV education and AIDS risk education programs in the Black community. *American Journal of Public Health*, 81(11), 1498–1505.

Thompson, V., & Morsanyi, K. (2012). Analytic thinking: Do you feel like it? *Mind & Society*, 11(1), 93–105.

Tversky, A., & Kahneman, D. (1983). Extensional versus intuitive reasoning: The conjunction fallacy in probability judgement. *Psychological Review*, 90(4), 293–315. http://doi.org/10.1037/0033-295X.90.4.293.

Twemlow, S. W., & Gabbard, G. O. (1984). The influence of demographic/psychological factors and pre-existing conditions on the near-death experience. *Omega*, 15(3), 223–234.

Ullman, M., Krippner, S., & Vaughan, A. (1973). *Dream telepathy*. New York: Macmillan.

Ullman, M., Krippner, S., & Vaughan, A. (1989). *Dream telepathy: Experiments in nocturnal ESP* (2nd ed.). London: McFarland and Company.

Unger, R. M., & Smolin, L. (2015). *The singular universe and the reality of time.* Cambridge: Cambridge University Press.

Uscinski, J. E., & Parent, J. M. (2014). *American conspiracy theories.* Oxford: Oxford University Press.

Utts, J. (1991). Replication and meta-analysis in parapsychology. *Statistical Science*, 6, 363–403.

Van de Castle, R. L. (1977). Sleep and dreams. In B. B. Wolman (Ed.), *Handbook of parapsychology* (pp. 473–499). New York: Van Nostrand Reinhold.

Van de Castle, R. L. (1989). ESP in dreams: Comments on a replication "failure" by the "failing" subject. In M. Ullman, S. Krippner, and A. Vaughan (Eds.), *Dream telepathy: Experiments in nocturnal ESP* (2nd edition) (pp. 209–216). London: McFarland and Company.

van der Tempel, J., & Alcock, J. E. (2015). Relationships between conspiracy mentality, hyperactive agency detection, and schizotypy: Supernatural forces at work? *Personality and Individual Differences*, 82, 136–141. http://doi.org/10.1016/j.paid.2015.03.010.

van Elk, M. (2015). Perceptual biases in relation to paranormal and conspiracy beliefs. *PLOS ONE*, 10(6), e0130422. http://doi.org/10.1371/journal.pone.0130422.

van Harreveld, F., Rutjens, B. T., Schneider, I. K., Nohlen, H. U., & Keskinis, K. (2014). In doubt and disorderly: Ambivalence promotes compensatory perceptions of order. *Journal of Experimental Psychology*: General. http://doi.org/10.1037/a0036099.

van Lommel, P., van Wees, R., Meyers, V., & Elfferich, I. (2001). Near death experience in survivors of cardiac arrest. *The Lancet*, 358, 2039–2045.

van Prooijen, J. -W., & Jostmann, N. B. (2013). Belief in conspiracy theories: The influence of uncertainty and perceived morality. *European Journal of Social Psychology*, 43(1), 109–115. http://doi.org/10.1002/ejsp.1922.

van Prooijen, J. -W., & van Dijk, E. (2014). When consequence size predicts belief in conspiracy theories: The moderating role of perspective taking. *Journal of Experimental Social Psychology*, 55, 63–73. http://doi.org/10.1016/j.jesp.2014.06.006.

Van Rooj, J. J. F. (1999). Self-concept in terms of astrological sun-sign traits. *Psychological Reports*, 84, 541–546.

Voas, D. (2007). Ten million marriages: A test of astrological "love signs". *Cathie Marsh Centre for Census and Survey Research.* Retrieved 22 August 2016 from https://astrologiaexperimental.files.wordpress.com/2014/05/voasastrology.pdf.

Von Grunebaum, G., & Callois, R. (Eds.) (1966). *The dream and human societies.* Berkeley: University of California Press.

Voss, U., Holzmann, R., Tuin, I., & Hobson, A. (2009). Lucid dreaming: A state of consciousness with features of both waking and non-lucid dreaming. *Sleep*, 32(9), 1191–1200.

Wagstaff, G. F. (1995). Hypnosis. In A. M. Colman (ed.). *Controversies in psychology* (pp. 21–35). London: Longman.

Ward, T. B. (1992). Structured imagination. In R. A. Finke, T. B. Ward, & S. M. Smith (Eds.), *Creative cognition: Theory, research and applications.* Cambridge, MA: MIT Press.

Ward, T. B., & Sifonis, C. M. (1997). Task demands and generative thinking: What changes and what remains the same? *Journal of Creative Behavior*, 31, 245–259.

Wason, P. C. (1960). On the failure to eliminate hypotheses in a conceptual task. *Quarterly Journal of Experimental Psychology*, 12(3), 129–140. http://doi.org/10.1080/17470216008416717.

Watson, N. (2013). *UFO investigations manual: UFO investigations from 1892 to the present day.* Yeovil, UK: Haynes Publishing.

Watt, C., & Kennedy, J. E. (2015). Lessons from the first two years of operating a study registry. *Frontiers in Psychology*, 7, 173.

Watt, C. A., & Morris, R. L. (1995). The relationships among performance on a prototype indicator of perceptual defence/vigilance, personality, and extrasensory perception. *Personality and Individual Differences*, 19, 635–648.

Watt, C., Watson, S., & Wilson, L. (2007). Cognitive and psychological mediators of anxiety: Evidence from a study of paranormal belief and perceived childhood control. *Personality and Individual Differences*, 42, 335–343.

Webster, R. (1990). *The mail order psychic.* Auckland, New Zealand: Brookfield Press.

Weiss, B. L. (1988). *Many lives, many masters.* New York: Simon & Shuster.

Weiss, B. L. (1992). *Through time into healing.* New York: Simon & Shuster.

Whinnery, J. E. (1990). Acceleration-induced loss of consciousness: A review of 500 episodes. *Archives of Neurology*, 47, 764–776.

Whinnery, J. E. (1997). Psychophysiologic correlates of unconsciousness and near-death experiences. *Journal of Near-Death Studies*, 15, 231–258.

Whitson, J. A., & Galinsky, A. D. (2008). Lacking control increases illusory pattern perception. *Science*, 322(5898), 115–117. http://doi.org/10.1126/science.1159845.

Whitson, J. A., Galinsky, A. D., & Kay, A. (2015). The emotional roots of conspiratorial perceptions, system justification, and belief in the paranormal. *Journal of Experimental Social Psychology*, 56, 89–95. http://doi.org/10.1016/j.jesp.2014.09.002.

Wiener, M., DeVoe, S., Rubinow, S., & Geller, J. (1972). Nonverbal behaviour and nonverbal communication. *Psychological Review*, 79, 185–214.

Willard, A. K., & Norenzayan, A. (2013). Cognitive biases explain religious belief, paranormal belief, and belief in life's purpose. *Cognition*, 129, 379–391.

Williams, L. M., & Irwin, H. J. (1991). A study of paranormal belief, magical ideation as an index of schizotypy and cognitive style. *Personality and Individual Differences*, 12, 1339–1348.

Wilson, I. (1987). *The after death experience.* London: Corgi.

Wilson, K., & French, C. C. (2006). The relationship between susceptibility to false memories, dissociativity, and paranormal belief and experience. *Personality and Individual Differences*, 41, 1493–1502.

Wilson, K., & French, C. (2014). Magic and memory: Using conjuring to explore the effects of suggestion, social influence, and paranormal belief on eyewitness testimony for an ostensibly paranormal event. *Frontiers in Psychology*, 5, 1289.

Wilson, S. C., & Barber, T. X. (1983). The fantasy-prone personality: Implications for understanding imagery, hypnosis, and parapsychological phenomena. In A. A. Sheikh (Ed.) *Imagery: Current theory, research, and application*, (pp. 340–387). New York: John Wiley and Sons.

Windt, J. M. (2015). *Dreaming: A conceptual framework for philosophy of mind and empirical research.* Cambridge: MIT Press.

Winget, C., & Kramer, M. (1979). *Dimensions of dreams.* Gainsville: University of Florida.

Winson, J. (1985). *Brain psyche: the biology of the unconscious.* Gardener City, NJ: Anchor Press/Doubleday.

Wiseman, R. (2011). *Paranormality: Why we see what isn't there.* London: Macmillan

Wiseman, R., & Morris, R. L. (1995a). *Guidelines for testing psychic claimants.* Buffalo, NY: Prometheus Press.

Wiseman, R., & Morris, R. L. (1995b). Recalling pseudo-psychic demonstrations. *British Journal of Psychology*, 86, 113–125.

Wiseman, R., & Smith, M. D. (2002). Assessing the role of cognitive and motivational biases in belief in the paranormal. *Journal of the Society for Psychical Research*, 66, 157–166.

Wiseman, R., & Watt, C. (2006). Belief in psychic ability and the misattribution hypothesis: A qualitative review. *British Journal of Psychology*, 97, 323–338.

Wiseman, R., Greening, E., & Smith, M. (2003). Belief in the paranormal and suggestion in the séance room. *British Journal of Psychology*, 94, 285–297.

Wiseman, R., Smith, M., & Wiseman, J. (1995). Eyewitness testimony and the paranormal. *Skeptical Inquirer*, 19(6), 29–32.

Woerlee, G. M. (2014). *Illusory souls*. CreateSpace Independent Publishing Platform.

Wolford, G., Taylor, H. A., & Beck, J. R. (1990). The conjunction fallacy? *Memory & Cognition*, 18(1), 47–53. http://doi.org/10.3758/BF03202645.

Wood, M. J. (2015). Some dare call it conspiracy: Labeling something a conspiracy theory does not reduce belief in it. *Political Psychology*. http://doi.org/10.1111/pops.12285.

Wood, M. J., & Douglas, K. M. (2013). "What about building 7?" A social psychological study of online discussion of 9/11 conspiracy theories. *Frontiers in Personality Science and Individual Differences*, 4, 409. http://doi.org/10.3389/fpsyg.2013.00409.

Wood, M. J., & Douglas, K. M. (2015). Online communication as a window to conspiracist worldviews. *Frontiers in Psychology*, 6, 836. http://doi.org/10.3389/fpsyg.2015.00836.

Wood, M. J., Douglas, K. M., & Sutton, R. M. (2012). Dead and alive: Beliefs in contradictory conspiracy theories. *Social Psychological and Personality Science*, 3(6), 767–773. http://doi.org/10.1177/1948550611434786.

Worsley, A. (1988). Personal experiences in lucid dreaming. In J. Gackenbach & S. LaBerge (Eds.), *Conscious mind, sleeping brain: Perspectives on lucid dreaming* (pp. 321–341). London: Plenum Press.

Yapko, M. D. (1994). Suggestibility and repressed memories of abuse: A survey of psychotherapists' beliefs. *American Journal of Clinical Hypnosis*, 36, 163–171.

YouGov (2011). *Psychics and mediums survey*. Published October 5 2011. Retrieved 1 November 2015 from https://d25d2506sfb94s.cloudfront.net/cumulus_uploads/document/2011-10-05/YG-Archives-Psychics-051011.pdf.

Zingrone, N., & Alvarado, C. (2009). Pleasurable Western adult near-death experiences: Features, circumstances and incidence. In J. Holden, B. Greyson, & D. James (Eds.), *The handbook of near-death experiences: Thirty years of investigation* (pp. 17–40). Santa Barbara, CA: ABC-CLIO.

Zuckerman, P. (2007). Atheism: Contemporary numbers and patterns. In M. Martin et al. (Eds.), *The Cambridge companion to atheism* (pp. 47–65). Cambridge: Cambridge University Press.

Zuckerman, M., Silberman, J., & Hall, J. A. (2013). The relation between intelligence and religiosity: A meta-analysis and some proposed explanations. *Personality and Social Psychology Bulletin*, 17, 325–354.

Zusne, L., & Jones, W. H. (1982). *Anomalistic psychology: A study of extraordinary phenomena of behavior and experience*. Hillsdale, NJ: Erlbaum.

INDEX